D0699232

RUSSIA UPSIDE DOWN

AN *EXIT STRATEGY FOR THE SECOND COLD WAR*

JOSEPH WEISBERG

PUBLICAFFAIRS
New York

All statements of fact, opinion, or analysis expressed are those of the author and do not reflect the official opinions or views of the Central Intelligence Agency (CIA) or any other U.S. Government agency. Nothing in the contents should be construed as asserting or implying U.S. Government authentication of information or CIA endorsement of the author's views. This material has been reviewed by the CIA to prevent the disclosure of classified information.

Copyright © 2021 by Joseph Weisberg

Cover design by Pete Garceau
Cover image © iStock / Getty Images
Cover copyright © 2021 by Hachette Book Group, Inc.

Hachette Book Group supports the right to free expression and the value of copyright. The purpose of copyright is to encourage writers and artists to produce the creative works that enrich our culture.

The scanning, uploading, and distribution of this book without permission is a theft of the author's intellectual property. If you would like permission to use material from the book (other than for review purposes), please contact permissions@hbgusa.com. Thank you for your support of the author's rights.

PublicAffairs
Hachette Book Group
1290 Avenue of the Americas, New York, NY 10104
www.publicaffairsbooks.com
@Public_Affairs

Printed in the United States of America

First Edition: September 2021

Published by PublicAffairs, an imprint of Perseus Books, LLC, a subsidiary of Hachette Book Group, Inc. The PublicAffairs name and logo is a trademark of the Hachette Book Group.

The Hachette Speakers Bureau provides a wide range of authors for speaking events. To find out more, go to www.hachettespeakersbureau.com or call (866) 376-6591.

The publisher is not responsible for websites (or their content) that are not owned by the publisher.

Library of Congress Cataloging-in-Publication Data
Names: Weisberg, Joseph, 1965– author.
Title: Russia upside down : an exit strategy for the second Cold War / Joseph Weisberg.
Description: First edition. | New York : PublicAffairs, 2021. | Includes bibliographical references and index.
Identifiers: LCCN 2021016405 | ISBN 9781541768628 (hardcover) | ISBN 9781541768635 (epub)
Subjects: LCSH: United States—Foreign relations—Russia (Federation) | Russia (Federation)—Foreign relations--United States. | United States—Politics and government—1989- | Russia (Federation)—Politics and government—1991–
Classification: LCC E183.8.R9 W429 2021 | DDC 327.73047086—dc23
LC record available at https://lccn.loc.gov/2021016405

ISBNs: 978-1-5417-6862-8 (hardcover), 978-1-5417-6863-5 (ebook)

LSC-C

Printing 1, 2021

For R

CONTENTS

A NOTE ON THE
SOVIET UNION/RUSSIA PROBLEM

Most writers who deal with the Soviet Union and Russia run up against the same word problem. Sometimes you mean one, sometimes you mean the other, sometimes you mean both. The most frequent solution I've seen is to just use "Russia" all the time. Since Russia was the most politically and culturally dominant part of the Soviet Union, and since half the time people called the Soviet Union Russia anyway, this works reasonably well, even if it's a little misleading.

But it doesn't work for me (except in the title of this book). I am referring so specifically to the Soviet Union or modern-day Russia, or both, over and over again, that the only approach I can find is to specify each time exactly which I mean. This is clumsy, and will likely drive you a little crazy, as it does me.

INTRODUCTION

America fought a long and hard Cold War against the Soviet Union, primarily because they were communist, atheist, and politically repressive.

We, of course, were the exact opposite.

So that all made sense.

Then the Soviet Union collapsed. In short order, Russia embraced capitalism, and Orthodox Christianity reemerged as a fundamental, state-approved component of Russian identity. The government remained politically repressive, but much less so than the Soviet party/state. Although these changes were fraught and enormously complicated, our fantasy of Russia transforming into a country more like ours was, to a substantial degree, realized.

Our relationship should have improved dramatically at that point, and for a few years it did. But then the United States and Russia slid fairly rapidly into a second cold war. Maybe it started with the U.S. invasion of Iraq in 2003, maybe it started with the Russian invasion of Ukraine in 2014. More likely, it didn't start on a specific date at all. But we have at this point spent a number of years in this new cold war. It is an angry, dangerous confrontation, and it has done a surprising amount of damage. We have wreaked havoc on Russia's economy. They have played a significant role in undermining our democratic process, and perhaps our society as a whole. It's not going well for anyone.

This book makes the case against our new cold war with Russia. It suggests that we are fighting an enemy with whom we have few if any serious conflicts of interest. It argues that we are fighting with ineffective and dangerous tools. And most of all, it aims to demonstrate that our approach is not working.

What we need is a whole new way of thinking about Russia, a completely new paradigm that will get us out of this conflict. I call this new way of thinking a "self-aware politics." I know those two words fit together awkwardly. "Self-aware" comes from the world of psychology, and has a whiff of New Agey-ness. It can be used judgmentally, implying some people "are" and some people "aren't." It is, undeniably, fuzzy. The word "politics" is weightier, more practical. Even when used conceptually, it's anything but fuzzy. As a word, "politics" doesn't want to be anywhere near "self-aware."

But the phrase "self-aware politics" has the advantage of being precise. It is what it says it is—a politics based on greater self-awareness. We usually ignore the psychological roots and dimensions of our personal politics. We think what we think, and we feel what we feel. In a self-aware politics, the focus is on how our psychology produces our beliefs and ideas. As we understand ourselves better, we understand our enemies better too.

I am nowhere near the pinnacle of self-awareness myself, as will no doubt be clear when you read this book. In fact, for someone who strives a lot—who is constantly trying to be better and do better—it has been its own challenge for me simply to accept that self-awareness is not another goal with a finish line, another thing to achieve. Nor is it primarily a spectrum, on which some are more self-aware and some less self-aware (though it is this to a degree). Mostly, self-awareness is an effort, a plan. I am trying not to call it a journey for the same reason the phrase "self-aware politics" rubs me half the wrong way, but let's face it, it's a journey.

The further I travel on the self-aware road—the more I come to understand how I was shaped, why I behave the way I do, how I feel and why—the more my politics shift, though not in a left or right direction. A self-aware politics leads to less judgment and more acceptance of people who believe different things. It makes it easier to let people and events take their course. Because after all, neither we as individuals, nor we collectively as a country, are responsible for the destiny of everyone and everything in the world.

This book, then, lies at the intersection of psychology—mine and yours—with history and politics. Mine and yours? I don't even know you. And yet I'm going to take a lot of what I've figured out about myself and extrapolate it onto you. That's because what I've discovered about myself, I believe, applies to many (or at least some) others too. I was a product of a common type of political upbringing in America, influenced both inside and outside of the home to believe we were the undisputed greatest country in the world—in fact, in all of history. We had flaws, but they were minor compared to those of other countries. Combined with certain aspects of my own psychology and family environment, this turned me into a hard-boiled cold warrior, a black-and-white thinker who saw the Soviet Union as the dangerous, tyrannical enemy of freedom, and the United States as the virtuous guardian of democracy and goodness. They were the bad guys, we were the good guys.

If you never saw the world this way, this book isn't really about you personally. But it is, I believe, still about "us." The black-and-white view of the Soviet Union that I had during the Cold War was shared by many, including most of those with political power at the time, and lay at the root of American foreign policy.

It seems to me that nearly identical ideas and beliefs about political good and political evil still guide our policy, such as it is, toward modern-day Russia. The key to ending the second cold war is to challenge these nuance-free, absolutist assumptions about who we are, and who the Russians are. I will not challenge them by declaring that every last piece of the old orthodoxy was wrong.

I am not trying to hammer home a new set of facts, designed to convince you that I am now right (and was wrong before). Instead, I hope to add nuance to the old assumptions, hopefully enough to undermine the binary thinking that produced the original Cold War and is now fueling a second one.

I will attempt to accomplish this by moving somewhat freely back and forth between the story of my own personal journey and a fairly wonky reassessment of Soviet history and Russian politics. I will likewise focus at times on the psychological and emotional underpinnings of my, and our, national prejudices against the Soviet Union and Russia, while at other times focusing on the facts and logic I used to fortify and justify my own animus. Eventually, I'll make a series of (sometimes) concrete suggestions for altering the national attitudes that have contributed to our disastrous relationship first with the Soviet Union, and now with Russia. These different angles on the problem are not independent. In fact, integrating these different ways of approaching the problem is intended to produce—to be—a self-aware politics.

HOW I GOT THIS WAY

HOME

I grew up in a liberal family on Chicago's North Side, not far from Wrigley Field. My parents were both active in local politics, and frequently hosted meetings at our house. These meetings took place after my bedtime, but I wanted to be close to the action instead of alone in my room, so I would crawl down the green-carpeted stairs and perch on the bottom steps, listening to the grown-ups talk. I didn't understand what they were saying, but I was pretty sure it was boring.

Although I didn't quite know what politics was, I had a vague sense that my mother's involvement in it was emotional, and revolved around envelopes and staying up late with friends, whereas my father's involvement was logical, and included going upstairs to bed while everyone else was still drinking coffee downstairs.

Politics—was it my parents' hobby? It seemed bigger than that. Almost a war they were fighting, against an enemy with strange, hard names like "Alderman Vrdolyak." It was also somehow connected with the pile of magazines on the window ledge of the bathroom I shared with my father. I started thumbing through these magazines when I was six or seven years old—*Commentary*, *The New Republic*, and *The New York Review of Books* (not exactly a magazine, but a thick, squat newspaper). I liked *Commentary* best because it had a heavy, almost sandpaper-like cover, with geometric shapes surrounding the article titles. *The New York Review of Books*, on the other hand, was difficult to open, close, and fold properly, and seemed to be sending the message that it was too busy with the subject matter inside to be bothered with fancy binding.

The large house we lived in was overrun with books. Certain rooms were essentially wallpapered with them, books jammed tightly into wall-to-wall, floor-to-ceiling bookcases. Some of the bookcases in the house were beautiful antiques, some were white particleboard. The bookcases were all full, but the books kept coming in, and never going out. My father would go to the yearly book sale at my school and come back with ten cardboard boxes brimming with books. My mother, usually not irritable, would complain bitterly as he hauled these boxes into the house, asking the question we were all wondering—where was he going to put them? But my father knew more than us about the elasticity of bookshelves.

When we traveled, in America or abroad, we always saw the sights and monuments, but none were more important than a local used bookstore. Wherever we were, traveling or not, if we passed a used bookstore, my father peeled off and went in. My brother and I were expected to follow. My mother did not hold a veto, but was allowed to go shopping until we were done. My father came out of these bookstores with books, every time.

Was he a book hoarder? He didn't seem tense or neurotic when buying or reading books—he seemed happy. He didn't take drugs, or gamble, or spend the family fortune on . . . new books. He just wanted to read.

And yet I wanted to grab him, to shake him and say, "Stop reading!" I felt like there was a pile of books separating us. (Is it any wonder I'm writing a book?)

The world of books and the world of politics were linked—they were not quite the same thing, but not quite different things either. Both were about words, and thinking, and were fundamentally boring. Although barely older than me, I knew my brother was not bored by politics and books. He was of that world. He read, it seemed to me, constantly. He spoke up during the never ending political conversations at the dinner table, where he had ideas and knew things.

I, on the other hand, wanted to watch television. They wanted to watch PBS, sometimes. When I was seven, and my brother eight, the three of them huddled together night after night in front of the Watergate hearings, which not only didn't count as television, but was an unfair monopolization of the TV set by people who didn't even like television.

My father, in fact, hated television. He gave my brother and me copies of an article written by his friend George Anastaplo, titled "Television Is More Dangerous Than the Atom Bomb." Anastaplo was a brilliant law professor who had been denied entry to the Illinois Bar in the 1950s when he refused to answer a question about whether he was a communist (which no one really suspected him of). When the bar tried to rectify its error and admit him years later, he refused as a matter of principle and was never able to practice law. This made him almost a version of my father, slightly improved by making a great sacrifice for integrity. A true hero for the Weisberg family. In any case, the article my father gave us, probably published in some bulletin of the University of Chicago, argued that, whereas an atom bomb might or might not be dropped on us one day, television was surely rotting the minds of Americans every day, particularly the young and impressionable. (My brother, often right in these matters, is dubious this ever happened, and wonders if instead my father once made an offhand comment about television being worse than the atom bomb. If my memory somehow conflated such a comment with the figure of George Anastaplo, good for it.)

If television was worse than the atom bomb, my father's firm rule that we were only allowed to watch two hours a week was both eminently reasonable and also a magnanimous concession to the unhealthy desires of young children. There was an exception for *Masterpiece Theatre*, which did not count against your time. I understood perfectly well that *Masterpiece Theatre* was a book in disguise, and as with the Watergate hearings, I only peeked in occasionally while my parents and brother watched.

For me, having to cobble together a two-hour block out *of Fantasy Island, The Love Boat, Charlie's Angels, CHiPs, M*A*S*H,* and *Good Times* was agony, repeated every week. In fact, I couldn't do it. I usually watched three or even three and a half hours of television a week, feeling I had betrayed my father in a deep and irredeemable way.

I thought I could get away with it because I didn't see any signs I was being monitored. So I was surprised one day when my father flew into a rage—almost the only time I ever saw him lose his temper—about the amount of television I was watching (which I think he intuited more than tracked). He unplugged the TV, wrapped the cord around the antenna, and carried it down to the basement. He then put a padlock on the basement door. I remember my mother standing there, trying to balance amusement with some compassion for me. Later, she would open the lock for me, and I would go down, plug in the TV, and stand watching it in the dark. What he had done turned out to be too much even for my father, and a few weeks later the TV came back upstairs.

My father was not severe, though. He was kind and gentle, which was why this outburst had a ridiculous element that I could detect. It didn't fit well with who he was. He enjoyed the world, despite certain private sufferings, and was both decent and full of compassion. All of this was evident in his relationships with his children, but also in how he spoke about his views and beliefs. He was an advocate for civic and civil rights, a part-time lawyer for the ACLU, an opponent of capital punishment. He had one conservative streak, the same one many other liberal Jews had—he thought the Soviet Union was a cruel and tyrannical country, and that America had to fight hard against it.

I became marginally more interested in what he was saying about the Soviet Union as I got older. There was something about

Russia that tugged at me. My father, like many parents, read aloud to my brother and me, but not surprisingly, he had his own ideas about what to read us. We were indulged with fairy tales and children's literature until I was about five, and then he switched to the classics of world literature. Although there were some nods to accessibility—we read a lot of Dickens—he was open about the fact that his choices primarily reflected books he wanted to read. This included a healthy dose of Chekhov, Dostoevsky, Tolstoy, Turgenev, and Gogol. And so a Russian world existed in my imagination from a very young age. This world was imperial, and romantic, and sometimes a little bit swashbuckling. Of all the books he read us, the ones by Russians were my favorites.

My own reading lagged. While my brother could be found, age ten, lying in bed with a Henry James novel, I did not move beyond comic books. This was the one kind of reading without merit. I loved Batman, Aquaman, the Fantastic Four, the Green Lantern. Some part of me understood this was a piece of childhood I had a right to.

Would I start reading on my own? It was a contest of wills. On the one side, my father, his love flowing through books, rarely pushing me directly, but his entire way of moving through the universe a never-ending pressure for me to once and for all start reading books. On the other side, four-foot-eight, big head of strawberry-blond curls, lonely, lover of television—I was less a complete underdog than a legitimate dark-horse contender, thanks to a deep and natural stubbornness that might win the day.

My long, slow defeat began at age twelve, when I picked up *From Russia with Love* at my school's yearly book fair. Its red cover, with both a gun and the word "love," stirred something in me. It went into the headboard bookcase behind my twin bed, previously occupied exclusively by knickknacks and joke books. One fateful night, I started to read it.

I say my long, slow defeat, because it wasn't a hundred percent clear this counted as reading. And Fleming was all I read for more than a year, Bond after Bond. I do not know how or where I then got the gray paperback of *The Spy Who Came in from the Cold*, but that did it. It was obviously less titillating than Bond, but le Carré's stories felt real, and opened up an entire fantasy world that I sensed I belonged in. It was also obvious that, if my father were to read this, it would pass muster. It was a real book.

I was entering my teen years. My political consciousness remained blurry. But at Sunday school, there was frequent talk about Jews in the Soviet Union, and the violent and dangerous communist colossus on the other side of the world that was crushing them. There was something like complete agreement between my synagogue, Ian Fleming, and John le Carré—strong evil forces were afoot in the world, and good people had to stop them.

According to le Carré, the most likely hero to stop them was . . . my father? Was it my father? George Smiley was an introverted intellectual. He was a version of my father. But didn't that mean he was also a version of me, me in the future? It turned out I had been groomed for this dirty but necessary work. It would be better to be James Bond, but that wasn't really a thing. George Smiley was a real thing.

By the time I started high school in the late 1970s, I'd developed a more overt political consciousness, centered on Israel, with the Soviet Union lurking in the background. This was partly the work of Sunday school and was aided by a trip to Israel, which might as well have been a summer at a Chinese reeducation camp. I do not mean that the conditions were harsh, or that any of us on the trip were forced to go there—although I suppose the familial and religious structures of our lives did force us, in a way. I mean that the real mission of the rabbis and group leaders and sexy young Israelis shuttling us around the country was to inculcate us with strong pro-Zionist beliefs. Their plan was to teach us Jewish history and Israeli passion, and send us home prouder of our heritage than we'd been before, ready to fight (or at least argue) for Israel as the historical and emotional embodiment of that heritage.

Back home, a junior in high school now, the Soviets and the Arabs were Devil #1 and Devil #2 for me. Although I couldn't exactly decide which was worse. Jews were in danger in Israel, where they needed more Jews. Jews were suffering inside the Soviet Union, which wouldn't let them (or not many of them) leave to go to Israel, where they could have been free and made the Jews already there safer. It was a vicious circle.

One day, my friend Anthony suggested to me that the Israelis were mistreating the Palestinians. I delivered a twelve-point lecture to him on the history of the Middle East, trying to prove so conclusively that he was wrong that he eventually just shrugged and walked off down the hallway.

AWAY

I headed off to college shortly before Ronald Reagan started his
second term as president. He called the Soviet Union an evil empire. He said that suppressing people was wrong. Better yet, he said
these great injustices had to and would end. It was a little unclear if
they would end on their own, because they were so morally wrong,
or if he would end them. Either way, I admired his willingness to
speak a clear, simple truth that I thought others shied away from.

As a freshman at Yale, I planned to major in English, because I
liked writing. Then I took a class in the history of the international
communist movement with Ivo Banac. We studied Yugoslavia,
Hungary, Czechoslovakia—the problems, the suffering, the tanks
crushing people's dreams were almost glamorous to me. It was like
George Anastaplo facing off against the McCarthyites, but in this
case, the bad guys had tanks.

I decided to major in history.

My sophomore year, I took a popular lecture course in Soviet
history with Professor Wolfgang Leonhard. Wolfgang was born in
Germany, and his mother was a communist. When Nazi persecution of communists in Germany increased before the war, they fled
to the Soviet Union. Wolfgang attended school there, and later
worked for the Communist Party. He was eventually sent to East

Germany as part of a group the Soviets put together to help administer the country after the war.

Wolfgang was magnetic, unpretentious, and had a wry, cheerful disposition. This man's mother had been a prisoner in the Gulag, he had gone from communist believer to decidedly not, but there was no trace of anger in his personality. His attitude felt like an act of politics itself, a statement that no matter how much suffering, injustice, and terror took place in the world, one could look at it and learn from it, without falling into the trap of bitterness.

Wolfgang was also the real thing, an actual apparatchik who'd escaped from behind the Iron Curtain and showed us what it was really like there. In his class, I loved the feeling of my political instincts acquiring a factual and intellectual basis. It was exciting to think and debate about whether Stalin turned the USSR into a brutal and violent country, or if Lenin had started them down that road. The best part was, there was no disputing that it had happened, that the Soviet Union had gone wrong. Even if Khrushchev had started to bring the country back toward some sort of normalcy, he was kicked out and the repression returned (if not to its former level).

The story was endlessly fascinating, deeply moving, but ultimately simple. There were good guys and bad guys. And the bad guys had run the Soviet Union for most of its history. That is what I heard. I remain unsure if Wolfgang led me in that direction—he was hard to pigeonhole, and not really the type to recruit people to his side.

I was eventually invited to join a small group of mostly graduate students who regularly visited Wolfgang in his rooms at the Davenport residential college. I'd smoke cigarettes while he smoked a pipe, and we'd talk about politics and the world. I felt grown-up, and a bit European. I was finding an identity as a student who smoked in my professor's room and had increasingly strong feelings about the politics of the Soviet Union.

I had something serious to do with my brain now. I was a person with ideas, and if there are stages in the development of an absolutist thinker, here is where those ideas became fixed. I desperately needed to combine all the old things I knew with all the new things I was learning, and to mix them in with passion and conviction, so that I could form myself, so that I could grow up.

As for my peers, I don't recall any who had positive feelings about the Soviet Union, but everyone I knew objected strenuously to Ronald Reagan. I kept fairly quiet about my feelings, and when I did talk about them, I emphasized that it was only Reagan's foreign policy I agreed with. In truth, I was living and thinking a bit behind Reagan. It was the mid-'80s, and my anti-Soviet fires were burning brightest just as his were calming down a bit. In all fairness, he said and did a lot of contradictory things, and it's somewhat clearer now than it was back then that he was softening.

In any case, the particulars of what was actually happening were not as important to me as believing what I needed to believe. Reagan said the Soviet Union was an evil empire. The details of when he said it, and when he backed off a bit, hardly mattered. I was animated—my body and soul were being animated, like never before—by the idea that there was an evil and dangerous empire out there, and we had to fight it. I had to fight it.

The summer after my sophomore year, I returned home to Chicago, where a friend reported to me that there was a rumor going around that I had turned into a racist. I had no idea if this rumor was widespread or not, or if anyone even believed it. But it was obviously upsetting, and bewildering. Why would anyone think that? After talking to a few people, I figured it out—I had been vocal about supporting Reagan's foreign policy. This meant, to some people, that I supported Reagan's social and economic policies, which were damaging to poor people and minority groups. And that meant I was a racist. I had no idea what to do about this. I didn't support those other Reagan policies. But I also wasn't focused on them. Overall, I realized I would have to fortify myself against what other people thought, if I was going to think what I thought.

During my junior year (according to my memory), the Russian poet Yevgeny Yevtushenko did a reading on campus. I'd never seen anything like the way he read his poems, declaimed them, in a loud and dramatic way, full of passion and sexuality. I was both attracted to and repelled by his performance. But instead of really hearing the poetry, I was mostly interested in whether or not Yevtushenko was compromising himself, collaborating with the Soviet authorities to secure perks and privileges, like the right to travel abroad and speak to American college students.

My judgments were not kind to Yevtushenko. I was in a constant search for who was good and who was bad, who was moral and who was not, who was being firm and who was compromising. I didn't have to face any of those choices in my life, but I had no sympathy for those who did.

Later that year, in a meeting during office hours with one of my writing teachers, with whom I had a friendly but fairly formal relationship, she suddenly blurted out, "You can be such an asshole." I was stunned. I was a friendly and polite young man, and had decent social skills. I was pretty sure people liked me, in a kind of general way. I had thought this teacher liked me. What was she talking about?

That same year, during parents' weekend, my father came with me to visit Wolfgang in his rooms. As the three of us talked, my father mentioned Lenin's famous quote about how the capitalists should be given enough rope to hang themselves. Wolfgang replied that Lenin had never actually said this. He was matter-of-fact about it, not at all rude or condescending. But my father placed great value on knowing things, and now he was wrong about a simple fact, in front of me and my professor. Because of how we were, we didn't talk about it later. But I sensed something tender in him, and felt badly. (My father, whom I know better now than I did when he was alive, was actually more curious than sensitive, and I doubt he minded Wolfgang correcting him.)

In my senior year, when the Soviet Union was starting to open up under Gorbachev, *People* magazine ran a cover story on what life was really like in the Soviet Union. They'd gotten access to a number of ordinary Russians, not party/government plants, and photographed their apartments. I thought the article was very good, and showed a side of life in the Soviet Union you didn't usually get to see. I felt nervous bringing the article to Wolfgang, because I didn't think anyone took *People* magazine seriously. But he returned the magazine to me a few days later and said he thought they'd done a very good job. He couldn't have cared less that it was *People*.

Wolfgang and another professor, Firuz Kazemzadeh, served as advisers on my senior thesis. The topic was "Popular Attitudes in the Soviet Union Towards Their Government" (I should have made that "Their System and Leadership"). I studied the issue by looking at the opinions of four different groups—dissidents, Western journalists, émigrés, and academics specializing in Soviet affairs. After reviewing what members of each of these groups thought, I concluded that I couldn't be sure how the Soviet populace felt. But I tended to lean in the direction of Wolfgang Leonhard, who thought about 15 percent supported the government, corresponding roughly to (though somewhat exceeding) the percentage of the Soviet population that belonged to the Communist Party.

Wolfgang told me the professor who served as the outside reviewer had let him know he didn't know what to make of my paper, but Wolfgang told him both he and Kazemzadeh liked it, so he gave me an A–. I didn't mind that the outside reader didn't get it—it was arguably not a piece of historical research (the basic requirement for the paper). I felt understood by my two advisers, which was enough for me. (I wonder if, to a certain degree, I am just rewriting this same paper almost thirty-five years later.)

After I graduated from college, I moved to Portland, Oregon, where I waited tables and studied Russian part-time at Portland State University. Several times a week, I'd get a glossy manila envelope in the mail from Radio Free Europe/Radio Liberty, stuffed with research packets on Soviet current events. I'd sit in the kitchenette of my studio apartment poring over this endless stream of papers, the desire to do something about Soviet repression getting stronger and stronger. This desire didn't coalesce into an actual plan, but my moral outrage, my anger, my indignation weren't satisfied by just learning and talking. Even if I couldn't verbalize it, I felt like I was a man of action. Not just a talker and a thinker.

After a year in Oregon, I spent a few months back home in Chicago, then went to Leningrad to study Russian for the summer. A few weeks after I got there, I went to meet with a man I'll call Ilya (not to protect his identity, but because I don't remember his name). Ilya was a refusenik—a Jew who had applied to emigrate from the Soviet Union, resigned from his job (required to apply for an exit visa), and then been refused permission to leave (thus, refusenik). I'd gotten his name and address from a Jewish relief organization in Chicago.

I knew that, after losing their jobs, some refuseniks had to stoke boilers in the basements of buildings to make a living. For many, this was a big step down, since they had been doctors, engineers, or university professors before applying to emigrate. Conflating some of these ideas, I was expecting to find Ilya living in something that resembled a boiler room. I was confused when his apartment was, in fact, fairly nice.

The relief organization had given me a Seiko watch for Ilya, explaining that he could sell it on the black market and then live on the proceeds for more than a year. As soon as we sat down, I handed the watch over. Ilya disappeared with it into a back room, then came back and started to tell me about his life in the Soviet Union.

As he talked, and I ate the cream puffs he'd laid out, Ilya casually mentioned that someone abroad had sent him a subscription to *Newsweek*. I knew you couldn't read Western periodicals in the Soviet Union, and I asked him if he'd gotten into trouble because of the subscription. Ilya seemed a little surprised by the question. He explained that every week he received a notice from the post office that the magazine had arrived. The notice would give an appointment time. He'd go to the post office at that time, and they'd let him into a special room where he could sit and read his *Newsweek*. As he explained this to me, it was clear there were no repercussions for any of this. The KGB didn't follow him home afterward. It sounded like no one cared.

This was confusing. The Soviet Union I had studied—the one I had traveled across the world to see—supposedly did everything it could to block Western books and magazines from getting into the country. If you got your hands on forbidden material, and of course especially if you circulated it, you could be sent to prison, or a psychiatric institution.

Of course, there were plenty of possible explanations for why Ilya was allowed to read *Newsweek*, and to live so comfortably:

It was 1988—Gorbachev was changing things.

Ilya was just one refusenik—a tiny sample size. He didn't necessarily represent the majority of refuseniks. (As one of the limited number receiving financial help from abroad through visitors like me, his material conditions were without a doubt vastly better than those of the average refusenik.)

Or maybe the wily KGB let Ilya live differently from other refuseniks in order to mislead visiting Westerners. He was a kind of *Potemkin* refusenik.

All of this occurred to me. But as I sat across from this smart, likeable man in his living room, a little bell was going off in my head—something wasn't adding up. I pushed whatever was bothering me into a dark corner of my brain, where it remained for almost twenty years.

After my trip, I moved back to Chicago, and got a job helping Soviet émigrés find jobs. I was restless and bored, and since what I'd actually wanted all along was to fight—to destroy the Soviet Union—I called the CIA and asked for a job application. A year and a half later, after a long series of tests, interviews, and then waiting for a security clearance, I moved to Washington and started my new job.

A few months after I arrived, I was taking a walk one night along an empty road running through the woods at the agency's semi-secret training base. The enormous compound was fenced and guarded, and I felt completely safe. That is what I thought—that no one could mug me or attack me there. I had joined something special, and being a part of it meant I would be protected.

Part of the CIA training program was a series of "interim" assignments in various parts of the agency. For my first one, I asked to be put in the division that spied on the Soviet Union. I wasn't sure a trainee would be let into this inner sanctum of an organization that was itself one giant inner sanctum. But it turned out that all the trainees got the assignments they asked for. Once you were in, you were in.

This was why I had come to the CIA, to take on the Soviet menace. And there I was, taking it on. Around a conference table my first day, my new supervisor told a group of us about his recent trip to the Soviet Union. The concrete in front of the Kremlin had been all torn up, and apparently had been that way for years. He said that he and his friends would have been able to fix it with a few hours and a quick trip to Home Depot. We all understood this did not bode well for the Soviet Union.

It was late 1990, and the Soviet Union was on its last legs. But it wasn't entirely clear at the time that the country was about to fall, especially if your job depended on fighting it. One afternoon, I overheard a group of senior officers in the hallway arguing about whether the agency should try to destroy the KGB while it had the chance. They were not all in agreement.

Later, in one of the training segments, I was driving through a small American city, an instructor next to me in the car. My job was to spot surveillance. I used the techniques I had been taught, and I identified the surveillant following me. I also recognized the driver, one of our instructors. Over the radio, thinking I was especially smart to pick up this level of detail, I said his name as I called out the surveillance. The instructor in my car scowled and rebuked me for saying someone's true name over the radio. No one had ever taught me not to do this, but it was supposed to have been obvious.

Another interim assignment—the group managing the CIA's covert war in Afghanistan. There was something rough about the officers here, some of whom had grown beards in the field, ridden horses, even worn traditional Afghan robes while on the horses. This was, essentially, what we all wanted to do. I was afraid of horses, but whatever. The Soviets had actually left Afghanistan by the time I worked in this office, so I was a little fuzzy on why we were still so active there, but I kept my questions to myself, and even more from myself.

During these office assignments, I would take a break and wander the floors of the two headquarters buildings, going from vending machine to vending machine until I found one with Hostess Snoballs in it. A friend who knew I did this would sometimes call me on a secure line—it was easier to call on a secure line than a regular one—and tell me if he'd spotted Snoballs on a particular floor of one of the buildings. This same friend and I saw an announcement on a bulletin board for a "Security Awareness Poster Competition," and we entered. Our submission was a Letterman-inspired "Top 10 List of Reasons to Be Security Aware," with entries like "Spies Are Everywhere" and "It's Fun to Be Security Aware." We thought there was an outside chance we would be fired. Instead, we received an Honorable Mention, which came with a surprisingly elaborate certificate, bound in white linen. We eventually realized that everyone who entered got the same award.

A little over a year after I joined the CIA, the Soviet Union collapsed. I had joined the CIA with the express purpose of helping to make this happen, so . . . now what?

At the training program graduation ceremony, I sat next to the agency's head of Human Resources. He told me most of my instructors had never actually recruited an agent. I wasn't sure what to make of this—was recruiting even harder than it seemed? Or maybe my instructors weren't good at it, even though they'd just spent all this time teaching me how to do it? Or maybe the head of Human Resources, who wasn't part of the operational side of the agency, didn't know what he was talking about. I couldn't figure it out. The instructors were almost cleanly divided between eager fast-trackers and tired-looking middle-aged men and women nearing the ends of what you could tell were disappointing careers. All the ones I liked were in the second category.

Back at headquarters, I received my first assignment abroad. I had a stack of books on my desk about the history and politics of the country I was going to. Another officer made fun of me for all the books, and said I was missing the point of what we actually did at the CIA. He wasn't unkind, and his jokes had a trace of respect for someone who would read so much. I knew he was wrong, that you would obviously do this job better if you knew more about the environment you were working in. But I didn't see any other desks with stacks of books on them.

I never went on my first assignment. I took a year off to take care of my father, who was dying, then came back and soon resigned. I didn't want to live abroad anymore, or maybe just didn't want to do the job. In a small white room, I had my exit interview. But there was no interview at my exit interview. Just papers slid across the desk for me to sign, including the original secrecy agreement from when I'd joined. It turned out there was another place to sign again just below the original signature, for when you left.

I drove out of the massive parking lot, knowing I would never, ever be back. It was a place that, once you left, you were not allowed to come back to (this turned out not to be true, but seemed completely obvious to me at the time).

THERAPY

A few years later, I stumbled into therapy. I say "stumbled," because since the death of my father, my life had taken on an odd sleepwalking quality. I still got out of bed in the mornings, I was still active and productive. But I was less vibrant than I had been before, less interested in things. My jokes were infrequent and sour.

Over the next few years, I learned about grief, and then the rest of the feelings and emotions. I'd known the words before—happy, sad, angry, anxious, elated, furious, lost, devastated, joyful, crushed, broken—I remember early on in therapy saying, "My father died. I'm sad. Isn't that what I'm supposed to feel? Sad? Well, I'm sad." But then I asked my therapist if there was something missing. He asked if I thought there was. I said I had a feeling there was.

It turned out grief wasn't about adjectives. It wasn't about words at all, and that was my only area of competence. Grief was about moments, experiences—watching a videotape with my father of the Marx brothers' *A Night at the Opera* that he'd asked me to rent, and seeing him go through the whole movie without laughing once. Days after his final chemotherapy session, when the doctor had said we'd have to wait and see, sitting next to him on the bed when he rolled onto his side, and seeing a tennis ball–sized lump protruding from his back. Touching the lump, then telling him about it, and the pause before he said, "Okay, we'll tell the doctor tomorrow." Grief was the strange sensation of being wholly re-created as soon as he died, and not knowing or liking the new me (who was made almost entirely out of grief). Some of this you could express in words, but you couldn't start there.

I was unprepared for this. Boy, had I been raised a thinker, and not so much a feeler. I had learned to motor through the world fueled by thoughts and ideas. I easily absorbed the basic rules of thinking—you had to be clear, you had to be honest, you had to listen to other ideas you didn't agree with. The biggest rule was that knowing more was good, and allowed you to be right. Being right was very important, maybe the most important thing of all. Decency, integrity, all the things you needed to make your way through the world (and that I experienced almost as feelings) required being right.

This need to be right is both a replacement for feelings and a killer of nuance and complexity. If your main need is to sort out which side you are on, to help you determine right from wrong, true from false, no matter how involved your thinking is, it can end up binary.

Where did my feelings go, exactly? In some cases, I was literally told not to have them—negative feelings were dismissed as bad, something to grow out of. All kinds of passions coursed through their subterranean worlds and came out as strongly felt ideas, often about books and politics (once I gave in and started reading). Some morphed into nervous, OCD-like habits, repetitive counting and tapping, carefully hidden (their remnants still alive today). Ask me how I felt, and you'd get "Good." Ask me how I felt after my father died, and I said, "Sad."

The quashing of my feelings, even though I wasn't aware of it, gave me a tremendous sympathy with others whose ability to express themselves was repressed. Specifically, I took the victims of repression in the Soviet Union—a country full of people not allowed to speak freely—and unconsciously turned them into versions of myself. They were suffering a similar fate, they were also being silenced. I was naturally sympathetic to the great mass of Soviet citizens silenced by their government because I was an American, and Americans particularly don't like that. But for me, it became a double sympathy. My anger about the repression in my own house was neatly displaced onto the Soviet leadership that was busy choking off the free expression of these other victims half a world away.

After all, I couldn't go to war against my parents. But I could go to war against the Soviet Union. We were already at war against them. They were my enemies, and I was prepared to destroy them. It was oddly comforting to have an enemy, to have my fears, resentments, and desire for change coalesce around something external. As long as my problems were reimagined outside of myself, I knew what to do—what to read, what to say, what to think—how, in my own way, to fight.

There were other ways in which my childhood blossomed into my anti-Soviet politics. For example, my family buoyed itself up with an unspoken and mostly unconscious sense of superiority. If we didn't get bogged down in the wild world of emotions, this was because we had more stability and balance than other families. Other families were screaming, yelling, divorcing. Letting their kids take drugs and watch as much television as they wanted. They were often, as a family, watching television during dinner.

We were different. We were not swept away by unruly and dangerous emotions. We were morally sound, even unassailable. This sense of superiority fit with, and for me was sometimes indistinguishable from, the American sense of superiority in the world. This political superiority came naturally to me, since I knew it at home too.

As I stepped into adulthood, it made perfect sense for me to join the CIA. With my feelings unknown and inaccessible to me—kept secret from myself—I was naturally disposed toward a secret life. A secret organization, in fact, turned these traits into virtues. The more experienced you were at keeping secrets—the better you were at secrecy—the more valued and successful you were in an intelligence organization. The CIA was a beautiful and perfect metaphor for the hidden life I lived anyway.

This is, of course, all a story I'm telling myself, about myself. It isn't true or false. Or rather, its basic truth for me lies in the pieces of life I remember that the story is built out of. And also in its utility, its success at helping me understand my life and my world. This understanding came from a long series of insights, which are both ideas that turn themselves into feelings, and also way-stations on the path of change. The process of working with these insights led me to feel more deeply—it worked alongside the relationship with my therapist, which functioned as both a real and a practice relationship for building human connection—really I need a whole book here. I'm trying to focus on therapy as it related to my politics, and it's not allowing me to give therapy its due. But anyway, all of this led me to feel more deeply, which led to feeling better.

This is not a book about therapy (per se), but I'll describe my experience one other way, or really, borrow my friend John's description. When he said this, I wasn't sure if he was talking about me, him, us, or lots of people, but he said the process of growth and change is like having an exoskeleton that keeps your unformed, gelatinous self inside. Keeps it from spilling out. And then you build for yourself—you learn to grow—a regular skeleton. Your insides start firming up around it. Eventually, your new skeleton lets you stand up without needing the exoskeleton anymore.

As I cracked open bit by bit—as my exoskeleton fell away (slowly, never entirely), the impression of its ribs on my skin a permanent reminder of who I am—I felt better. I left behind the extreme secrecy I'd lived with not just at the CIA, but my entire life. I also started to slide away from the iron-clad political certainties of my youth, as I had moved away from other certainties about my family and myself.

Discovering the complexity of my own feelings also led me to the complexity of human feelings in general. If I was like this, so was everyone, in one way or another. We were all driven by a universe of feeling, all sometimes caught in tangles of our emotions with our thoughts and ideas. In this rich and complex universe, binary thinking lost its utility. It obscured the world instead of illuminating it.

It's hard to say more precisely how therapy affected my politics. My political views did not particularly flip or flop. But I came to understand that politics was emotionally based. That people's beliefs came from somewhere, and that it was all flawed, like everything else. I became a little less judgmental, a little less certain. (Was it this judgmentalism and overcertainty that my college professor had picked up on when she called me an asshole? Had she said what my friend Anthony was too kind to say a few years earlier?)

One day, midway through his illness, I was pushing my father through the grocery store in a wheelchair. It was a big trip for him, he rarely had the energy to go out. He seemed entranced by the symmetry and color of the products, and he commented on how beautifully the cereal boxes stretched out down the aisles. This was not his usual talk.

He asked me to slow down. Tired, irritable, in a hurry to go see my friends, I started passive-aggressively pushing the wheelchair so slowly that we were barely even moving forward. After a few moments, my father got the message and said, "Okay, okay, we can go now." I feel sad about this, sad that I did it, but I don't feel guilty. I do not hold myself responsible. What the fuck did I know? I was lost in my own tunnel of misery, struggling through a sorrow I couldn't name or discuss, or fully feel. When your own world is obscured like that, you behave in strange ways. You do nasty things. You don't have the tools to do anything else.

This is all relevant here. A self-aware politics aims to arrest our strange behavior before it happens. Or at least shortly thereafter. Knowing what you are feeling is a tool for living a full life, but do not sell it short as a tool for altering your behavior. For making it less weird.

Somehow despite all the new insights and feelings I got in therapy, despite my new appreciation for how my anti-Soviet views had formed, my monolithic view of the monolithic Soviet state remained intact. Part of this was, probably, the result of a partial turning away from the issue, of the Soviet Union no longer occupying a central place in my daily life and thoughts (not to mention no longer existing). There may also have been a certain laziness—having rethought so much, did I have to rethink this too? But most of all, I had spent so much time, so much life, earning my knowledge and beliefs about the Soviet Union—I did not want to let them go.

CHERKASHIN

Then, in 2004, a former KGB officer named Victor Cherkashin published a memoir called *Spy Handler*. Cherkashin had run two of the most devastating moles in the history of U.S. intelligence, CIA officer Aldrich Ames and FBI agent Robert Hanssen. It wasn't the stories in the book about Ames and Hanssen that grabbed me, though. It was Cherkashin's description of his KGB colleagues.

Many of these Soviet intelligence officers sounded just like me and my friends from the CIA. They were patriotic, loyal, and believed in their country. They had a high degree of integrity. They liked their work. And many, like Cherkashin, were friendly, social guys you'd want to have lunch with.

The CIA actually hired for this specific attribute, because outgoing, social types supposedly made for the kind of intelligence officer best suited to recruiting foreign agents. My friends and I at the agency were mostly gregarious, glad-handing, and extremely comfortable in social situations. People liked us, people wanted to be our friends. Our training program was almost a competition to out-outgoing each other. And yet it was genuine. We really were a positive, cheerful bunch.

So it made sense that the KGB also hired in part for these social qualities, since they also needed officers who would be able to go out and get foreigners to like and trust them, officers who could use their personalities to recruit spies. But the way Cherkashin described his colleagues still shocked me, because I'd assumed the KGB was looking for other qualities in its officers, like blind loyalty to the state and a capacity to be cruel. Although I had read serious accounts of the KGB and its activities, my sense of KGB officers themselves had been formed by reading James Bond books and perhaps even more by watching the Bond movies. The one who really stuck with me was Jaws, the giant, metal-toothed villain from *The Spy Who Loved Me*. Jaws wasn't actually in the KGB itself, but I remembered him that way, and I think it was this childhood vision that I internalized, slightly modified by a certain amount of more realistic information (I didn't think KGB officers were giants with metal teeth). Le Carré's villains were less overblown, but still rapacious and serving the dark cause. They were even more dangerous models for me, since they seemed so realistic.

By the time I joined the CIA, I knew to pay lip service to the idea that we had certain human qualities in common with KGB officers—they could also love their children—but I also knew they worked tirelessly against humanity, thus making them inhuman. For me, KGB officers never emerged as individuals in any way separate from the evil things their organization did.

In *Spy Handler*, they emerged. They became real people. Even the cynicism and careerism Cherkashin described, which seemed to affect a wider swath of KGB officers than CIA officers (though there are certainly cynical and careerist CIA officers), felt familiar, and human.

As I struggled with the new and discordant information in Cherkashin's book, I found myself thinking back to my meeting with Ilya in Leningrad, at this point almost twenty years earlier. I remembered his subscription to *Newsweek*, and how it had surprised me. Now other things about the scene started to bother me too.

Why was a twenty-two-year-old American being sent to smuggle gifts (the black-market Seiko, which I'd been instructed to hide carefully in my luggage) into the Soviet Union? Why was I being asked to face off against the dreaded KGB? And why was the KGB, for its part, so utterly uninterested in me? For that matter, why did the Soviet state allow me to meet with a refusenik in the first place?

All these years later, I finally understood what those warning bells had been trying to alert me to. I had seen with my own eyes that the post-Stalin Soviet Union was different from my own dark vision of it. It was a more open country than I realized, and repression there was not as pervasive and systemic as it was portrayed in the West.

Much of what I thought about the Soviet Union still seemed true. They had imprisoned people for their political convictions, put dissidents in mental institutions, tortured people who wouldn't recant their anti-state views (or views that weren't even anti-state, but simply pro–human rights).

None of this cruel and inhumane treatment of any portion of the population was morally defensible. But my sense of the Soviet Union as a country where everyone was miserable, suffering, repressed, and hostile to the political system now seemed off-base. That meant the fundamental formulation I'd used for labeling and understanding the Soviet Union—that it was an evil empire—just wasn't right.

EVIL EMPIRE

My deeply held conviction that the Soviet Union was an evil empire was a two-legged stool that eventually fell over. Still, the fact that it stood for so long on just two legs is a testament to the stubborn strength of those legs. One leg was built out of complex psychological forces, the other out of facts and logic. I have, and will continue to, ping-pong between these two sources of my conviction in an effort to demonstrate how they worked together to create something as powerful as an absolutist belief system.

Here, I'll focus on the psychological leg of the stool again, how my black-and-white vision of the Soviet Union sprang out of two specific issues in my personality. One, I was imbued with a sense of my own (and America's) superiority, which made me a more self-righteous, less empathetic person. And two, I had a desperate need to have enemies, bitter political foes I could fight with and could look down upon as the embodiment of everything I wasn't.

Let's start with my sense of superiority. I've already described the sense of superiority in my family, how our remove from our feelings made us believe we were better than people who were controlled by their emotions. It was important for us to be better than other people in this way because we thought you couldn't navigate the world while screaming, crying, and losing sight of reason.

Superiority, then, was necessary for survival in a complicated world. But you couldn't say you were superior, and more important you couldn't think it. That would be arrogant. So my own sense of superiority manifested as a belief that the United States was superior, that it was good and the Soviet Union was bad. (I was an American, so if America was better, so was I.)

I could easily prove this American superiority, because I saw the whole world through the lens of American virtues—freedom of expression, freedom of religion, democracy, all of our strengths. If those were the points of comparison, we beat the Soviets by a landslide. I wasn't exactly unaware of the extreme poverty in the richest country in the world, or of our murder rates, but I didn't count them in this particular debate.

I simplified the Soviet Union in the same way, but in reverse. I saw only its bad sides, while ignoring all of its good sides. I literally had no sense of any Soviet good sides. When Soviets themselves enumerated them, I believed they were either lying or deluded. So in the moral contest between the United States and the Soviet Union, the deck was stacked—it was our good sides versus their bad sides.

My relationship to the Soviet Union, then, was judger to judged. I was good (America was good). The Soviets were bad. I needed them to be bad in order to understand that I was good.

Mix all of that together, and I had an enemy. Something to hate. Something to define myself against. My need to make and retain enemies didn't just help me feel like a good and moral person, though. I also needed an enemy in order to feel passion, in order to have something to fight against. This gave my life clarity and purpose.

The whole thing fell apart if the enemy wasn't really, truly bad—if they had even a few fully human or relatable qualities. The enemy had to be evil. So I also dehumanized the Soviets (see earlier discussion of my intractable perception of KGB officers as something close to killer robots).

Where was my empathy? Where was my ability to relate to other human beings? They were wholly reserved for my enemy's victims.

I don't think my own psychology and worldview have any greater political significance. Unless—meaningless cog though I am, I represent a fairly substantial number of other cogs. I suspect this is, at least to some degree, true: that my own sense of superiority, and my need to make enemies, were both fairly common. Only the reader can say if they, too, were motivated by these factors, but I doubt I was alone. And I think these tendencies, in a collective way, helped to fuel the Cold War.

After all, the Cold War was a competition about who was better, us or them. As a nation, in word and policy, we systematically focused on Soviet failings and were blind to their virtues. President after president defined "them" as the enemy and used their flaws as a way to reflect American virtues back to us.

Is there a case to be made that this overpowering rejection of the Soviet Union was simply reality, that they actually were that awful, while we were that good? Is there any possibility our sense of superiority was justified? I used to justify it by focusing on the tremendous internal political repression in the Soviet Union, an area where we shone. We didn't have that kind of repression.

But did this really make us better than the Soviet Union, or just different? At least in the twentieth century, patterns of violence suggest that some countries tend to take their anger and aggression out on their own people, and some countries take it out on others. The Soviets had the Great Purge and the Gulag; we had Vietnam and a long list of other foreign countries that were devastated by our actions and policies. Although there were significant counterexamples for both the United States and the Soviet Union, the general pattern was that the Soviets tended to let their violence loose on their own citizens via significant internal repression, and we let ours out on other countries through foreign wars and military actions.

Was the scale of Soviet atrocities somehow bigger than the scale of American atrocities? Is this what justified our sense of superiority? How can you decide which was bigger, which was worse, between slavery and the Gulag? Between collectivization and the near-extermination of Native Americans? Between Afghanistan and Vietnam?

Still, wouldn't it have been better for the Soviets if their country had been a liberal democracy? Wouldn't a free press and the right to speak one's mind without risking prison have been obviously better? They could have asked the same about us. Wouldn't a Marxist America have avoided the catastrophe of slavery or, later on, embraced civil rights sooner and more fully?

If you still think we were "better" than the Soviet Union, I'd suggest that some of our own moral failings are simply on a different timeline from Russia's. Look at slavery compared to Stalin's atrocities against his own people, roughly a hundred years later (counting from the end of slavery). Or discrimination against gays in the United States decades ago versus discrimination against the LGBTQ community in Russia today. It's odd that we would be so judgmental, and consider them so awful, when we've been there too.

Neither country was innocent. But our constant judging of the Soviet Union, our need to declare ourselves the obvious winner in a moral competition, made us believe we were better. And this blinded many of us to our own flaws and weaknesses. All our judging actually made it harder to see ourselves. To understand that we were flawed and human too.

THROUGH THE FOG,
I SEE A COUNTRY

EIGHT THINGS I MISUNDERSTOOD
ABOUT THE SOVIET UNION

I f you didn't live through the first Cold War, it may be hard to understand how intensely I (and many other Americans) feared and hated the Soviet Union. It was a country as big and powerful as we were, but it stood for the opposite of everything we believed in. It was as if someone had designed a country specifically to threaten us on every level. The Soviets were strong enough to annihilate us, they were aggressive enough to challenge us everywhere, and they wanted to create a world based on the opposite of our most deeply held values.

My Cold War anti-Sovietism was built on the rock-solid certainty that the Soviet Union was an evil empire, but also on a firm belief that I completely understood this dangerous adversary. I had studied the Soviet Union carefully, and I could look at virtually any aspect of the country and see its rotten core. This was obviously valuable. You have to know your enemy.

But as a general rule, all of my knowledge, all of my certainty, had been built on very limited information. As a result, most of what I thought about the Soviet Union turned out to be skewed, confused, or only partially true. As I've said, my conviction that the Soviet Union was an evil empire was a two-legged stool, one leg psychological and one leg logical—the logical, fact-based leg was a series of profound misunderstandings about the Soviet Union, what it was and how it worked.

Picking apart these misunderstandings was a large part of how I eventually moved past my black-and-white way of seeing the Soviet Union. After I opened up psychologically, I dug in intellectually, used all the tools of reason and logic I'd spent my life developing. I never turned against reason and logic, even if I'd previously misused them to prove things to myself that I wanted to believe. My struggle has always been to integrate facts and logic with feeling and emotion, not abandon them.

I've chosen eight specific misunderstandings I had about the Soviet Union to look into here. I don't claim they were the only ones. But taken together, they represent most of what I was failing to see about the Soviet Union, and they also reveal the shaky foundation of my conviction that the Soviet Union was evil.

It's important to note that I am arguing here against my own misguided perceptions. When I write in the coming pages that the KGB, for example, was not an evil behemoth as much as a complex bureaucracy, not everyone thought it was an evil behemoth. My beliefs about the Soviet Union were always on the extreme side. But whereas the psychological issues behind my great hostility toward the Soviet Union may or may not have been common American issues, I feel more certain that the views about the Soviet Union in the following pages were widely shared. These were facts, ideas, and beliefs that I read, heard, and saw all the time. They circulated constantly in our culture. I was not alone in believing these things, and I was probably not in the minority, either. At least some of these ideas were also shared by many of those who played a guiding role in formulating American policy.

A self-aware politics requires not just examining where beliefs come from, but the sturdiness of any reassessment. I will poke and prod at my reassessment for the rest of this book—near the end, I will investigate it with a therapeutic buzzsaw—but it's also important to ask whether my reevaluation of the Soviet Union represents an overcorrection. Am I, this time around, seeing the Soviet Union through rose-colored glasses?

You will have to decide that for yourself. I know that my previous view kept me from anything approaching real understanding, and prevented me from responding thoughtfully to the challenges in our relationship with the Soviet Union. The facts and ideas I'll present in the coming pages, which I encountered mostly in the years after I read *Spy Handler*, burst my bubble. They do not disprove every last thing I had thought before, do not negate all previous facts. But they allowed me to start seeing the Soviet Union with greater depth and complexity.

Let's look at these misperceptions, one at a time, and see how they hold up to scrutiny without my old anti-Soviet bias, without a need to be superior to the Soviet Union. I'll begin by looking at the KGB, because it was a particular object of fascination for many of us, and because everything evil about the Soviet Union seemed to crystalize in the form of its dreaded secret police.

1. THE KGB WAS LESS AN EVIL BEHEMOTH AND MORE A LARGE, COMPLEX BUREAUCRACY

If the Soviet Union was an evil empire, the KGB was generally considered its cruelest instrument. At home, the KGB spied on everyone, tortured and imprisoned dissenters, and made sure the police state remained secure. Abroad, it spied on its enemies, never hesitating to lie, cheat, and steal to accomplish its goals. The consensus in the West was that it not only behaved this way abroad more often and in a less moral manner than its enemies, but it did so in the service of a brutal and unjust cause.

That's why I was confused when I read *Spy Handler* and found KGB officers who seemed like decent, likeable people, and who also liked the KGB. How could people like Cherkashin and his colleagues work for and believe in such an evil organization?

Here are some things I learned that helped me develop a more well-rounded understanding of the KGB, a complex organization that did some terrible things, but could also inspire the loyalty of decent people. (To clarify, I am writing about the post-Stalin KGB, my conclusions here do not apply to the NKVD, its infinitely bloodier predecessor.)

The KGB Was Not Corrupt

In a 2015 interview, Charlie Rose asked Vladimir Putin about charges by presidential candidate Marco Rubio that he was a gangster. Putin answered, "How can I be a gangster if I worked for the KGB? That simply has no basis in reality." My earlier self would have taken this for a cynical lie, and an almost comic one at that. And I suspect most viewers took it this way, both because the Western view of the KGB is wholly negative, and because it can be hard to distinguish between Putin's lies and his sincere comments. But by the time of this interview, I knew enough about the KGB to understand that Putin was referring to a real tradition of integrity and incorruptibility in the organization.

The party, the government, the military—all were notoriously corrupt in the Soviet Union (I am discussing only financial corruption here). Bribery was everywhere, a basic part of how the system functioned. But even in this environment, the KGB stayed fundamentally honest and largely uncorrupted. Former KGB officers who have written about their experiences, even defectors who turned against the KGB and the Soviet Union, describe a moralistic organization with both cultural and institutional protections against corruption. After the fall of the Soviet Union, when some Russian journalists were uncovering everything they could about KGB malfeasance, there was little sense of systemic corruption at the heart of the organization. Generally speaking, you could not bribe the KGB.

There were exceptions. Especially in the republics farther from Moscow, local KGB chiefs sometimes abused their authority, walking a line between taking bribes and something closer to extortion. Even in the capital, KGB officers used their influence to get the children of the *nomenklatura* (the Soviet ruling elite) into the best universities, and accepted gifts afterward (it's hard to say if this would even register as corruption in the Soviet Union, but if we're examining just how sparkling clean the KGB was, it needs to be mentioned). In the same vein, while abroad, KGB officers bought foreign goods and then sold them on the black market at tremendous profit back home, which was technically illegal but also a widely accepted practice among Soviets who traveled outside the country.

But overall there was much less corruption in the KGB than in other bodies of the Soviet system, and the organizational culture stressed professionalism and integrity. Decent people could work there and reasonably believe they were dedicating themselves to a fundamentally honest organization. For several years beginning in the early 1980s, the KGB even led a major anti-corruption drive in the Soviet Union. This effort stemmed from KGB Chairman (and later General Secretary) Yuri Andropov's often repeated, undoubtedly sincere, and reasonable belief that corruption was out of control and posed a serious threat to the entire Soviet project. Although primarily targeting the massive and powerful food trade organizations in Moscow, the anti-corruption drive was seen as a first step in taking on the broader nationwide corruption that was crippling the Soviet economy.

The KGB actually lost this multiyear struggle with the grocers, distributors, managers, and bureaucrats of the vast and powerful food-supply network and their widespread and corrupt allies throughout the party and state machinery. This was arguably a harbinger for how difficult it was going to be to reform the Soviet economy as a whole later on. The KGB's effort could almost be seen as a kind of early failed perestroika from the right (or the left? Right and left as terms become muddled in Soviet politics).

I will repeat frequently that I am not trying to whitewash, oversimplify, or glorify the KGB. I am trying to understand it, and to challenge the oversimplification that it was all bad. The KGB definitely wasn't seen as all bad inside the Soviet Union. Popular feelings were mixed. Some respected the organization, and there was broad-based support in later years for its attempts to take on corruption. Others hated the KGB, both for its extensive internal surveillance and its heavy-handed and sometimes brutal repression. Even true party believers, who shared most of the core values of the organization, often disliked and feared the KGB. It was too powerful, and there was always the chance it could come after you.

The KGB Spent Most of Its Time and Resources in a Bizarre and Self-Destructive Effort to Spy on the Soviet Population

It's hard to figure out exactly what the KGB's roughly 700,000 employees in the post-Stalin era did (this number may have been a few hundred thousand lower by the time the country collapsed). In the West, we generally focused on their brutal mistreatment of dissidents—outright torture, incarceration in psychiatric institutions, and forced treatment with psychotropic medications. These were horrible crimes and human-rights violations. But they only took up a small amount of the KGB's manpower and resources.

The KGB had an array of scientific research institutes, did analysis on foreign countries and the Soviet Union itself, guarded the nation's borders, protected the leadership, and of course handled foreign espionage. It's impossible to put an exact number on all of this, but the border troops were the largest contingent, at approximately 200,000. Foreign espionage may have taken up as few as 12,000 KGB employees (this was where Cherkashin worked). There were countless support staff—drivers, secretaries, and so on. At an estimated ratio of four non-officers to every officer in the KGB, that's still around 175,000 KGB officers out of the 700,000 we started with. For comparison's sake, the CIA and FBI combined probably have around 60,000 total employees today.

It's easy to understand how it took so many people to carry out the work of the secret police in Stalin's time. NKVD officers were constantly arresting people, killing people, and generally wrecking the country. But what were the secret police so busy doing in the post-Stalin era, and why did it take so many of them?

In all likelihood, the vast majority of the KGB's time and energy went into a kludgy, bureaucratic, self-defeating effort to spy on Soviet citizens. One estimate is that 220,000 KGB officers worked at running a vast network of informers throughout the country (so this would be slightly higher than the 175,000 officers in our other estimate). These officers had to find, recruit, meet with, and then write reports on their meetings with informants not only in major cities but every small city, town, and province in the country. The KGB also ran informants in virtually every factory, every military unit, and almost every other group or organization in the Soviet Union.

It's hard to know if all these meetings and all this report writing actually filled up the days in the lives of these officers. I find it easier to imagine them also sitting around for hours at their desks, wasting time like so many other Soviet workers. But regardless of how much time it took to run all these informers, the vast effort expended, the uselessness of almost all the information collected, and the mind-numbing work for the KGB officers who managed this network all attested to the stupidity and mediocrity of the enterprise.

Here's an example of how it worked, far removed from my fantasies of the all-powerful and evil KGB. Ken Alibek was a junior scientist in the massive, top-secret Soviet biological weapons program in the late 1970s. In his memoir *Biohazard*, he tells the story of how he developed a lab technique for weaponizing *Brucella*. His scientific work was a success, but he made a major bureaucratic error. Although he'd been given orders from his superiors in Moscow to undertake this project, he'd failed to inform the KGB detachment at his lab about what he was doing. This violated a regulation. He and his superiors were in trouble because of this oversight.

Alibek and a colleague were called to the regional KGB headquarters in Berdsk. The KGB commander there, meeting alone with

Alibek, asked him why he'd undertaken his project. When he said he'd been following orders, the KGB officer accused him of being a fascist, since fascists excuse killing people by saying they were following orders. The KGB officer got louder and louder. Finally, he said he could forgive Alibek, but that he needed his help. He explained it was in Alibek's favor that he'd just joined the party. Many of the other scientists at his lab hadn't joined the party, and as the officer explained, this meant the KGB didn't know what kind of people they were or if they had doubts about the Motherland. Alibek could help them figure this out.

Now Alibek understood what was going on. He stated out loud that the officer was asking him to be an informer. The officer responded no, more like an assistant. Alibek declined, and even mocked the officer slightly. The officer then said that Alibek would be sorry for thinking this was a joke. But in fact, this one meeting was the end of it. Alibek went on to have a meteoric rise, and ended up as deputy director of Biopreparat, the Soviet agency in charge of biological warfare.

The power to decline such offers without repercussions seems to have been the norm. In other cases I've heard or read about, KGB officers were sometimes more persistent, but there were rarely consequences for turning them down.

Instead, the KGB relied primarily on inducements to get people to cooperate. If you became an informant, you got certain benefits in return. A factory worker who agreed to inform on his fellow workers might get a promotion. Others might get a child into a preschool, or an apartment they'd been waiting for. Yevgenia Albats is a journalist who began writing about the KGB for the Soviet press in the early Gorbachev years. In her book *The State Within a State*, she tells about a waiter who wanted a job in a different restaurant, and was placed there the day he agreed to become an informer. In a poor society, where life was hard, these inducements were powerful enough that it was fairly common for people to volunteer to become informants.

Still, it wasn't all about inducements. Many people cooperated out of fear, not knowing they could turn the KGB down. And sometimes, the KGB did resort to threats. It was easy for them to ruin people's careers, or prevent them from traveling abroad (a serious problem for people whose jobs required foreign travel). They might threaten the same consequences for the family members of people resisting recruitment. The KGB officer who tried to recruit Alibek was using an implied threat of something even worse when he accused him of being a fascist.

How many informers were there in the Soviet Union? Albats interviewed former KGB officers who said the quota for an officer was to recruit two a year. One officer told her he'd recruited four or five a year, which apparently wasn't uncommon. Albats says that Eastern European services generally ran about 1 percent of their population as informants, and using that as a rough baseline, she suggests the Soviet Union may have had at least 2.9 million citizens reporting to the KGB. If several hundred thousand KGB officers working in this area were recruiting one to two new informers a year, even counting for attrition, it's easy to imagine getting to several million, so this figure makes sense.

Albats also points out that there was an entirely different category of Soviet citizen who cooperated with the KGB, called "reliable people." This was not a recruited informant per se, but someone whom the KGB had a more informal relationship with, and who was not compromised in the same way an informer was. "Reliable people" could be anything from a telephone operator to a plant director to someone who worked in a housing office or someone who was in charge of a personnel department. These people had friendly chats with the KGB as opposed to more formal meetings. Some reported to a superior at work who wasn't in the KGB, but who in turn passed their reports on to someone who was. "Reliable people" weren't paid. Many would have been surprised to find out the KGB formally labeled them this way. (The terms here can be confusing, because these "reliable people" were, of course, another kind of informant.)

Much of a "reliable person's" work consisted of writing up reports about people they worked with, and Albats suggests this could have seemed to many of them like part and parcel of ordinary life in the Soviet Union. Some also may have cooperated because there was no other way to advance in their chosen field, or in order to get permission to travel abroad (where they reported on foreigners they came in contact with).

One KGB source told Albats he believed the number of reliable people and informants together in the Soviet Union was close to 30 percent of the population, and another KGB officer told her it was as much as 60 to 70 percent of the population. Alibek, the bioweapons scientist, had a close friend in the KGB who had multiple supervisory positions, and ultimately rose fairly high in the organization. He once casually told Alibek that 1 in every 10 Soviet citizens unofficially reported to the KGB (let's assume he was talking about informers and reliable people together—everyone seems to agree that reliable people were far and away the larger category). Yet another estimate suggests that with about 220,000 KGB officers running informers, and each officer having a total of about twenty in their caseload, there had to be at least 4.5 to 5 million informers, or 3 to 4 percent of the country's adult population.

It's hard to know what to make of these estimates. The best I can do is this: I find the estimates of informants in the range of several million to be convincing. The estimates that informants and reliable persons together comprised 30 to 70 percent of the population are harder to evaluate, but the upper range at least seems dubious. Soviet bureaucracy could be absurd, but it wasn't fully dystopian—it's hard to believe the country had more informants than non-informants. Practically speaking, I also can't see how several hundred thousand KGB officers could have run or even maintained contact with 70 percent of the Soviet population of around 265,000,000 (taking a very rough average from the population of the 1970s and 1980s). Does this become a plausible number if you cut it in a little less than half to get to 30 percent of the population? Could 200,000 or so KGB officers have at some point recruited or compromised and then serviced 80 million informants and reliable people? That would mean each officer having roughly 350 unique meetings a year—if they met each of the informants/ reliable people only once a year. And that doesn't account for how they all got recruited or compromised in the first place. Maybe the level of reporting required of these informers was so low—possibly just telling their KGB officers almost anything they'd heard their fellow citizens say—that these kinds of numbers are possible. But I don't see it.

If you start shaving it down to around 10 to 20 percent of the population, it starts looking plausible to me. That's still a shocking number, but it's in keeping with the general sense that Soviet society was infiltrated by a vast number of informers.

I wouldn't put too much faith in my back-of-the-envelope math, though. I don't know how the KGB's actual procedures worked. And once you have several million informants in your society, and many millions more cooperating with the secret police in a somewhat less formal manner, it may not even matter if the total number is 15 million or 25 million or 50 million. Whichever the figure is, it's staggering.

You have to really imagine this whole enterprise to get it. This was a country physically much larger than ours, with a population roughly the same size. Hundreds of thousands of secret police officers were spread throughout the entire land, "recruiting" people from all walks of life who had literally nothing of value to tell them. Imagine this happening in your office, your club, your factory—happening everywhere. These informers had to report some gossip back to their KGB contacts, who in turn wrote it in files, where it rarely affected anything or was even noticed again. These tentacles were spread all through society, and everyone knew it, and everyone was used to it. But it was less a grand terror, less Orwellian, and more a stupid, dull waste—a vastly bloated bureaucracy making work for itself. (Obviously there were times when informants were more dangerous than this, especially when real regime opponents were more carefully targeted.)

When I say this effort was mostly stupid and bureaucratic, I'm not saying it was harmless. The secret police, as an agent of the state, turned against its own people, in the name of protecting the state from them. The effect on Soviet society was serious and profound, creating an entire culture where people knew they were being watched, knew there were informers in their midst. It was dangerous to speak openly in public. This undermined society in profound ways.

But it didn't exactly match my long-held perception of life in the Soviet Union. I thought that a steely net had been woven around a fully hostile population. But it was really a sad, ineffective net of informants undermining a population that wasn't particularly hostile to begin with.

The inner workings of this system were fairly well understood by at least some Western historians and experts on Soviet affairs. But the bureaucratic and almost pathetic part of the KGB that ran informers was given far less attention than the much smaller part of the organization that harassed, arrested, and sometimes tortured dissidents. It often seemed that the goal, conscious or unconscious, of mainstream Western media (television networks, prominent newspapers and magazines) and the particular scholars they interviewed or quoted was to portray an iron-fisted police state, not a complex, bumbling, self-destructive one.

As for the smaller part of the KGB—smaller in scope and resources—that grossly mistreated dissidents, it's worth taking a minute to consider their strategy and tactics. Post-Stalin, the KGB still had the repressive capacity to deal with dissidents much more harshly than they did—they knew who most of them were. They could have quickly rounded up almost every dissident and put them in jail, or killed them, or exiled them all to the provinces, anytime they wanted to. There just weren't that many dissidents in the country in the first place, probably numbering in the thousands, or even the hundreds for those most active in confronting the authorities.

As outlined earlier, the general assumption in the West was always that more extreme measures weren't taken to solve the dissident problem because the Soviet leadership was afraid of looking bad to the rest of the world. This likely was a part of the reason they didn't take comprehensively harsher measures against dissidents. But there were other possible explanations. When the dissident movement took shape in the mid-1960s, the Soviet leadership and the KGB were just a decade out of a period of horrible, brutal repression under Stalin, and there was clearly a need and a desire to be something different, to no longer be executioners at the head of a traumatized society. Or maybe the leadership and the secret police were trying to find a balance between avoiding that kind of Stalinist brutality while also retaining and using repressive powers they weren't sure they could survive without.

I read an interview with one former KGB leader who claimed the service was trying to protect the dissidents from Western intelligence services who were exploiting them, that it was not persecuting them for their beliefs. This is a startling claim, almost painful to hear in the way it distorts the truth. And yet it also hints at something in the worldview of the Soviet leadership that is worth understanding—they probably believed that the dissidents enjoyed certain basic rights under Soviet law, including the right to think freely. It wasn't that simple to just arrest them all, or throw them out of their apartments with their families, or exile all of them. I'd always assumed the authorities could do whatever they wanted in the Soviet system, but that wasn't quite true. Like all Soviet citizens, dissidents had the right to meet with each other, to meet with Westerners, even to meet with Western journalists. They could, even in the minds of the KGB and the leadership, express themselves to some degree without the consequence being immediate and automatic arrest.

But free thought couldn't be allowed to challenge or harm the state's interests. And so there were red lines in terms of what dissidents could say publicly, or say to Western journalists. These red lines weren't always clearly defined, but they weren't entirely muddy, either. When they were crossed, the likely penalties were very harsh, and could in some cases lead to torture and death (at some point along the way, dissidents were generally given an option to desist and recant in order to avoid severe punishment).

This is an important place to reiterate that I am in no way trying to minimize the cruelty of official Soviet repression against the country's dissidents. I'm trying instead to say that it didn't exactly match the vision of it I had as a cold warrior in the last decades of the Soviet Union's existence. The Soviet state was brutal and cruel to the dissidents. But there was a complicated push-pull between those in power and those fighting that power, laws that guaranteed some rights that were somewhat respected in certain ways, some official reluctance to employ the harshest levels of punishment and repression. Manuscripts, letters, reports of human-rights groups were regularly smuggled out of the country, all kinds of literature was smuggled in, dissidents in prison were able to get guards and visitors to carry letters and updates out into the Soviet Union, which then sometimes made their way out to the wider world. The repressive capacity existed to stop or at least substantially reduce all of this, with more extensive searches and harsher punishments, but it wasn't fully employed.

Instead, after Stalin, an odd kind of ecosystem developed that made dissidence extremely costly and dangerous, but usually survivable—in fact, most dissidents survived the system they were fighting against. They suffered, but they won a kind of victory without dying, which says something about the system they were fighting against. None of this is to excuse what the Soviet authorities or the KGB did, but to note that the system functioned according to certain norms, and to some degree rules and laws, and that as repressive and horrible as it was, it was less total, less repressive, less brutal, less murderous than I had imagined.

There's really no reason or specific evidence to believe that the authorities' reluctance to use all the repressive capabilities at their disposal was caused entirely by a fear of looking bad or harming their international reputation. Again, this was likely part of the reason, but the authorities' actions and words also suggest some level of humanity and underlying decency, perhaps. Their actions and words suggest those in power were not all good or all bad, that they were sometimes befuddled and uncertain what to do, that they were eager not to be Stalinist. In other words, the totality of what the KGB and party/state leaders did and said suggests they were a far cry from the total monsters I had thought they were.

I would add at least one more possible reason the KGB didn't take even harsher measures against all dissidents. The KGB was entrenched in a system, and their job in that system was dealing with the malcontents. What would they do if the problem was actually solved? What function would they serve? The KGB needed their enemies in order to be useful themselves.

The KGB's work against dissidents was distinct from, but also of a piece with, its main occupation of spying on the Soviet people. But it was that broader spying on the Soviet populace as a whole that had the greater effect, that constituted one of the Soviet Union's primary dysfunctions. We have our own comparable dysfunctions—comparable in scope, not in the particulars. What goes on in our cities' poverty-stricken neighborhoods, for example. How the richest country in the world allows such suffering, violence, and inequality to exist. Or maybe the recurrent mass shootings of children in our schools, and our inability to respond effectively. Maybe these dysfunctions will eat us up, as the Soviet Union's dysfunctions destroyed them. Maybe not.

KGB Officers Had a Wide Range of Feelings About Their Work

I read a story somewhere (unfortunately I cannot remember where) about a KGB officer who was leading the interrogation of a Soviet dissident. When he ran into a colleague in whatever the KGB version of their break room was, he told him that he had to send the dissident to a mental hospital, when he knew even better than the man himself that everything he was saying about Soviet society was true (as a KGB officer he had better access to the real facts about Soviet society than most citizens). He was so disheartened by what he was doing that he was being driven to alcoholism. (We used this story more or less verbatim in an episode of *The Americans*, a TV show I created about KGB officers living undercover in the suburbs of Washington, DC, in the 1980s.)

Not everyone who worked at the KGB was a bad person. There were officers there who did terrible things, those who did good things, and probably a great many who would be best described as cogs in the vast bureaucracy. Some of these officers clearly had a sense their work was problematic, and some believed in it wholeheartedly as a way to protect their society. In a sense, this is obvious, because the KGB was in reality a fully rounded, three-dimensional secret service.

The KGB's Foreign Arm Was Not Particularly Brutal

The KGB's foreign intelligence service recruited foreign agents to spy on its rivals (and allies), and engaged in widespread propaganda efforts. It recruited agents with an eye toward political intelligence, just like the CIA, and was also focused on finding agents who could help it steal technology, which it needed to help the backward Soviet economy.

Despite its fearsome reputation, the KGB only engaged in widespread murder abroad during wartime. For the KGB, this meant Afghanistan, where they carried out targeted killings. It's not unusual for intelligence agencies to become more violent during wartime. During Vietnam, the CIA coordinated the Phoenix Program, a counterinsurgency campaign against the Viet Cong that used targeted assassinations as a tool, and more recently, the agency engaged in targeted assassinations as part of the war on terror.

The KGB Was Fairly Permissive with Western Visitors

The original warning bell that tried to alert me I was misunderstanding something basic about the Soviet Union came during my meeting with the refusenik in Leningrad whose physical and emotional condition didn't match what I expected. When I eventually came to reevaluate this encounter, among the things I wondered was why I'd been so blithely sent off to smuggle contraband into the Soviet Union. No one would have asked me to bring drugs into Turkey.

As noted earlier, I went to the Soviet Union in the summer of 1988, three years into Gorbachev's tenure as general secretary. Things were loosening up, and although the Soviet state and the KGB were still conducting some operations against refuseniks and dissidents, the pace and severity of these operations was quickly diminishing. Still, much of the official permissiveness I saw on that trip actually went back a long time. Western visitors had been meeting with refuseniks and dissidents throughout Brezhnev's, Andropov's, and Chernenko's time in power, usually without being thrown out of the country. Many Westerners—journalists and academics—were in fact allowed to travel, live, work and study in the Soviet Union. For the most part, no one ever laid a hand on them.

That doesn't mean no visitors were ever harassed. According to Alex Hazanov, a historian and expert on how the KGB treated foreign visitors to the Soviet Union, a fair number of Westerners who visited refuseniks in the 1970s and '80s were spied on, especially those meeting with leaders of the movement. Some members of the intelligentsia formed friendships with Westerners, and then informed on them to the KGB. Visitors could find themselves arguing in the street with apparently concerned citizens who were in fact KGB plants. In a more threatening vein, visitors were occasionally assaulted by men the police would later claim were "hoodlums," but who had in fact been instructed to carry out the attacks.

And sometimes Westerners were kicked out of the country, even forced to appear in crude propaganda in the Soviet media before leaving.

For the majority of Westerners, who were not kicked out, this harassment was what they talked about when they came back home. I remember reading countless stories, both when I was growing up and later when I was immersed in Soviet studies, about journalists and other travelers being followed by the KGB, experiences they recounted almost as badges of honor. But few of these stories ended with anything that could be termed serious harassment, which was rare compared to the overall number of Western travelers to the Soviet Union.

The Westerners themselves, though, usually saw any permissiveness by Soviet authorities as self-serving. They believed official concerns about bad publicity and world opinion explained any instances of less brutal or repressive behavior. Hazanov suggests something slightly different—that the Soviets allowed so many Westerners to visit because they needed the cash that visitors brought into the economy, and because the state was dependent on technological and scientific exchanges to gather information and know-how. All of these explanations for Soviet permissiveness were probably at least partially true.

And we certainly shouldn't get carried away in feeling grateful for Soviet permissiveness toward Western visitors to their country. The real harassment was saved for Soviet citizens themselves. Refuseniks and dissidents were monitored closely by the KGB, and meeting with Westerners, even though it wasn't illegal, was dangerous. If Soviet citizens created other problems—for example, by distributing political leaflets, or sending letters protesting against the state to the West—then meeting with Westerners, particularly journalists, could be used as evidence of anti-Soviet agitation and propaganda and added to the list of crimes if they were arrested and tried.

The KGB Was Not That Different from the CIA

When I was first starting to think about politics as a teenager, if someone suggested the United States acted just as badly at times as the Soviet Union did, usually someone would shout, "Moral equivalence!" at them. "Moral equivalence" meant you were making a logical and moral error by comparing anything the Soviet Union did with anything we did. Since our motives were good, and theirs were bad, even identical actions were not "morally equivalent."

People used the charge of moral equivalence in the new genre of aggressive, pundit-fueled talk shows on TV. I heard it at home, where my generally broad-minded father sometimes used it. I can't exactly say my peers were attacking each other with cries of "moral equivalence" in the schoolyard, but it almost felt that way.

The problem is that the brain naturally compares like this. When you criticize another country for something they've done, your brain wants to consider what you do that's similar. This mechanism helps you look at yourself and think, Hey, if what the other country is doing is so bad, maybe we shouldn't be doing it either. Or conversely, it can make you realize, if you're also doing something that they're doing, maybe that thing isn't so bad after all.

The idea that almost anything a democracy does is okay, but if a communist country takes almost identical actions it's not okay, made little sense. Just as it made little sense when the Soviets claimed they could do anything because they were fighting for communism, and we were wrong to take similar actions in the name of democracy (or as they saw it, capitalism and imperialism). Moral equivalence (or in today's arguments "whataboutism") is just another fancy way of saying we're the good guys and they're the bad guys.

It's easy to see where the idea of moral equivalence comes from. We have frequently used the same brutal methods and techniques for acting in the world that other countries use, but it's hard to face this. So we came up with the idea of moral equivalence to defend ourselves against our own brains, which are saying, "Wait a minute."

Honestly comparing our behavior with that of other countries is in fact the best and most obvious way to see ourselves clearly and accept that we, too, are deeply flawed. It's also the best way to get perspective on the KGB.

So let's compare.

The CIA has a long history of politically and morally questionable acts. But it's hard to argue that any are as bad as its torture of terrorism suspects in the mid-2000s. When I was younger, the United States was able to clearly and easily set itself apart from nations that engaged in torture. Throughout the Soviet era, the fact that the KGB used torture was one of the reasons we considered them evil. Now we were doing it.

Current figures suggest 119 people went through secret CIA prisons. About 20 percent of them had no ties to terrorism. There were cases of mistaken identity, bad intelligence, simple soldiers from the battlefield who had the bad luck to end up in CIA custody, mentally ill foreign fighters, very young foreign fighters. About a third of these people were clearly tortured (including at least one man who was arrested by mistake and had no connection at all to terrorism or the wars being fought at the time). They weren't all waterboarded, but they were beaten, subjected to sleep deprivation, bathed in ice water. They were caused grievous and intentional suffering.

The CIA did this. But it is also a well-meaning organization dedicated to protecting the national interest, and full of decent people. It contained people who would torture other people, and others who were strongly opposed to that torture. These people coexisted with each other, worked together, and stayed loyal to their organization, despite having such profound differences.

As for the CIA bureaucracy, it allowed torture, accepted it, and when it was over, would not turn against those individuals who carried it out.

If you want to understand the KGB, you can look at the CIA to see that an intelligence organization can torture people and it doesn't mean the entire organization is evil, it doesn't mean everyone who works there is bad.

This is not a perfect analogy. Torturing terrorists—or people you think are terrorists—isn't exactly the same as torturing dissidents. And although it was surely low in both cases, I don't know exactly what percentage of the CIA workforce participated in torture, or how it compared to the percentage of the KGB workforce that participated in torture.

But if we look only at the horrible things done by the KGB, it's the same as looking at the CIA and only seeing the people who carried out torture or took other morally compromised actions, like overthrowing foreign governments. To be consistent, if we choose to see only the terrible things the KGB did, we should look only at the terrible things the CIA did too. But if we see the CIA as complex, with good and bad sides, we have to do it for everyone.

I'm not sure either the CIA or KGB ever struggled enough with what they'd done. It is fair to say that the NKVD, along with Soviet society as a whole, did struggle with the nightmarish brutalities of Stalinism, and despite mixed results, the KGB at least emerged a much less brutal organization. Likewise, our society struggled with what the CIA did in the war on terror, and we did put a stop to it, though many continue to argue it was acceptable and necessary, and President Trump actually publicly encouraged more torture. Perhaps a fuller reckoning will come in time.

I have pointed out previously that much of the KGB's work, rather than protecting the Soviet Union, was actually self-defeating, and did a tremendous amount to undermine the state. For example, running such a vast number of informers surely made the populace feel that it wasn't trusted by the authorities, which in turn must have undermined faith in the party and government. My friends and former colleagues in the CIA, whom I like enormously, are also engaged in work that I believe is largely, though not entirely, self-defeating for our country. The damage done by the KGB was principally directed inward, against the Soviet people. The damage done by the CIA is mostly directed outward, focused on foreign countries, where it recruits spies to produce secret intelligence supposedly of value to the U.S. government. But the damage is ultimately done to us too. I believe that most (not all) secret intelligence collected by the CIA is of little value (more on this later). But the suspicion and anger created around the world by CIA espionage, both among foreign governments and foreign populations, has fueled worldwide resentment of the United States. CIA spying, along with covert actions that have undermined and toppled governments, are obviously not the sole cause of this resentment, but they are major contributing factors.

This spying represents both the heart and soul, and a significant percentage of the work, done by the CIA. There is other positive and important work done by the agency—counterterrorism operations that have prevented acts of terror, analysis that has helped our leaders understand the world and formulate policy. But espionage is the bread and butter of the CIA. Some of it may be useful sometimes. But it is a mistake to take it on faith that the successes and benefits of espionage outweigh the enormous damage it does.

On balance, the CIA and KGB were in many ways more similar than different. Both were large organizations that did many different things. They both inspired the loyalty of good and decent people, who worked to protect a state they believed in. And they both had their share of cynics, careerists, people who just needed a job, and people whose feelings about the organization they worked for were complex and could change over time.

Other Views of the KGB Shouldn't Be Dismissed

There is a completely different way of looking at the KGB, essentially a more sophisticated version of the idea that the KGB was an evil behemoth. In *The State Within a State*, Yevgenia Albats argues that the massive and pitiless violence unleashed and nurtured by the Russian Revolution corrupted a generation of people, and then was passed on to those who came after. The words and deeds of Lenin and his cohorts were so brutal that young people at that time, including the ones who would become Stalin's interrogators and executioners, grew up without a moral compass, without a sense of right and wrong. All they saw during the revolution itself, the civil war, and the period after was brutality and killing. Naturally they repeated it, with the NKVD as the primary tool. The KGB modified but hardly shook off this legacy.

Albats makes a strong case, which I'm oversimplifying. I don't entirely disagree with her argument about the KGB's predecessor, the Stalin-era NKVD. It explains much of what went on in that era, and the psychology of many of the interrogators. But it doesn't explain everything. Although the secret police would never be able to separate itself from the legacy of what it did under Stalin, the KGB was not the same as the NKVD. The level of brutality carried out by the post-Stalin KGB was vastly reduced, a consequence of titanic social and political changes in Soviet society, and perhaps of a latent decency and humanity inside the secret police. A new generation of officers came in, and it was now possible for a large share of them to be good and decent people.

Albats doesn't see the KGB this way. For her, it was an all-powerful organization that fought its way to the pinnacle of Soviet power, and then did whatever it had to in order to remain there. She believes the KGB was responsible for Khrushchev's ouster as well as Gorbachev coming to power. She notes how high party officials moved in and out of the KGB, and concludes that they remained creatures of the organization even after they left it and were serving in influential party posts. Her belief in the KGB's power and influence on society then, and the Russian intelligence service's power and influence now, knows almost no limits.

It's hard to come up with an analogy to help understand this way of looking at the Soviet Union and Russia. Maybe we could think about the way some people view corporations in America as all-powerful. They point to the money corporations give to politicians, and the way people move between corporate jobs, lobbying, and government. Is it possible that, behind the scenes, these people, essentially always representing their corporations, exert so much influence that they're responsible for most legislation? That their hand in choosing presidential candidates is ultimately decisive?

Whether you believe that corporations have thoroughly corrupted our system or not, we can probably agree that they are a huge power base in our country. They wield their power largely for their self-interest, and while wielding this power, many in corporations probably think they're doing it for the nation's own good. They believe that healthy and wealthy corporations are good for the economy, which is good for the nation.

We can probably say all these same things about the KGB. It was a huge power base, it wielded its power in part for its own self-interest, and many people who worked there believed this self-interest was synonymous with their nation's interests. But we can still question if the KGB's power was so broad-based that the organization became the ultimate power in Soviet society. The same holds true for the current Russian security services, often considered to be secretly running Russia.

However we assess the KGB's power, there is no question that it was used in part to spread fear and intimidate people. Former KGB officers and current Russian intelligence officers (as well as anyone in any security service in the world) would do well to read Albats's book and listen to her simple and plaintive cry that they are frightening her. They should accept her general assessment of the damage they're doing, and modify their behavior accordingly. If KGB officers and leaders had listened to the many available critiques of their behavior earlier, they might have saved the Soviet Union (it would have taken a lot to save the Soviet Union, but the secret police radically redefining how to protect the country might have played a role).

I Might Have Joined the KGB

Once I started to see these different sides of the KGB—it had a certain integrity, officers had a range of feelings about their work and the organization, it was in many ways similar to the CIA—I found myself wondering if I would have joined the KGB if I'd been born in the Soviet Union. After all, if KGB officers like Cherkashin weren't that different from me, couldn't I have ended up in the KGB the same way I ended up in the CIA?

Aleksandr Solzhenitsyn runs a version of this same thought experiment in *The Gulag Archipelago*. He says it wouldn't have been that hard for someone like him to wind up in the NKVD, which recruited at the regional technical schools that people like him went to. Although no one was forced to join, there were many advantages, and some pressure was applied. Students also knew very little about the secret police and everything that was wrong with it. At this early stage in a person's life, Solzhenitsyn thought it took a certain force of will and intuition to resist them. If a young man did join, Solzhenitsyn believed a series of almost ordinary decisions they would make in the course of their work at the NKVD could turn a perfectly decent person into a brutal interrogator.

Solzhenitsyn sees how almost anyone could have ended up both joining the secret police and then engaging in its worst behavior. I suspect my particular psychology might have predisposed me to join the secret police if I were a Soviet citizen. Although I thought I joined the CIA to fight against totalitarianism, I now think I was there less because of politics and more because I unconsciously wanted to live a secret life, to be in a secret society that fought against a hated enemy. That may have held true whoever the enemy was, in whatever country I was born in.

I'm not dismissing the idea that I might have been a dissident in the Soviet Union, or perhaps most likely of all, just kept quiet and tried to fit in. Growing up Jewish in the 1970s in the Soviet Union might have extinguished any desire for a secret life serving the state. But the idea that I might have ended up in the KGB doesn't seem preposterous to me. These are my people. I was only in the CIA for three and a half years. I'm not trying to lay claim to a long and meaningful career there, but this is who I was until I was almost thirty years old. It's who I was really from a very young age—a person full of secrets. Someone who was muddled up in that way. Yes, I was (and am) also a believer in freedom—freedom of speech, freedom of conscience. That's why I always had such a strong feeling for Soviet dissidents. But I was also a member of a secret service. I have a great sympathy with others who followed this path—no matter what they did, or what country they served.

If you're inclined to dismiss my chances of getting into the KGB because I'm Jewish, it's worth noting that although there were very few open Jews in the KGB, there were Jews. Often they took the name of their non-Jewish parent, but everyone still knew they were Jewish. By identifying as Russian, at least on the surface, they showed they were trustworthy—they weren't going to support Israel or embarrass the state by sticking up for the Jews.

There were also at least some openly Jewish officers in the KGB in the later Soviet period (or at least one). My friend Sergei relayed a story he heard about a Communist Party conference at the KGB in 1978. At the beginning of the conference, someone read out details about the participants. Out of 800 delegates, about 600 were Russians, more than fifty were Armenians, and so on. And then the speaker read out that there was one Jew (an open and official Jew, that is). The man, whom everyone knew and liked, stood up and bowed as everyone applauded.

Of course, the need for most Jews to even partially hide their identity indicates some broad level of anti-Semitism in the KGB. But this wasn't necessarily the personal and broad anti-Semitism we tend to assume was prevalent in the Soviet Union. It was more likely the complex, multilayered, partly institutional kind of anti-Semitism that was hardly unique to the Soviet Union, and which I'll discuss now in detail.

2. THE SOVIET UNION WAS NOT AS ANTI-SEMITIC AS MANY OF US THOUGHT

With the exception of rabidly anti-Semitic states like Nazi Germany, it is difficult to assign a value to a country's level of anti-Semitism— to determine that country A is not anti-Semitic, country B is somewhat anti-Semitic, and country C is very anti-Semitic. State anti-Semitism is a combination of official policies, societal attitudes, specific incidents, and unwritten rules. It is both concrete and ab-stract, and far too complex most of the time, to allow for easy labels.

This section, then, is not meant to determine whether the So-viet Union was an anti-Semitic state, or to quantify precisely how anti-Semitic it was. Rather, I will review the history of the Jews in the Soviet state, look at official policy toward the Jews, consider specific incidents and widespread attitudes, and compare it all to my judgments about Soviet anti-Semitism at the time (and here again I will argue that my opinions represented those of a fairly broad swath of the American public, as well as most of the political elite). I will also compare anti-Semitism in the Soviet Union to anti-Semitism in the United States. None of this will answer the question of exactly how anti-Semitic the Soviet Union was. But it will, hopefully, demonstrate that many of us made judgments that were off-base, and that a different way of evaluating anti-Semitism in the Soviet Union can reveal deeper truths about both that coun-try and our own.

I would summarize my early education in Soviet history, vis-à-vis the Jews, this way: For some mysterious reason, there were a lot of Jews in powerful positions in the early days of the Soviet Union. Stalin got rid of most of them, and near the end of his life, afraid that Jews were conspiring against him, railed against a 'Doctors' Plot' of imagined Jewish assassins. Before he could purge countless

Jews on this pretext, he died, thank God. But in subsequent years, the Soviet Union remained very anti-Semitic, never letting Jews into positions of power again, and repressing them in all sorts of ways, culminating in the plight of the refuseniks. It was both the leadership of the Soviet Union and the Soviet (or at least Russian) people themselves who were anti-Semitic.

It was easy to believe all of this because it accorded with certain moral and political assumptions about the Soviet Union. The main knocks on the "evil empire" were that it put people in jail for speaking their minds, sent dissidents to psychiatric institutions for opposing the government, didn't let people leave the country, prohibited the free exercise of religion, et cetera. Obviously a country like that was also going to be inherently and viciously anti-Semitic. It went with the territory. Even a cursory look at the history—and particularly a cursory look at the history—made it clear Russians had always been anti-Semitic anyway, long before the Russian Revolution. Jews had been slaughtered in pogroms, confined to the Pale of Settlement. This type of anti-Semitism didn't just go away—naturally it had carried over into the Soviet Union.

Where exactly did this version of the history of the Jews in the Soviet Union come from? I studied Soviet history, but I never took a class in the history of Soviet Jews specifically, so my teachers never did more than touch on the topic. In the more general classes I took, when it would have been normal to wonder why so many Jews were active in the revolution, or why Stalin helped arm the Jews who were fighting to establish the state of Israel, I never dug deeper. The answers to these questions were not secrets hidden in the archives, only to be revealed after the fall of the Soviet Union. They were out there. I could have started to question these assumptions after I first met a refusenik in Leningrad living relatively comfortably, or at least living very differently from how I'd expected. But there was a political fog keeping my curiosity from being piqued—I wanted the Soviet Union to be simply and clearly anti-Semitic.

Let's briefly review the history of the Jews in the Soviet Union—or rather touch on some key points and trends in that history—without the assumption of rabid anti-Semitism I carried with me in my earlier studies. We'll examine both official state ideology and policy, and popular societal attitudes, which are intertwined in enormously complex ways.

Considering the long history of violent, brutal anti-Semitism in Russia and Ukraine, Jews would've been crazy not to support the Bolshevik revolution. Bolshevik ideology, clearly articulated in the writings of its early leaders, strongly condemned prejudice based on ethnicity. The revolutionary movement was openly friendly to Jews, as it was to women and oppressed groups in general. It served in many ways as a kind of liberation movement. In his masterpiece *The Jewish Century*, historian Yuri Slezkine argues that this liberation was more than political, it also allowed young Jews in the shtetl who joined the Bolshevik cause to rebel against the backwardness of their parents and against the confines of Judaism itself, to rebel toward modernity. (The revolution had a similar effect on many non-Jewish peasants too.)

The Bolshevik egalitarian ethic wasn't just expressed in words and ideas, it was concrete. Pogroms—organized riots and massacres against Jews—were common in the Russian Empire, and were still taking place sporadically during the Russian Civil War that followed the revolution, mostly carried out by the whites who opposed the Bolsheviks (but in some cases by the Red Army). But within a few years after the end of the war, the Bolsheviks had put an end to this practice, after centuries of organized violence against Jews in Russia condoned or ignored by the state. We should think of the Soviets as the government (or the Bolsheviks as the party) that ended pogroms.

Jews were such devoted and militant Bolsheviks that quite a few of them joined the Cheka, the secret police organization formed shortly after the revolution. The Cheka used a deliberate strategy of hiring Jews in Ukraine and sometimes Russia to use against state enemies that the Jews would consider anti-Semites. Tapping into this well of anger in oppressed and victimized minorities gave the Cheka more reliable personnel to carry out the extreme levels of violence it employed in its work. The Cheka used Latvians against their common enemies to similar purpose. When victims of oppression are given power in this way, they're often doubly reviled in the end. People have fixated for years on why there were as many Jews as there were in the Cheka, and scapegoated them for the horrible excesses of the secret police.

In the same vein, the state used Jews in the early 1920s to carry out confiscations of church property, which the famed Russian writer Maxim Gorky claimed was a deliberate use of anti-Semitism to divert anger away from the Bolsheviks and onto the Jews. The final Russian pogroms took place in several towns after these confiscations.

This was a complicated dance, to say the least. The state protected and advanced Jews, but sometimes used them in ways that increased popular anti-Semitism. Although a low percentage of Jews were Bolsheviks, a high percentage of leading Bolsheviks were Jews, which also played into anti-Semitic prejudices in the country. Trotsky was probably the most visible target of this anti-Semitism, although people who actually knew and worked with him seemed to dislike him primarily because he was arrogant, not because he was Jewish.

The complicated mix of state tolerance intersecting with popular anti-Semitism continued into the mid-1920s. For example, many of the traders who thrived under Lenin's New Economic Policy (which I'll discuss in more detail later) were Jewish, and this led to some overt anti-Semitism, at times actively fueled by lower-level party officials.

Still, beginning after the revolution and continuing as Lenin's rule gave way to Stalin's, an enormous number of Jews who were discriminated against and couldn't get an education in Tsarist times were now able to go to university. They were part of a broader mass movement of poor people who were picked up and brought into the higher echelons of society by Soviet power. They advanced immeasurably in the early years of Stalin's reign, and in many ways integrated into the mainstream of Soviet society.

Early on, Stalin himself spoke out clearly and convincingly against anti-Semitism, following the Bolshevik line but using language that felt personal and real. He seems in private to have occasionally made anti-Semitic remarks, and sometimes to have made fun of Jewish mannerisms and the way Jews talked. By itself, in the context of the time, this anti-Semitism may have indicated little more than a mild prejudice. In general, I'm not a big fan of excusing abhorrent attitudes and behavior because they were common at a certain historical time. There were always some people who knew better. And if you weren't one of them, you should take the rap. Still, historical context is useful when trying to understand the role prejudice may have played in a particular person's life.

Robert Conquest, one of the earliest and most renowned chroniclers of Stalin's terror, says that overt persecution of Jews was not allowed during the first part of Stalin's rule. But he suggests Stalin was an anti-Semite, his prejudice based on ideology, not race. In other words, the problem with Jews wasn't that they were Jews, it was that they were bourgeois, or religious, or Zionist, or active in the Bund (a Jewish socialist party).

In the late 1920s, Stalin created Birobidzhan, an ostensible Jewish homeland in the Soviet far east near the Chinese border (later the administrative center of a larger Jewish Autonomous Region). I won't go into the fascinating history of this place, which never became anything remotely resembling the kind of national home that federal republics were for some other nationalities. Suffice it to say, Birobidzhan did not prosper or become a true Jewish republic.

A long and brutal period of increased political violence began in the Soviet Union in the 1930s. Over the next decade, Stalin murdered many of the Jews who were among the original leaders of the revolution, and killed or replaced others who rose high in the party/state apparatus after the revolution. The victims included Leon Trotsky, Grigory Zinoviev, Lev Kamenev (half-Jewish), Genrikh Yagoda (who converted to Christianity), and Maxim Litvinov (who was re-placed but not killed). But these men were probably not targeted because they were Jewish. Stalin's main problem with Zinoviev and Kamenev was that they threatened his absolute power, not that they were Jews. The same was true for Trotsky, whom Stalin hated for many reasons. Stalin continued to have many close associates who were Jewish, and he didn't seem to have problems with them, or at least not problems related to their Jewishness.

Stalin's anti-Semitism was complex, then, and not clearly much of a driving force. In his early years in power, he may even have been less prejudiced than much of the Soviet population, in which con-siderable latent anti-Semitism remained. Latent because Russia's more blatantly anti-Semitic history had been in a sense cut off by the revolution and the communist/Marxist belief in equality. But during the Second World War, the older and more vicious kind of anti-Semitism returned. In historian Timothy Snyder's book *Black Earth*, he writes a devastating account of Soviet citizens' collab-oration in the Holocaust on Soviet territory during the German occupation. Traditionally, it was thought that the Germans did most of the dirty work of killing Jews inside the Soviet Union, but Snyder has unearthed a sad and brutal story of active participation, largely by Ukrainians, Belarusians, and people from the Baltics, but also every other nationality present in Nazi-occupied areas of the country, including Russians.

Is this collaboration a story of Soviet anti-Semitism, though? I don't mean to split hairs. In one way, of course it is—Soviet citi-zens were assisting in genocide. But everything being done to the Jews was anathema to Soviet ideology and practice. It never would have happened and nothing like it ever did happen to the Jews on Soviet-controlled territory. The Holocaust on non–government controlled Soviet territory during World War II was enabled by the reemergence of old forms of anti-Semitism in disparate peoples, and was not fed or created by any specifically Soviet anti-Semitism promulgated by the party or the leadership.

Ronald G. Suny, a historian and early proponent of seeing Soviet society in more nuanced terms, makes the point that the Soviet Union ended the Holocaust. A fair number of Western historians have long pointed out that the Soviets don't get the credit in the West they deserve for their outsized role in defeating the Nazis. But the fairly obvious corollary that they were responsible for ending the genocide against the Jews had never occurred to me. It's a fair point. When the Soviets beat the Nazi army off Soviet soil and then back through Eastern Europe, it ended the Holocaust. The Red Army discovered and freed the survivors from the death camps along the way—in his book *Bloodlands*, Snyder points out that the most frequently circulated Western photographs suggest it was American forces that accomplished this, but in fact the Allies only liberated Nazi concentration/work camps. These camps were so horrible it was probably hard to imagine there were even worse camps, but in fact there were death camps dedicated solely to extermination, and every one of these was liberated by Soviet forces (along with the cities, towns, and forests where mass shootings of Jews took place). It's true that ending the Holocaust wasn't the motive for the Soviets to fight, but does that matter? It was a crucial side-effect of a huge and unimaginably costly and virtuous battle waged by the Soviet people and the Soviet authorities, in which the country suffered staggering losses. Why shouldn't they get credit for it?

At the end of the war, probably the most blatantly anti-Semitic period in Soviet history began. A campaign launched during the war to get Jews out of sensitive positions in the state apparatus now spread to other institutions. This was likely fueled by Stalin and powerful elements in the state bureaucracy feeling that Jews had too many connections abroad and couldn't be trusted. Information about Jewish heroism during the war was suppressed, with many Soviets claiming that Jews were the first to flee to the rear and the last to go to the front. With official state practice no longer acting as a check on anti-Semitism, and in fact now with official encouragement, this grassroots anti-Semitism spread quickly. According to historian Vladislav Zubok, this widespread anti-Jewish feeling was also a part of a broader Russian nationalist movement. Russian nationalism was, by definition, xenophobic and against any non-Russians. It made it harder for many non-Russians to believe in communist internationalism, and alienated them from the state.

A few years after the war ended, a wave of even more blatant quasi-official anti-Semitism began. The Jewish Anti-Fascist Committee, a group formed to agitate for Soviet policy and interests during World War II, was secretly attacked, and later destroyed. Various Jews in official and quasi-official positions were publicly attacked as "cosmopolitans," which became a code word for Jews. Even more Jews were expelled now from jobs and various institutions, including positions in the state/party bureaucracy, where they were replaced with Russians. The authorities never came out and directly attacked "Jews." But the revolutionary stand against racism and anti-Semitism had always battled a popular strain of anti-Semitism, and now the balance was shifting, with Stalin on the wrong side.

This anti-Semitic wave became worse in 1948, when Golda Meir arrived in the Soviet Union as the ambassador from the new state of Israel. She was met by tens of thousands of Jews in the streets when she visited a synagogue. Stalin, who was already suspicious of everyone—that was who he was—felt this meant Jews were not loyal. According to historian Joshua Rubenstein, Stalin had known he could trust Jews against Hitler, but what about in the new Cold War?

In 1953, near the end of Stalin's life, the media became brazenly anti-Semitic, and started attacking a group of mostly Jewish doctors, claiming they were plotting with Western intelligence agencies to murder Kremlin leaders. Again according to Rubenstein, all propaganda about the 'Doctors' Plot' actually stopped a few weeks before Stalin's death, not with his death as is often suggested, meaning that Stalin himself must have stopped it, for whatever reason.

Nevertheless, if Stalin had lived, the 'Doctors' Plot,' as it came to be known, might well have proved to be the opening salvo in an assault on the Jews similar to assaults on other groups he carried out, with mass deportations and a complicated type of disenfranchisement from Soviet society. In a way, had this happened, it would have resembled a kind of pogrom. But were the initial steps Stalin took against the Jews really different from the attacks on other groups he didn't trust, except that in this case a full-scale assault wasn't ultimately realized? Stalin's moves against the Jews took place in a sea of his prejudice and hatred and paranoia of almost everyone.

It's also interesting that with all the groups that were targeted and attacked in various ways throughout Stalin's reign—Poles, Finns, Latvians, Estonians, Lithuanians, Koreans, Romanians, Greeks, Chinese, Chechens, Crimean Tatars, Volga Germans, not to mention kulaks, the party, the intelligentsia, and more—Jews as a group never made the cut until the very end. Of course, many Jews were executed and sent to camps as members of other groups that were being purged and brutalized, ranging from the party elite to the bourgeoisie. But how is it that Jews were never specifically targeted as a group until near the end of Stalin's life? In the West, when you study Soviet history, Stalin's attack on the Jews is often pointed to as yet another proof of Soviet anti-Semitism. But in a way it was also a sign of how well Jews were integrated into society. Of course Jews suffered horribly, but they suffered right along with everyone else, as members of other groups Stalin went after. It's not the sign you want of being well integrated into society, but it is one nonetheless.

In Vasily Grossman's novel of the Stalin era, *Life and Fate*, the author describes a character, presented as quite normal in this regard, who thought about being Jewish for the first time after the war started. Before that, he'd never thought about being a Jew, his mother never once spoke to him about it, and at Moscow University not a single student or professor had ever mentioned it. This gives a sense of how assimilated at least some urban Jews were in the Soviet Union almost twenty-five years into the revolution. In another scene in Grossman's book, a Russian officer complains about better-qualified Russians losing out on promotions to minorities, singling out Jews, Kalmyks, and Armenians. It reads like a scene in America during almost any recent era, with people complaining about minorities getting preferential treatment, and hints at a complex kind of prejudice, strikingly modern and familiar.

The late 1950s and early 1960s were similarly complex. Khrushchev seems to have been afflicted with some of the anti-Semitism of his time, and since he was unusually forthright, he didn't hide it. He repeatedly stated that Jews were disloyal and couldn't be trusted. Even if these feelings were rooted in genuine doubts that some Jews had about the system (in large part because of anti-Semitism), the idea that Jews as a whole were disloyal was false and anti-Semitic. Khrushchev also stated that Jews were extreme individualists incapable of collective effort and discipline, and he complained on numerous occasions about the number of Jews in responsible or powerful positions in the communist parties of the Soviet Union and Eastern European states.

Khrushchev's actual policies were a mixed bag. On the one hand, he put a conclusive ending to the official wave of anti-Semitism that preceded and included the 'Doctors' Plot.' On the other hand, he closed many of the country's remaining synagogues, and continued to prohibit many aspects of Jewish cultural life (this was part of a broader antireligious campaign, in which he also closed down churches). Khrushchev also launched campaigns against economic crimes that seemed to disproportionately target Jews.

More broadly, Jews were by now largely excluded from the party/state hierarchy, with several notable exceptions—the military/industrial complex, sectors working on nuclear energy, and the Academy of Sciences. In part because their parents had been able to make it all the way to the top, this generation of Jews couldn't accept these limitations. Many became proponents of greater liberalization and started developing deeper Jewish identities and a desire to emigrate. In a vicious circle, this in turn caused even more exclusion.

In the late 1960s and 1970s, after Khrushchev's ouster, large numbers of Jews started petitioning to emigrate to Israel. Often, they were members of the intelligentsia and had relatively high-status jobs—many were doctors or engineers—until they requested permission to leave. Then they were ostracized.

In other words, Soviet society, broadly speaking, accepted these Jews until they declared they didn't want to be part of the society anymore. I'm not suggesting this acceptance was universal, or that Jews weren't treated badly at all unless they requested to emigrate. But this was one pattern—Jews being accepted until they declared they didn't want to be part of the group anymore.

I don't think Soviet society shunning refuseniks was viciously anti-Semitic. The Soviet Union in its final decades was a barely functioning socialist country, its economy almost in shambles. But most people had jobs, and although pay was very low, the state provided free healthcare and education. Food prices were kept low, and some meals were provided at the workplace. That was the deal. The system didn't provide for people at a high level, in fact it barely provided for them. But it was an understood and at least somewhat functional system. If you declared that you wanted to pull yourself out of the system, it makes sense that the government would say, "Then you no longer have this job," and it makes sense that some in society would resent you. It's not an enlightened attitude, it's not a great way to do things, it's not what I would do—but it's not necessarily targeted at Jews in a way it wouldn't have been targeted at any other group that tried to leave (as it happens, no other group had the same combination of historical and political factors to make mass exodus a possibility).

Of course, not letting people leave your country is a problem. It was a flaw in the Soviet system. But this rule applied to everyone. The stated goal was in fact to have Jews stay. This didn't mean the authorities loved Jews. Most likely, they feared a brain drain, and also didn't like sending the message that some Soviet citizens considered another way of life in a different country to be better. But there's no denying the simple fact that the Soviet state wanted Jews to stay, not go. Sometimes refuseniks could even return to their previous jobs if they withdrew their requests to emigrate.

This isn't to say anti-Semitism played no role in the authorities' fight against the refuseniks. Sometimes state efforts to propagandize against Zionism veered into the traditional anti-Semitism of the Russian nationalists in the party. But these anti-Jewish feelings were mostly buried post-Stalin until the early 1970s when Jews who wanted to leave started organizing and acting as more of a dissident group.

The refuseniks on the whole were incredibly brave, and fought a long and hard battle under extremely difficult circumstances. But it wasn't a black-and-white battle against anti-Semitism. Despite much of what I was told in synagogue and what I read in the American press at the time, some Jews were leaving because they were desperate to live freely and safely as Jews, but many were primarily looking for greater economic opportunities in Israel or the United States. Of course, you could want to leave for both reasons. But the refuseniks, their supporters worldwide, and the U.S. government focused on the anti-Semitic side, and played down the economic side. It didn't sound good to say you were applying to leave because you wanted to live a more financially secure life somewhere else.

Hazanov has a fascinating take on how the KGB viewed refuseniks. Much of the work of convincing Soviet Jews to leave was planned by Israeli and later American organizations that deliberately exploited holes and weaknesses in the Soviet system to encourage their fellow Jews in the Soviet Union to emigrate (smuggling in literature, for example). This was exactly in line with the KGB's view of the world. Foreigners were coming into the country, and smuggling in material and intellectual support for opponents of the regime, who were then becoming politically organized and making the country look bad to the world. It looked to the KGB like a conspiracy because in part it was one—a conspiracy in a country that was prone to imagining conspiracies.

According to Hazanov, when Soviet media or Soviet officials railed against Zionism, this is to a substantial degree what they were talking about—literally the Zionist movement coming in and turning their own citizens against them, trying to get them to move to Israel. It was not really code for anti-Jewish feelings, or even automatically anti-Israeli feelings. Even the side of the Soviet state's anti-Zionism that was centered on Arab rights was probably much less important to them than what was happening at home. It's hard to say exactly where and when the state's anti-Zionist rhetoric veered into anti-Semitism, just as it can be hard to determine where that line is today in anti-Israeli attitudes around the world.

Although nurtured by Israeli and American organizations, the refusenik movement was also homegrown—it grew and thrived because it had both grassroots and significant outside support. These forces combined, and ultimately a subset of Soviet Jews said, "We're out." In total, 200,000 to 250,000 emigrated from the USSR, between 10 and 20 percent of the Jewish population. Many other Soviet nationalities followed suit a few years later when their republics declared independence in 1990 and 1991, although these groups didn't actually have to go anywhere to leave the Soviet Union. The fact that so many Jews were allowed to leave was a preview of the response to these other groups. This was no longer a regime that was going to take the harshest measures to force people to remain part of the system.

As for the actual treatment of refuseniks, the one I met in Leningrad is instructive, I think, of the broad experience during the Brezhnev era and after. Ilya was much better off than the average refusenik because he had contacts in the West, which resulted in Seiko watches, and therefore money, alleviating the primary concern of a potential émigré who has lost his job. Still, like most of the others, after he was fired (through forced resignation) from his job, the authorities kept their hands off of him. The general oppression of refuseniks was limited to ostracization, including loss of jobs, with the notable exception of those who became leaders and spokespeople, who were likely to get harsher treatment, including prison sentences. It's important to note that most of the hundreds of thousands of Jews who emigrated were never refuseniks at all—during the years of high emigration, instead of being refused, they applied and were allowed to leave (though you were far less likely to get permission to emigrate if you were from the central cities in Russia and Ukraine—most of those given permission were from outlying republics in Central Asia, as well as Georgia and Lithuania). The number of refuseniks at any given time tended to be in the thousands, maybe as high as ten thousand, and concentrated in big cities.

Ultimately, several hundred thousand Jews were allowed to emigrate, under both Brezhnev and Gorbachev. Should this be understood as a humanitarian concession, as flexibility by the Soviet regime? For Brezhnev, the decision to let a significant number of Jews leave was likely influenced primarily by a desire to mollify the West during détente. Gorbachev was also probably influenced by a desire to improve relations with the West, but also likely just felt it was the right thing to do.

Gorbachev was a new kind of leader in virtually every way, and there wasn't a hint of anti-Semitism about him. As for Russia's two post-collapse leaders, Yeltsin showed no signs of anti-Jewish feeling. Neither has Putin. Both were products of the Soviet state.

With the history at least somewhat fleshed out and expanded from my early limited view, let's look now at the assimilationist goals of Soviet ideology and practice, and how they affected the Jews. This is a particular area in which Jews felt, and indeed were, victimized, but in which it is harder to say if the culprit was really anti-Semitism.

The Soviet state had a clear goal for all ethnic minorities, including Jews. They were expected to assimilate, to become Soviets first and foremost. A fundamental project of the Soviet state was the creation of a new kind of Soviet person, and the state demanded that everyone work toward this goal. Pressure in this direction ebbed and flowed, and at various points certain groups were allowed and encouraged to maintain their ethnic identity while also becoming Soviets. But the Soviet Union was always an assimilationist state. It was a huge melting pot, and if you didn't want to melt, or couldn't quite grasp the exact degree you were expected to melt, there was trouble.

In their account of the history of Birobidzhan, *Where the Jews Aren't*, journalist Masha Gessen suggests that the Soviet Union hurt Jews in part by keeping them from knowing anything about being Jewish. Most never got a chance to embrace their unique culture and religion. In fact, the state made everything so hard for Jews that many wanted to lose their Jewish identity just for the sake of an easier life.

This was the Soviet assimilationist project at work. We are now in an era where a state pushing for assimilation is seen as threatening and prejudiced, but the roots of the Soviet effort were idealistic (as was the American offer for immigrants to jump into its own melting pot, originally contingent on leaving behind the parts of ethnic heritage that kept people from melting in).

These are not simple issues. As we have seen, the Soviet state made efforts to help and advance Jews, while simultaneously forcing them to assimilate in ways that made many Jews feel singled out and victimized.

Assimilation and official demands to assimilate were further complicated by the complexity of Jewish identity in the Soviet Union. What, exactly, was a Soviet Jew? In the Soviet Union, the state answered this question—a Jew was a member of a nationality.

If you were Jewish, it said so on your internal passport, under the heading "Nationality." Every ethnic group, including Russians, had their nationality marked on their passports.

The decision to include nationality in internal passports was initially made to help ensure that minorities could be identified and then included in party and government posts in their national republics (where they weren't minorities, but were still at risk of being displaced by native Russians). This was part of a broad effort at inclusiveness in the early multiethnic Soviet state. The registration of nationality on passports did make certain types of anti-Semitic (and anti-other minority) prejudice easier later on—for example, it was simpler to discriminate against a job applicant if their passport made it clear they belonged to an ethnic minority. But the original intent of the stamp was not anti-Semitic.

It was, however, indicative of the state's complex and ambivalent feelings about national minorities. Historian Terry Martin has labeled the early Soviet Union an "affirmative action empire." Martin says that this affirmative action empire actually supported national minorities over majorities in certain ways. But he also argues that acceptance of the needs and goals of national minorities was more a concession by the Soviet leadership than a heartfelt goal. They understood nationalism was a potent tool for political recruitment, and felt that if they didn't exploit it themselves, at least until proletarian consciousness took over, it would be used against them.

This official and doctrinal ambivalence affected all the national minorities, but arguably was experienced in its own unique way by Jews. The Soviet state's relationship to Jews rested on a central assumption that they were (and are today in Russia) the same type of national group as Ukrainians or Tajiks or Georgians. It's true that Jews were an ethnic group, but their status as a Soviet "nationality" was less clear cut. Most Soviet Jews were culturally Russian (and like most Russians at the time, had let go of their religion). This wasn't true of the other nationalities, although elements of Russian culture were absorbed by many groups.

Jews were also different from the other large nationalities who had ancestral homelands inside the Soviet land mass, which became their national republics or autonomous regions. Perhaps the Jews were most like the Crimean Tatars or the ethnic Korean population of the Soviet Union, who also lacked a national homeland (the Tatars had one, but it was effectively abolished during World War II when the entire Tatar population was forcibly deported to Central Asia for alleged collaboration with the Germans). Still, there was no nationality quite like the Jews. They were, mostly, their own thing. Jews had a singular place in Russian and Soviet history, culture, lore, and prejudice. Among other things, they were uniquely prominent in the big cities, and made up a substantial part of the intelligentsia (where they thrived despite anti-Semitism). This gave them an outsized and complicated role in society.

Of course, Jews themselves often struggle to figure out if they're a religion, an ethnic group, or both. But if Jewish identity anywhere can be confusing, Soviet Jews seemed particularly torn about it. At least abroad, they were often referred to, and referred to themselves as, Russian Jews. But these are two separate nationalities, at least according to the system they grew up in. You couldn't be a Russian Chechen or a Russian Ukrainian. Maybe calling themselves Russian Jews was part convenience—shorthand for a Jew from Russia—but it was also in part an expression of the dual and muddled nature of their identity.

By giving a definitive answer to what Jews were—a Soviet nationality like the rest—the Soviet state was off to a troubled start in its relationship with its Jewish citizens. It was excluding them from their own Russianness, and demanding their identity be fixed, when for Jews, it wasn't.

———

On a practical level, critics charged the Soviet Union with many different kinds of official anti-Semitism, but the claim I have heard most frequently was that Jews were discriminated against in higher education. Every Soviet Jew I ever met had a university degree, but I didn't pay attention to this for a long time, until it eventually occurred to me that something didn't make sense here. Were Jews kept out of higher education or not?

The best schools in the country did have unofficial quotas that put a cap on the number of Jews who could attend, and many Jews went to lesser schools than their academic skills and talents should have qualified them for. But as Artemy Kalinovsky, a historian whose family emigrated from the Soviet Union when he was a child, pointed out to me, these weren't exactly "Jewish" quotas. They applied to all the ethnic minorities. The goal of these quotas was actually to ensure representation for everyone in higher education and in Communist Party jobs. This generally meant minorities received significant preferences for spots in university and party/government jobs in their national republics, and also had some spots reserved for them in "central" institutions like Moscow State University.

The problem here for Jews is obvious. Unlike most of the other national minorities, they didn't have a home republic in the Soviet Union (Birobidzhan was a strange experiment, and never had huge numbers of Jews living there). To compound the problem, a lot of Jews wanted to go to college, always more than the quotas allowed for.

Also, as was often the case with Soviet policies, the well-intentioned motivation for these quotas lost some of its initial force over the years, and quotas were sometimes used simply to keep the number of Jews in certain institutions low. Social science and law faculties at some top universities were essentially closed to Jews, although the science faculties weren't (a Jew may have had to significantly outperform a non-Jew to get a spot there, but they could get in). Most of this applied to finding a job after school too. Jews were sometimes funneled into professions with a shortage of personnel. Some prestigious workplaces, like a top laboratory, if they already had a few Jews, wouldn't take another one. In the post-Stalin era, Jews were outright barred from political leadership and the senior officer ranks of the military. Some of these forms of discrimination weren't laws or official policies, but closer to accepted norms or unofficial policies. It's hard to say what instigates this type of norm, because individuals have different reasons for complying. Over time, open prejudice morphs into institutional prejudice, and motives become even harder to discern.

But after university, Jews still became doctors, professors, scientists, engineers. And relative to their percentage of the population, there were proportionally many more Jews than non-Jewish Soviet citizens with university degrees, in these prestigious jobs, living in major cities.

We're certainly familiar in this country with the vagaries and complexities of affirmative action, the cross-currents of discrimination, remedies for discrimination, and reverse discrimination all at play. The formal and informal Soviet quota systems did contain a level of discrimination, but overall this certainly didn't prevent Jews from going to college at all, and didn't deny them access to a variety of good jobs. Viewed in context, this type of discrimination was less vicious and less pervasive than I had always imagined it to be, and did not support my vision of the Soviet Union as virulently and almost unabashedly anti-Semitic.

———————

Although popular anti-Semitism was intertwined with state prejudice in complex ways, it was also its own unique phenomenon. Many Jews suffered day-to-day prejudice in the Soviet Union— taunting on the streets, scorn, ridicule, and sometimes beatings. Robert Conquest suggests the motives for popular anti-Semitism in Soviet society were mixed. Sometimes it was xenophobia, sometimes indulgence in the general denunciatory habits of the country, and sometimes people just wanted to take the money and jobs of Jews.

It has to be said that many Jews lived peacefully with their fellow Soviet citizens in the post-Stalin era, and earlier. I have heard and read endless true stories of street-level anti-Semitism in the Soviet Union, but also endless stories of close and enduring friendships between Jews and non-Jews. In the earlier and perhaps later years of the Soviet Union, the egalitarian state ideology was arguably much more powerful and influential than the hatred some had for Jews.

Although the state probably deserves credit for significantly restraining popular anti-Semitism during much of Soviet history, it's sometimes impossible to fully separate state from popular prejudice against the Jews. Gessen illustrates this difficulty when they describe the semiofficial behavior that made it harder for Jews to get into certain universities in the post-Stalin period. Jewish applicants were asked an extra "coffin" question during their application exams. These questions seemed almost impossible to answer, and when Jewish applicants got them wrong, they were denied admittance. Gessen tells about a private tutor who figured out these questions were actually unsolvable, and to give this as the answer during the exam—to say the question was unsolvable—constituted an undeniably correct answer. When this tutor's Jewish students answered the coffin questions this way, they passed the test. This suggests to me that anti-Semitic individuals and groups could baldly discriminate against Jews, but if the victims of this prejudice found a way around anti-Semitic tricks, the persecutors were powerless in the face of official Soviet doctrine, which didn't allow outright discrimination.

Of course, discrimination will always find some way to rear its head. In *The Gulag Archipelago*, Solzhenitsyn relates the story of how, during the uprising in the Steplag prison camp in Kengir in 1954, rumors spread of a Jewish pogrom about to break out in the camp. One of the leaders of the uprising announced that those spreading the rumor would be publicly flogged, and the rumors stopped. But this kind of hatred breaking out during a prison-camp revolt, when all were united in a common purpose that had nothing to do with Jews, shows how spontaneously anti-Semitism can and will crop up.

How different was Soviet anti-Semitism from American anti-Semitism?

If we go back to the nineteenth and first half of the twentieth century in America, Jews were heavily discriminated against (I'm mostly following historian Robert Michael below). The period between World War I and World War II, and particularly the 1930s and 1940s, probably saw the most anti-Semitism in American history. Although Theodore Roosevelt appointed the first Jewish cabinet officer at the beginning of the 1900s, by the interwar period, many government officials, from secretaries of state to chiefs of staff, were blatantly prejudiced, and made anti-Semitic comments openly. Anti-Semitism focused on the alleged role Jews played in undermining Christianity and a Christian nation, but also included direct political attacks on Jews for their alleged responsibility for the Bolshevik revolution. Stereotypes about Jewish control of finance became more prevalent as the country slipped first into depression and then moved toward war, a war that some claimed was primarily about Jewish interests.

As Jews streamed into universities during this era, quotas (sometimes unofficial) sprang up, for college, medical, law, and dental schools. Jews were also discriminated against in myriad professional fields. Jobs were sometimes advertised for Christians only, and a majority of employers wouldn't hire Jews.

Among the immigrants pouring into the country in the 1930s and 1940s, Jews were among the most hated groups. Battles over anti-immigration legislation involved blatantly anti-Semitic language and ideas. The Ku Klux Klan, viciously anti-Semitic in its stated goal of preserving a Christian nation, had members who were judges, governors, and congressmen. Michael offers a number of disturbing statistics: one public-opinion research organization found in 1942 that only 1 percent of Americans thought Nazi hatred of Jews was bad. During the war years, one poll suggested that 70 percent of respondents would have supported a campaign against Jews in the United States, or refused to take a stand against one. An expert in prejudice estimated that in the mid-1940s, 5 to 10 percent of the population was virulently anti-Semitic, and about 45 percent mildly bigoted against Jews. It's hard to know how accurate these various polls and surveys were. But the picture they paint of the 1930s and 1940s broadly matches anecdotal evidence, as well as the open anti-Semitism in parts of the press and among many public officials at the time.

Still, President Roosevelt had several Jewish advisers, and some Christian groups and prominent citizens stood up and loudly condemned anti-Jewish attitudes and practices. Things were getting better by the 1950s, and many Jews were thriving by the 1960s. Polls showed anti-Semitism was still prevalent, but lower than before. By 1960 almost all universities had stopped using quotas to deny admittance to Jews, and Jews moved decisively into the middle class.

Jews in America were now outstripping Jews in the Soviet Union in their professions and status. They still weren't often reaching the heights that some Jews reached in the revolutionary period and into the 1920s in the Soviet Union, when they were at the very top of the political elite there. Arguably, the United States of the 1950s and 1960s, full of Jewish professionals, but still suffering a real degree of discrimination, somewhat resembled the USSR of the 1970s. Does that put the USSR twenty years behind us in remedying anti-Semitism? It's hard to say, because the types and levels of prejudice are so complex, and because the USSR went backward in certain ways after the early 1920s. Actually, it went forward, backward, and forward again.

Was, or is, the United States anti-Semitic? In some ways, obviously. And in some ways it was and is the opposite of anti-Semitic—a land of great opportunity for Jews, a country that has been at the vanguard of opposing anti-Semitism.

Both of these things were also true about the Soviet Union. In fact, the Soviet Union was like a lot of other countries—it struggled with anti-Semitism, but doesn't deserve to be held out as anything like a particularly egregious practitioner of it. It was no more anti-Semitic than many other places, and less so than plenty of others. Was it average, for a country? That scale doesn't exist, and I don't know how to create it. I only know the Soviet Union wasn't as bad as it was often made out to be.

Of course, no one ever told me about the part of the USSR that fought anti-Semitism. And I never sought out that information, because I was so mad at them—the charge of anti-Semitism was another cudgel I could hit them with.

3. A MAJORITY OF THE SOVIET POPULATION PROBABLY DID NOT WANT THE SOVIET UNION TO COLLAPSE

In 1987, while I was writing my college thesis, which expressed skepticism that there was any real level of popular support for the Soviet government, I read a book published a few years earlier called *Rethinking the Soviet Experience* by Stephen Cohen. I remember one part of Cohen's argument clearly from all those years ago. He disagreed with the prevalent Western belief that an unpopular Soviet government (or more accurately party/government) was ruling over an oppressed and cynical populace. Cohen thought the Soviet authorities had an unwritten pact with the population whereby they provided the basics of a welfare state (jobs, food, pensions, medical care), and in exchange the population accepted their legitimacy. (Rereading Cohen now, I see he suggested this pact also involved providing—or at least promising to provide—national defense, internal stability, state-sponsored nationalism, and material improvement for each generation). At the time, I thought Cohen's ideas were interesting but naïve.

Cohen caught me by surprise again in his 2010 book, *The Victims Return: Survivors of the Gulag After Stalin*, when he wrote that among his close Russian friends—every one of them a former dissident or the child of a dissident—not a single one was glad that the Soviet Union had collapsed.

This was hard for me to believe. I knew that some Soviets regretted the collapse of the Soviet Union, but I thought they were mostly die-hard communists. How could former dissidents wish the country had survived? And if even dissidents and their children did feel this way, what did that suggest about the vast majority of the Soviet population, who had never been particularly sympathetic to the dissidents? Were most of them sorry the country had fallen apart?

It's important to note that a significant number of Soviets were in fact glad the Soviet Union dissolved. Among the non-Russian nationalities, some were less nationalistic than others, and there was never a universal opinion about independence from the Soviet Union. The Baltic republics of Lithuania, Latvia, and Estonia, along with Georgia and Armenia, stood out as the republics with the strongest concentration of pro-independence opinion, almost certainly a substantial majority.

In March of 1991, as the Soviet Union was fraying at the seams, it held a referendum to determine who wanted to stay in the union, and who didn't. The referendum was complicated, and many consider the results suspect. In Russia, for example, in addition to the primary question about preserving the union, there was another question about whether the Russian Republic should have a popularly elected president. These two questions were essentially sponsored by Gorbachev and Yeltsin, respectively—Gorbachev wanted the union to survive, and Yeltsin wanted to be a strong, popularly elected president of Russia. Since both questions were approved by significant majorities, some have suggested the vote on remaining in the union lacked credibility, especially in Russia, since you can't have it both ways. But why couldn't you have it both ways?

Russians easily could have wanted the Soviet Union to remain intact, but with the Russian Republic getting more autonomy and power, and instituting popular presidential elections.

In the Central Asian republics, both participation in the vote and the yes vote to preserve the union were officially reported to be near 90 percent. These feel like old Soviet-style numbers, with near universal participation and almost unanimous agreement. Nevertheless, while independent election observers reported some anomalies, they also reported that the vote appeared to represent the general mood and position of the populace.

All three Baltic states, along with Georgia, Armenia, and Moldova, refused to participate in the referendum, which certainly reflected how it would have turned out in those places—high levels of nationalism meant most people in those republics wanted out of the union. But not only was that just six of the fifteen Soviet republics, they were all relatively small, and together represented far less than six-fifteenths of the Soviet population or landmass.

Of the remaining nine republics, all voted decisively to preserve the union. The vote to stay in the USSR hovered around 70 percent in most of them.

Clearly, there were many Soviet citizens who didn't want the country to dissolve. This wouldn't have been a surprise to anyone in the Soviet Union. But it was a surprise to me. The fact that so many inside the country valued it, and cared about it, was something I hadn't understood.

What had I missed?

Former Soviets, and former Russians in particular, can go on at length about why they didn't want their country to disappear. For starters, most Soviets were patriotic, like people everywhere. For all its problems, the Soviet Union was their country. At the same time, it was a very unusual country, with a very unusual ideology based on high ideals that promoted radical equality. Even if there was a distance between this ideology and Soviet reality, many Soviets believed in the country's basic values and goals. There was also a feeling, for many, of being in it together. Even if they knew their country was deeply troubled, even if many of its ideals had been corrupted, they were all in the same boat.

For many, their regret about the country's collapse seemed to grow over time, as they failed to make successful transitions to new lives in their newly independent, very different countries. In Russia, unhappiness over the Soviet collapse was reflected in how unpopular Gorbachev was, since he was blamed for what happened (I knew people didn't like Gorbachev in post-Soviet Russia, but I missed the fairly obvious explanation for why).

As for Cohen's point, that even his dissident friends supported the survival of the Soviet state, this is more complicated. During their long struggle with the Soviet authorities, some dissidents wanted the Soviet Union to fall away and to be replaced by a liberal democracy, or a group of liberal democracies. But others did want it to survive. Many stated very clearly time and again that they wanted to reform the system, not do away with it, and that they were working well within the bounds of Soviet law in their efforts to accomplish this. I believed these claims about "reforming" the system as opposed to destroying it were just a strategy, a way the dissidents tried to shield themselves from the authorities by claiming their goals and actions were within the bounds of Soviet law (it was a strategy for some, but for others reflected their true goals). It was especially easy for me to assume the dissidents all wanted to do away with the Soviet Union since they disliked the same undemocratic and repressive things about the system that I did.

In addition to purely political beliefs, dissidents had a concrete personal reason to oppose the collapse of the Soviet Union. Dissidents usually came from the intelligentsia, which meant they were taken care of by the Soviet state. As professors, doctors, and engineers, they had relatively privileged lives inside Soviet society, and never had to worry about where their next paycheck was coming from. The collapse of the system meant the end of this life. Even if that life wasn't easy or perfect, it had its benefits, and many of its most severe drawbacks were fading in the Gorbachev era—there was far less direct repression, and far fewer restrictions on intellectual freedom.

It's hard to say which dissidents were really looking for the dissolution of the Soviet Union, and which ones only wanted the system to change. Once Gorbachev came to power, many dissidents strongly supported him. This was what they'd been waiting for. But other dissidents were suspicious of him, and openly critical. Were the suspicious dissidents just skeptical of Gorbachev himself and his approach to change, or was the issue that it wasn't the reform of the Soviet Union they actually wanted, but its collapse?

My own sense that the dissident movement was monolithic and fully committed to the end of the Soviet Union demonstrated how poorly I understood the complex feelings of the Soviet population as a whole. I had always assumed, when the United States constantly put pressure on the Soviets to stop imprisoning and otherwise harassing dissidents, that we were essentially speaking for the people of the Soviet Union. I assumed the dissidents were their leaders, the bravest among them. This was hardly the case.

I identified with and admired the Soviet dissidents of the 1960s to the 1980s—Andrei Sakharov, Yuri Orlov, Vladimir Bukovsky and the rest (Solzhenitsyn was a case unto himself, and none of this applies perfectly to him)—and it was hard for me to come to terms with the fact that they were never heroes to a large number of people inside the Soviet Union. Most Soviets weren't interested in the dissidents, and many considered them troublemakers, or worse. They were only heroes to a portion of the intelligentsia, which was itself a small percentage of Soviet society. After the collapse of the Soviet Union, greater access to information about the role and history of the dissidents didn't increase their popularity, and few considered them central to the political upheavals that brought first reform to the Soviet Union, and then the end of the state. On the bright side, this meant the dissidents weren't blamed for the collapse of the Soviet Union either.

I have to admit being somewhat depressed by mainstream Soviet and later Russian attitudes about the dissidents. Imagine if the civil-rights leaders of the 1960s in the United States had significantly fewer followers than they actually did, and weren't considered heroes by so many of us today. What if their accomplishments weren't taught in our schools? What if there was no sense at all that they'd been instrumental in transforming our society for the better?

Of course, our civil-rights leaders did change the course of a nation. The impact of the dissidents is harder to measure. They were one of the only segments of society that wouldn't go along in the Soviet era, that said no to those in power. Did their protest put important pressure on Soviet authorities? Did they keep the entire system somewhat flexible, and ultimately more capable of change? Or were the dissidents really just a marginal group?

If I were to ask myself now the same question I asked in my senior thesis—did the Soviet population support their government?—I would answer that the question is too simplistic. Even in America it would be a tricky question. Support for any current administration is usually mixed here, while support for our system of government has traditionally been broad. This same distinction was important in the Soviet Union, where support for the system was probably much, much higher than it was for most individual leaders in the post-Stalin era. The discrepancy between what the idealized system was supposed to be and the compromised version people were living under added to the complexity of people's feelings. Overall, a better question would have been "What are some of the complexities in the ways the Soviet populace thought and felt about their system of party/government and their leadership?" (Not quite as catchy.)

Regardless, it is clear there was stronger and more broad-based support for the idea of, existence of, and survival of the Soviet Union than I understood at the time. That support flew in the face of most of what I assumed about the feelings of the Soviet population, and meant my uncompromising views on the Soviet party/ state's lack of legitimacy were wrong.

4. SOVIET LEADERS AFTER STALIN WERE NOT DOLTS— THEY WERE BRIGHT, CAPABLE, AND OFTEN IDEALISTIC MEN

My interest in Soviet politics began at the end of the Brezhnev era, so I watched as Andropov and then Chernenko followed him as general secretary, each lasting barely over a year in the post before dying. I remember the feeling in the air at the time, that an incompetent gerontocracy was running the Soviet Union.

The idea that these next-to-last Soviet leaders were incompetent, enfeebled old men was based in part on fact. Brezhnev was much more astute and capable (and presented in the American media that way) in his younger years, when he first ascended to power. He did degenerate, and was clearly too infirm to run the country in his later years. Andropov also came off in the American press as more formidable at the very start of his time in power, but then quickly became ill. Chernenko was in poor mental and physical shape almost the entire time he was general secretary.

Eventually, though, the more youthful and capable versions of these men were forgotten in the West, and they came to be seen only as a bunch of tottering old geezers, hanging on to power because that's what totalitarian rulers do. In my mind, these men were and had always been doltish, incompetent cynics. Their final decay only helped reveal what they had always been.

These were mostly misconceptions. Brezhnev, Andropov, and Chernenko were bright, capable men, and arguably also idealistic men who did bad things, or maybe complicated men with good and bad sides. You got to the very top of the Soviet leadership structure for many reasons, but you couldn't do it without being smart and capable. Even if these men weren't political geniuses like Lenin and Stalin, they were men with strong abilities. In trying to understand them, I had made a mistake in focusing only on their final years.

Although I'm focusing on leaders during my lifetime, I'll start with a story I like about Khrushchev.

In *The Gulag Archipelago*, Solzhenitsyn writes about a man he met in prison who used to be Khrushchev's driver. This man had also driven for many other high-level Soviet officials. The only one of them he liked was Khrushchev. He felt all of the others acted like they were better than him, which made them bad communists, and hypocrites. Khrushchev, on the other hand, used to invite him to sit and eat at the table with his family. He was a true man of the people.

After Khrushchev was ousted by his fellow leaders, Brezhnev became first secretary of the Communist Party (later called general secretary), the most important leadership position in the Soviet Union (in my descriptions of Brezhnev, Andropov, and Chernenko, I'm largely, but not entirely, following Dmitri Volkogonov, a Soviet general who became a historian with an early and unusual level of access to Soviet archives). Brezhnev had risen through the ranks of the party bureaucracy in various high-level posts around the country, with his mentor, Khrushchev, helping him along. Later, Brezhnev played a key role in the plot to replace Khrushchev. When Brezhnev found out he'd been chosen as his old mentor's (possibly temporary) successor, he was surprised, and told a friend on the Politburo he wasn't sure he was up to the job.

Brezhnev was chosen from a pack of potential leaders to follow Khrushchev in part because he was likeable. He knew how to compromise instead of ruling by fiat, and he could listen to other opinions and change his mind. He wasn't an angry or vengeful person, and wanted everyone to be happy. Like Reagan, he would be moved by a stranger's plight and reach out to help them. He also helped his friends and his old comrades whom he fought with in the war. In cases where he helped family and friends too much, it led to substantial cronyism. But it also showed a level of care and concern for old friends who could have easily been forgotten. In a generally scathing indictment, Volkogonov calls Brezhnev a kind of anti-Stalin, because he solidified his power through social, friendly relationships instead of fear and terror.

Brezhnev, who had lived through the chaos and devastation of the Second World War, mostly wanted stability (as did the other members of the Politburo). And he didn't just prize a calm and peaceful environment for himself and his friends. The man I saw as a half-senile, angry cold-warrior desperately wanted to secure a legacy as a world peacemaker. In his early years as Soviet leader, he believed he could reach accommodations with the West and play a major role in advancing the cause of peace. He was a key driver of détente, and wanted to join forces with the West in both spreading peace and avoiding nuclear war. He tried to forge close, personal relationships with both Nixon and West German chancellor Willy Brandt, and at one point presented Nixon with an almost wide-eyed plan for how the Soviet Union and the United States could combine forces to actually enforce peace around the world (I am naturally in sympathy with this way of thinking, in favor of approaching intractable problems with idealistic solutions that many would consider politically naïve).

A decade and a half into his tenure as Soviet leader, when the Politburo debated whether or not to invade Afghanistan, minutes of the meeting show that Brezhnev considered the pros and cons intelligently, and realized the trouble the Soviet Union was getting itself into (as did many other members of the Politburo). He didn't make the right decision to avoid the war, but got sucked into its vortex the same way America's best and brightest were sucked into Vietnam. But he was still a thoughtful leader who was able to carefully consider what he was doing before making his grand mistake. Brezhnev may not have been a genius, or an original thinker. But he was no fool.

Brezhnev also seems to have played an instrumental role in the Politburo's decision to drop the development of plans to intervene militarily in Poland in response to the Solidarity movement. He was apparently eager to avoid another military intervention after Afghanistan, a mess he felt others in the Politburo had gotten him into.

In his later years, Brezhnev accepted endless state prizes and medals, and seems to have become vain and lazy. He also probably suffered from an addiction to sedatives. He stayed in power as his health failed, and became something of a caricature of what an old civilian-military autocrat might look like. This wiped out most memories of his competence and intelligence when he was younger, and at the same time fixed an image in the political imagination of a fading Soviet leader. The changes he went through represented an actual decline in first his moral strength as a leader, and later his actual mental capacities. It was also bad PR, both at home and abroad.

Although his background is a bit murky, the next Soviet leader, Yuri Andropov, seems to have grown up poor, and then was orphaned either at thirteen or, according to other sources, at seventeen (most sources agree that his father died years before his mother). Andropov worked a series of manual-labor jobs, went to school, and was active in Communist Party organizations. Andropov's hard work, along with the priorities and ideals of the Communist Party and the Soviet state, allowed a poor orphan to prosper.

After he became head of the KGB in 1967, Andropov fashioned the secret police into a guardian of ideology, and focused it on doing preventative work, through surveillance of the population and monitoring of public opinion, instead of using mass incarceration to exert control (of course, it wasn't just him guiding the way; the transformation of the secret police was part of a broad historical movement).

During his tenure at the KGB, although he was a driving force behind the invasions of Hungary, Czechoslovakia, and Afghanistan, Andropov opposed military intervention in Poland during the rise of the Solidarity movement. He reportedly told a subordinate that "the quota of interventions has been exhausted." He also understood that the Soviet Union had to focus on its internal problems at this point, including food shortages, and the possibility that labor strikes could spread from Poland into the USSR.

Even before this, Andropov had led a major anti-corruption drive as KGB chairman (and continued it later as general secretary). He felt corruption was strangling the Soviet economy, and threatening the entire nation. He took on high-ranking officials and the powerful food trade organizations in Moscow. His goal was nothing less than to save the country, since he believed honesty and integrity in its economic structures were vital to its future. Andropov and the KGB lost this battle, but it's hard not to be on his side against the many corrupt bureaucrats he was fighting against.

Many of the people who worked for Andropov at the KGB liked and respected him. They described him as having a superior intellect. His writing often suggests he had a keen intelligence, and some of it reads differently from the dry and repetitive memos that post-Stalin Soviet leaders had others write for them. In his book *Lenin's Tomb*, journalist and *New Yorker* editor David Remnick quotes Gorbachev adviser Alexander Yakovlev as saying that he considered Andropov the most dangerous of the late Soviet leaders because he was the smartest one. Andropov was also widely considered to be polite, modest, and well read.

In 1981, believing the United States was preparing to launch a nuclear first strike against the Soviet Union, Andropov launched Operation RYAN, in which KGB *rezidenturas* around the world were tasked with finding evidence and details of this planned attack. How could someone as intelligent as Andropov be this paranoid? In part, high levels of paranoia were typical during the Cold War on both sides. Soviet leaders were perhaps also especially vulnerable to paranoia because their country had been caught by surprise by the Nazi invasion of 1941 (or at least had been caught somewhat by surprise, as I'll discuss later).

Andropov ran the KGB for fifteen years, but was only general secretary for fifteen months before he died. As general secretary, he launched a law-and-order campaign, in line with the anti-corruption drive he began as KGB chairman. Among other efforts, the campaign tackled "absenteeism" from work. Andropov had police and volunteer vigilantes confront people who were in stores during working hours and ask why they weren't at their jobs. This is hard to understand for those of us in the West, where you aren't legally required to work. But in the Soviet Union, Andropov was enforcing the law, and he surely saw himself as playing a basic role in protecting society and ensuring it was functioning properly.

Some think of Andropov as a kind of pre-Gorbachev reformer, since he understood the mess the country was in, at least to some degree, and made an effort to address it. Already under Brezhnev, Andropov was warning of tough times to come, based on a realistic appraisal of the Soviet economy. He understood the country was in trouble and tried to act. His anti-corruption drive was a good idea, but it only focused on one side of the nation's economic problems, ignoring all the other issues that came along with a command economy.

Volkogonov believed Andropov couldn't break out of his Leninist worldview, and only came up with the same old solutions for Soviet economic malaise, like getting people to work harder, strengthening the role of the party, and taking stronger administrative and organizational measures. Even his anti-corruption drive was probably doomed because of these limitations.

Of the three post-Khrushchev leaders before Gorbachev, starting with his time at the KGB, Andropov was probably the most responsible for the panoply of brutal measures used against dissidents, including putting them in psychiatric institutions. Of course, Brezhnev and the rest of the leadership were involved in all of this repression too. But Andropov led the way. It's common to find him described as vicious, and this side of his legacy explains why.

Let's think again about Andropov's background. He was orphaned at thirteen (or seventeen). He worked his way up through the Communist Youth League and various jobs. He rose and rose in the ranks, through hard work and merit. His journey is hardly different from that of a self-made American (though in the American Horatio Alger story, an underprivileged background is an impediment to overcome, whereas in the Soviet Union, a proletarian background conferred a status that helped one rise in the bureaucracy, especially during the early and mid-Soviet periods).

Naturally, then, Andropov became a great and true believer in the Soviet system, which proved itself to him in every way. The Soviet leadership was filled with similar success stories, men who had worked their way up from the very bottom. Why wouldn't these people be true believers in the system that created them? Why wouldn't they view anyone who was threatening it as an enemy? Dissidents were trying to undermine a system that men like Andropov had every right to believe in. At least, this is one way of looking at it. It doesn't justify the inhumane methods used to combat those dissidents. But it does suggest that something beyond malice and a thirst for power lay at the heart of this fight.

An early reformer trying to fix the problems of the country that had made it possible for a poor orphan like him to become general secretary? A KGB chairman who imprisoned those who spoke out against that system, and sometimes put them in psychiatric institutions? Andropov was complex, human, and not all bad or all good.

On his deathbed, Andropov wrote that Gorbachev should succeed him—more evidence that Andropov wanted reform. Instead, Chernenko became general secretary. Chernenko is widely considered the most drab, ineffective, and sclerotic of the bunch, the pure embodiment of a bureaucrat. He's often reduced to a joke because he was already in his early seventies when he became general secretary, arguably looked even older, and like his predecessor quickly became infirm. Most stories about him involve how sick and mentally out of it he was as general secretary.

The portrayal of Chernenko as drab and intellectually limited was probably more true than the unflattering perceptions of other Soviet leaders, but it was still at least somewhat exaggerated and misleading. Chernenko made his career through years of successful work as a powerful bureaucrat. He solidified his power base from deep inside the party structure as head of the General Department of the Central Committee. The General Department had control of the party's secret archives and was responsible for the flow and often the creation of paperwork. In any society as bureaucratic as the Soviet Union, this kind of accumulation of power through stewardship of the intricate levers of the system takes a real degree of intelligence.

Chernenko worked his way higher and higher, over decades, and ultimately made it all the way to the top. His abilities shouldn't be dismissed as simple cunning or clever political maneuvering. Chernenko was able to get people to trust him, and to develop a deep knowledge of how a complex and subtle system worked. He had the political and social skills to become Brezhnev's favorite. Of course he used political maneuvering, and perhaps at times ill-gotten knowledge, to his advantage as well.

Maybe as a leader, Chernenko was still a mediocrity, someone with no vision or ability to see the trouble the Soviet system was in. But here's one story that suggests there was another side to him. It comes from the book *Afgantsy*, by Rodric Braithwaite, a former British ambassador to the Soviet Union. During the war in Afghanistan, an officer in the field named Leonid Shershnev wrote and sent Chernenko a highly critical report about how and why the Soviets were losing. It revealed how badly the war was going, a fact that was being largely covered up. Although no other officers would sign onto the report, it did, miraculously, make its way to Chernenko's desk. Chernenko wrote on the report, "Shershnev is not to be touched."

Chernenko obviously understood that this officer could and probably would be retaliated against for telling the truth. And in fact, even with the general secretary's express admonition to leave him alone, the military still found a way to get him. Shershnev simply wasn't promoted, until he eventually left the army out of frustration.

This one story hints at the possibility that the generally accepted wisdom about Chernenko isn't entirely true. Whatever his faults, Chernenko was a person, not a caricature of a senile old bureaucrat.

Like all Soviet leaders, he was a man who wanted the best for his country, and would use his power to protect someone who spoke truth to power.

———————

For most of my life, I believed the United States was a true meritocracy, as demonstrated by Lincoln (or Clinton) rising to the presidency. In comparison, I thought the Soviet Union was a kind of malevolent party-led bureaucracy, where success was determined primarily by cronyism combined with a willingness to fake extreme loyalty. But the fact that the much-maligned Brezhnev, Andropov, and Chernenko were all intelligent and highly capable demonstrates that there was a more significant meritocratic side of Soviet politics and society.

The origins of every post-Lenin Soviet leader also reflects a higher level of meritocracy than I had recognized. Stalin's father was a cobbler, and he grew up extremely poor. Khrushchev was the son of peasants. Brezhnev's father worked in a steel mill. Andropov grew up poor and was orphaned at a fairly young age. Chernenko grew up poor in Siberia, his father a miner. Gorbachev came from a poor peasant family.

None of this is to say the Soviet system was meritocratic across the board. It was also bureaucratic and corrupt, and family and professional ties played an important role in advancement. And obviously, all kinds of extremely talented people were weeded out of the system if they wouldn't conform. But merit determined success in many areas, and played a fundamental role in who made it to the very top. Soviet leaders weren't born into power or privilege. This pattern might not have survived if the Soviet Union had lasted. The *nomenklatura* was becoming increasingly entrenched, and passing on its rights, privileges, and to some degree its jobs to its children, as upper classes do in all societies. Would the next generation of Soviet leaders have been comprised of children of the *nomenklatura* instead of children of peasants and workers?

If I was wrong about Brezhnev, Andropov, and Chernenko being mediocrities who climbed to the top through a combination of careerism, ruthlessness, and working in a system that weeded out talent instead of promoting it, was my belief that they were terrible human beings another wrongheaded absolutist judgment?

None of these men were mass killers. They weren't political geniuses either. They had to rule without either of these tools at their disposal. Were they basically ambitious and idealistic politicians who did some bad things? Could even fundamentally decent men allow the kind of repression and brutality that still took place in the Soviet Union after Stalin?

Many of our founding fathers owned slaves, most (or arguably all) of our presidents presided over a nation where minorities were repressed and brutalized. More recently, our presidents started unnecessary wars that resulted in massive numbers of civilian casualties, one of them explicitly sanctioned an active program of state-sponsored torture, and in several other cases they allowed targeted drone strikes that invariably resulted in innocent civilians being killed. Were these still decent men?

The truth is, I'm torn about what kind of people Brezhnev, Andropov, and Chernenko were. Idealistic? Complicated? Men with good and bad sides? The only thing I'm sure of is that I want to move away from the uncomplicated view I used to have of them as clearly horrible people. They followed Lenin and Stalin, who were both unabashedly brutal, and who both sanctioned high levels of political killing, in Stalin's case so high that he became one of the greatest political murderers of all time. Brezhnev, Andropov, and Chernenko also followed Khrushchev, who exposed and ended Stalin's terror, but had participated in those same horrors and carried on a significant level of repression afterward. All three ruled with a level of brutality infinitely closer to Khrushchev's than to Stalin's. Repression is always bad, but I don't think this makes them monsters. Focusing only on their bad sides is part of a process of dehumanization, common when creating and dealing with "enemies."

Brezhnev, Andropov, and Chernenko grew up with a different value system than I did, inside a different political system. They had goals and worldviews that matched their experience. They were all believers in their system, and wanted their country to thrive. To varying degrees, they made the mistake of accepting or promulgating repression to defend their system. But that is a fairly common story of leadership. If we believe moral errors made by otherwise decent men are what defines them, we should apply that standard to our leaders as well. If we believe moral failings in our leaders are elements of complex people with good and bad sides, that should be the standard applied to Brezhnev, Andropov, and Chernenko too.

5. THE SOVIET WAR IN AFGHANISTAN WAS NOT A SIMPLE ACT OF COMMUNIST AGGRESSION; IT WAS A COMPLICATED WAR THAT LOOKED A LOT LIKE OUR OWN FOREIGN INTERVENTIONS

I was fourteen when the Soviets invaded Afghanistan. I understood our enemy had done something bad, and we weren't going to the Olympics as a result. But as I came into my own politically a few years later, I became outraged over this brutal and unjust war. The Soviet monolith was marching on as usual, attacking innocent people who were fighting bravely for their freedom and independence. The USA was trying to blunt the communist advance, with the mysterious, powerful, and awesome CIA at the vanguard of the battle.

Just over a decade later, on one of the CIA training program's interim assignments, I went to work at the Afghan Task Force. Just the name—"Afghan Task Force"—was exciting. A task force was obviously important, and slightly military. It was filled with purpose and urgency. True, the Soviets had finished withdrawing from Afghanistan over a year earlier. But the communist government was still in place there, and this was what the Afghan Task Force was fighting against at that point (I guess).

Shortly after starting at the task force, I was assigned to help with the arrangements for a somewhat complicated covert plan I am not allowed to publish the details of. I can say that it involved meeting with a man who was traveling to the United States from abroad, whom we were going to enlist in our efforts. The day the man arrived, I met up with two officers from the agency's Office of Security, and we went to get him at Dulles airport. When the officers flashed their credentials and we walked straight through security without any screening, it felt like my life was working out the way I wanted.

The man who stepped off the plane was slight, spoke very little English, and was naturally charming and likeable. We took him to meet a translator and a group of people who were going to work on our project. It's obviously difficult to tell this story without the story itself. But what remains for me in any case is less what we were doing and more what it meant to me. I went back to headquarters on top of the world, feeling like much more than the chauffeur I actually was.

Many years later, while researching a storyline on Afghanistan for *The Americans*, I read Braithwaite's *Afgantsy*, which is a masterpiece of seeing things from the other side. It's impossible to read it without recognizing how similar the Soviet experience in Afghanistan was to our own experience in Vietnam.

Americans generally believed the Soviets invaded Afghanistan because they were intent on spreading communism to the Middle East, were looking for eventual access to a warm-water port (ultimately through yet another country), and planned to take or at least control Persian Gulf oil. All of this has been disproved by the minutes of Politburo meetings from the time. The primary reason the Soviets invaded Afghanistan was to keep a faltering, allied communist government in a neighboring country from switching sides in the Cold War. But because they needed loftier goals to launch a war, Soviet leaders also convinced themselves they had humanitarian motivations. They could prevent civil war and chaos in Afghanistan. And they could modernize the country, not just economically but culturally and socially. They looked at their own Muslim population in the Soviet Central Asian Republics and decided that since they'd succeeded in modernizing these societies— among other advances, making their women some of the most liberated in the Muslim world—they could do the same thing again in Afghanistan. Some of these humanitarian goals, used to justify a strategic decision, closely paralleled our own a few decades later in Afghanistan and Iraq.

Many in the Soviet leadership recognized they were wading into a quagmire, but they marched forward against their own better judgment. According to Braithwaite, the war had significant popular support at first, including from a lot of young Soviets, who were patriotic and wanted to help the people of Afghanistan by spreading (or securing) communism there. I was startled that a meaningful percentage of Soviet youth supported the war. I assumed the population in general was disaffected, and didn't support anything the leadership did. At the very least, I thought the population had retreated into political apathy (if not downright hostility), and that these feelings were strongest among the country's youth. But it's now clear from multiple sources—interviews conducted by journalists and historians, personal stories, the complicated referendum referenced above, and generally just a better understanding of the Soviet world—that there was at least a complex level of broadbased support for the Soviet system, and that this support existed among the younger generation too.

Popular support for the war waned as the conflict dragged on, casualties increased, and prospects for victory dimmed. Even the censored Soviet press couldn't successfully hide any of these realities from the Soviet people. According to Braithwaite, soldiers would bring the bodies of their dead comrades back to their families in small towns across the Soviet Union, and in multiple instances near riots broke out as aggrieved families and neighbors lashed out at the soldiers carrying out this terrible duty. In addition to how profoundly sad this was, it demonstrated that the Soviet press was less able to mold a truth that everyone believed in than I'd thought it was. It also showed that central authority in the Soviet Union wasn't as dominant or complete as I'd assumed. I never could have imagined that anyone would dare threaten violence against the Red Army, or come close to rioting against the Soviet government.

Braithwaite's book, like Cherkashin's, challenged my understanding of the Soviet Union. If people supported the war initially, it meant they were more patriotic, and the party/government had more support, than I realized. The Politburo was also less devious and more complicated than I thought. I had no idea the leadership would allow near riots to take place without responding brutally. Finally, Braithwaite describes how citizens wrote letters to newspapers, some of which were printed, complaining bitterly about the terrible losses they suffered as a result of the war. This was the first time I realized the Soviet press, rather than serving as a one-way outlet for propaganda, also played a role as an outlet for the frustrations of the citizenry.

I told myself that I wanted to fight the Soviets in Afghanistan because they were making war on and brutalizing a good and independent people. I particularly admired the Mujahideen, who courageously fought back even when they were hopelessly outmatched at the beginning of the conflict. When the White House released a photo in 1983 of Reagan sitting in the oval office with a group of traditionally clad Mujahideen, I deeply respected these tough, exotic-looking men.

But the Mujahideen and the Afghan people were actually invisible to me. I had no real idea who I was supporting—who these people were that I wanted American arms and money to flow to— just as I had no meaningful sense that I was supporting the killing of young Soviet soldiers, real people I would have related to if I'd known them.

The Soviet war in Afghanistan was a terrible and brutal mistake, like most wars. But it was also a mistake for us to supply the money and arms that killed so many of the young soldiers sent on that tragic journey. The war should have been left to run whatever course it was going to take, without us. My belief that we were going to liberate the freedom-loving people of Afghanistan was both a naïve fantasy and a rationalization, an excuse to fight my favorite enemy. It was based on almost zero knowledge of Afghanistan, the Afghan people, their history, aims, or desires.

During this period, I frequently went to eat at what we called the "International Conflicts Mall" in Arlington, Virginia. The tiny strip mall had an Afghan, a Cambodian, and a Vietnamese restaurant all right next to each other. Eating at the Afghan restaurant made me feel immersed in the culture I was involved with (making war on). It made me feel serious and respectful toward Afghanistan.

6. STALIN WAS A MONSTER, BUT HIS
SUPPORTERS WEREN'T ALL CRAZY OR EVIL

Stalin was a vicious mass murderer whose death toll was on the same scale as Hitler's, and who arguably destroyed his own country. But he was extremely popular during the twenty-five-odd years he led the Soviet Union, a revered, father-like figure to most of his people. Even today, polling suggests 70 percent of the Russian population believe Stalin played a positive role in Soviet history, and just over half the population think positively of him as a person.

How is this possible? How could such a brutal killer (of his own people) engender such positive feelings?

In my early studies of Soviet history, I was always bewildered by this. Some historians and commentators explained it by saying that Soviet citizens were wildly misled. They supported Stalin because they didn't really know what he was doing. But this isn't exactly right. Many Soviets could see the death and destruction happening all around them with their own eyes. True, they lacked access to even a remotely truthful account of the extent of Stalin's crimes, but many had a basic idea. In any case, much of the truth came out after Stalin's death. At that point, his support diminished somewhat, but remained strong.

Were Stalin's supporters then (and now) delusional? Were they evil, or stupid? I used to think some fatal flaw in their collective and individual characters explained their feelings about Stalin, but that doesn't satisfy me anymore. Tens of millions of people—more, even—supported Stalin, then and now. Dismissing them as crazy or otherwise flawed is an excuse for not trying to understand them.

I am going to try to understand them here. This is a dangerous business. To truly understand Stalin's supporters, I will have to engage seriously with their arguments about Stalin's accomplishments and personal strengths. When dealing with a mass murderer, this pulls focus away from their horrible crimes and all the suffering they caused.

In order, then, to keep the focus where it belongs, and to make clear what we're up against in trying to understand Stalin's supporters, I'll begin with an accounting of his crimes.

The Crimes

Stalin killed and imprisoned millions of Soviet citizens, creating an endless stream of completely innocent victims throughout his time in power. Most of these were workers and peasants, although Stalin deliberately decimated the party elite as well. The waves of repression ebbed and flowed, but never stopped.

The numbers are staggering, hard to even conceptualize. Probably around 15 million Soviets overall were incarcerated at some point in the camps of the Gulag. Two to three million of them died, from exposure, exhaustion, overwork, illness, and sometimes execution. Around three-quarters of a million people were killed during the repressive frenzy of the Great Terror between 1936 and 1938. (This doesn't include those who died during the forced deportation of around 6 million ethnic minorities, and other "special exiles.")

Looking at what many consider original overestimates and correcting for later archival research, here's how Ronald G. Suny compiles the numbers: 10 to 11 million lives "destroyed" in the 1930s, approximately 3.8 million sentenced for counterrevolutionary activity or crimes between 1930 and 1953, of which 786,000 were executed, and at the end of Stalin's reign, 2.5 million prisoners and 3.8 million in special settlement or exile. Another 5.7 million killed in collectivization (following Stephen G. Davies and R. W. Wheatcroft), mostly victims of famine as Stalin forced the nation's farmers onto collective farms, upending the entire agricultural system of a largely agrarian society.

Anne Applebaum, a journalist and historian, points out in her brilliant and comprehensive *Gulag: A History* how imprecise any accounting is, both because there's so much left to learn and also because the number of victims borders on the uncountable—there are just too many categories. For example, elderly parents of men who were sent to the camps died of starvation, and might have been provided for had their children been free. Orphans of Stalin's victims died of diseases in poorly equipped orphanages. And even when statistics do manage to count victims accurately, Applebaum suggests that they still can't ever reflect all of the misery and suffering inflicted on families.

There are many theories about why Stalin killed and imprisoned so many people. Some suggest he was emulating Ivan the Terrible, keeping his populace afraid in order to keep them in line (the pioneering historian Sheila Fitzpatrick fleshes out this notion by saying that Stalin saw the old party bosses as the equivalent of feudal lords, and himself as the modern Ivan the Terrible who had to destroy them in order to build a modern state with a new subservient nobility.) Others argue that Stalin wanted to replace the party elite with newer and more loyal cadres. Still others believe that, with the Second World War coming, the fear of internal and external enemies played into the worst impulses of a leader who was suspicious and paranoid by nature. These interpretations aren't necessarily exclusive—historians who highlight one explanation often agree with several of the others as well.

In his multivolume biography of Stalin, historian Stephen Kotkin argues that the political terror in particular was caused by the combination of the Communist Party's conspiratorial worldview, which saw the world as composed of two enemy camps, with Stalin's dark mind and great political ability. Describing that dark mind, Kotkin says that Stalin saw himself as the only true guardian of the revolution and anyone who opposed him as creating weakness and disunity. It was his job to protect the socialist state, and whatever he had to do to accomplish this was justified. Stalin believed that pitying your enemies would be foolish and sentimental, even ignorant, since the laws of history were clear. On an immediate rather than grand scale, Kotkin believes the key drivers of the terror were Stalin's obsession with the criticism of collectivization, his obsession with Trotsky, and concerns about the independence of his inner circle. In other words, as he led the state on a path of historical development that he couldn't allow to be thwarted, he felt undermined and threatened by others with power.

Despite the insane level of repression Stalin carried out, many of his actions were obviously sane and competent. Some historians have come up with an approach that tries to see him as a more rational actor. J. Arch Getty was one of the early historians to look at Stalin this way. He argues that the purges of the Communist Party ranks in the mid-1930s were, at least in part, a response to local officials asking Moscow to get rid of corrupt local leaders. It was hard for the Soviet leadership to know what was really going on far from the center, but charges of incompetence and corruption were believable, and Stalin responded. Getty also believes Stalin felt threatened on a number of levels: a new constitution had recently turned everyone into citizens, potentially giving them more power; Stalin thought that Lev Kamenev, Grigory Zinoviev, and other leaders were likely conspiring against him because, as a Bolshevik himself,

Stalin knew Bolsheviks were by nature conspiratorial; the provinces had to be empowered so that local leaders could govern, but they were getting too powerful, and provincial leaders were lying to him about their economic situation; and in a recent census, a huge number of Soviets had admitted that they didn't like communism and did like Christianity.

Another theory holds that Bolshevik governance required unity, but that meant dissent was kept quiet, so the leaders didn't know what people really thought. In order to find out where popular opinion really stood, the state surveilled the population more heavily, and encouraged denunciations. This led to arrests, interrogations, and mass incarceration. The leadership was also afraid that conspiracies would grow because so many people had been hurt by the party. Victimization itself created a link between those hurt by collectivization and those hurt by incarceration for political activities. This spelled danger.

James Harris, a historian at the University of Leeds, challenges a common and long-held assumption that the terror was primarily about Stalin and his goal to increase his power. In *The Great Fear*, he argues that the Bolsheviks looked at earlier revolutions, including France's, and saw they had failed because the revolutionaries had underestimated the ferocity of the counterrevolutionary response. The Bolsheviks were determined not to make the same mistake. This extreme (though understandable) anxiety about missing the signs of counterrevolution meant they didn't believe their security services when they reported that things were actually okay. Instead, the Bolshevik leaders insisted the security services find the conspiracies they were sure were out there. They ended up creating a whole system to produce information that said things weren't okay, and then they believed that information.

According to Harris, this manufactured information fit with and then also amplified information about real threats. For example, Stalin received intercepts of internal Japanese communications arguing that Japan should invade the Soviet Union, occupy the country up to the Urals, *and make contact with forces opposed to Stalin inside the country* (emphasis mine, and probably Stalin's too). He also obtained a transcript of Churchill (out of office at the time) saying that the Soviet Union's growing industrialization was a grave danger to all of Europe, and that European countries had to create a bloc with the United States against the USSR. All of this information fed into Stalin's fears about internal opposition and the world's determination to destroy the Soviet Union. In fairness, Churchill's views did represent widespread sentiment. There were kernels of truth to many of the conspiracies Stalin saw.

Harris details still more deep anxieties for Stalin: Kulaks who had been incarcerated during collectivization were now coming back from their terms in prison, and were potential opponents; the nationalities might not support the regime in time of war, which Stalin knew was coming. Despite the strength of the Soviet state, Stalin felt under siege.

Harris's approach leans into the relatability of historical actors. He dispenses with the idea of a clinically paranoid Stalin, and explains how his suspicious, conspiratorial view of the world formed. For me, this is particularly convincing. But really, all of the above explanations for Stalin's brutality are extremely thoughtful. Still, we have limited experience that can help us understand such a high degree of brutality stemming from exaggerated insecurity, suspicion, and fear. We are used to seeing violent race hatred spark such levels of violence. But Stalin's motivations were much more complicated than Hitler's, for example, and we'll never know with any certainty why he did what he did.

––––––––––

In addition to the murder and mass incarceration of ordinary citizens and members of the party elite, from the late 1920s through the 1930s peasants also suffered and died in unimaginable numbers during Stalin's collectivization. Collectivization was the mass movement of the nation's peasants from their small, independent plots of land onto larger farms where the land was assigned to the collective, and the farmers as a group owned the output. Stalin thought the system of individual ownership of small plots of land was terrible at providing grain for the market, and perhaps more important, not in keeping with the country's communist ideals.

At this stage, well over half the Soviet population was made up of peasants. This is a complicated category of victims, because most died as a result of famine brought on by collectivization, but many were also arrested, deported, and sometimes executed for resisting this enormous shift in their social, economic, and political lives. The nonfamine victims were similar to any of Stalin's other targets—he thought they were conspiring to stop him, and he responded with violence. But the millions who starved were a different matter.

Most peasants didn't want to give up land they owned to become collective farmers. So the authorities forced them to. This became a vicious war on a half-real, half-imagined class of wealthier peasants called kulaks, who were supposedly spearheading the resistance. Kulaks were declared class enemies, which essentially meant anything could be done to them. Entire families were deported to distant parts of the country. Many died during these long and brutal journeys, and people continued to die after they arrived in isolated locations that often had barren lands and barely any food or shelter.

Many peasants slaughtered their livestock to keep from being declared kulaks, or because they didn't want their animals to become the property of the collective farms. This led to an enormous reduction in the nation's stock of farm animals. The government was confiscating grain and sending it to the cities and even abroad, while peasants who had any surplus grain often hid it. As more peasants were moved onto collective farms, agricultural productivity plummeted further.

All of this resulted in poor harvests and severe food shortages. Famine spread across Ukraine, Kazakhstan, the North Caucasus, much of the Volga valley, the Urals, and some areas in the north. Estimates of how many died range from 2.5 million to more than

7 million people. In the midst of this misery, some turned to cannibalism—there were reports of parents killing one child to feed them to another, and of bands of starving people targeting orphans to kill and eat.

Some historians have argued that Stalin intentionally created the famine to weaken resistance to collectivization. More recently, Kotkin has argued this older interpretation is incorrect. While Stalin's policy of collectivization certainly caused the famine, he didn't starve the peasants on purpose to get them to submit. In fact, he agreed to send food and farming equipment to the hardest-hit regions. According to Kotkin, even Robert Conquest, who originally charged Stalin with creating an intentional famine, later withdrew this assertion.

Is it possible to understand why Stalin and his supporters, even in pursuit of their communist ideals, accepted collectivization's massive cruelty and suffering (beyond Stalin's obvious high tolerance for cruelty and suffering)? Fitzpatrick suggests the Bolshevik revolution actually kept going through the late 1930s, instead of ending in 1917 after the Bolshevik takeover, or after the civil war ended in 1921. This means that both collectivization and the surge of terror in the mid-to-late 1930s were actually a part of the revolution. This is one way to understand the tremendous violence and upheaval of collectivization—revolutions are extremely violent, and revolutionaries will often do anything to achieve their ends. Since collectivization was a fundamental value of communism and was supposed to be a practical solution to economic problems, Stalin, an extremist even for a revolutionary, was going to go through with it no matter what.

It's worth comparing collectivization to what we did to the Native Americans starting several hundred years earlier. Obviously the goals were different—appropriating land as opposed to creating a state-controlled socialist farming system—as were the underlying attitudes toward the victimized populations. But in some ways the experiences were similar. The means we employed to conquer Native American land were not for the most part intentionally genocidal (though they were at times), but they used many of the same brutal tactics that collectivization did—forced relocations, outright killings and massacres, state power and propaganda used to whip up popular sentiment against innocent people. And the effect was similar: famine, mass death, and incalculable suffering.

In a sense, both projects accomplished their goals. White Americans got what they wanted. We took over the whole country, and we're still here. Although the glamorization of the conquest of America and the destruction of Native American populations has been to some degree replaced, or at least challenged by, a more thoughtful approach to this brutal history, concern about what was done is hardly universal or even widespread. Cartoonish images of Native Americans on baseball and football team uniforms (thankfully in decline) suggest a nation still uninterested in facing what happened, and willing to forgive ourselves and our forebears for what they did. But we're surprised that some in Russia have forgiven Stalin.

Did Stalin's crimes reach the level of genocide or holocaust? Genocide refers to the extermination of a national, racial, religious or ethnic group, while holocaust usually refers specifically to the Nazis' mass murder of Jews or more generally to large-scale, intentional mass slaughter. Historians don't usually use those words when they're discussing what happened under Stalin, probably in part because there wasn't a single ethnic group targeted for destruction. Stalin's victims were sometimes singled out as members of religious or ethnic groups, but not by any means always, and not with the specific intent to exterminate. Still, the sheer number of deaths—those executed for alleged political crimes, those worked and starved to death in camps, those who died in forced migrations during collectivization, those who died in the famines that resulted from Stalin's policies—add up to millions of people (some think the total number is around 10 million, others estimate it's double that). The word "extermination" was used frequently in state propaganda during this mass assault, a violent exhortation and description of the plan for fighting against class enemies, including the bourgeoisie and the kulaks. "Class enemies," of course, was not an ethnic group, and was also hard to define, largely because it was so preposterously broad. "Class enemies" was used as a catch-all to justify attacking almost anyone the authorities wanted to.

Whether or not we define Stalin's murders as a genocide or holocaust, it seems to me that Stalin presided over a movement around the borders of a holocaust against those he called class enemies. I say around the borders of a holocaust rather than engaging in a holocaust because, despite the language of extermination, and the level of violence and killing, the actual intent was probably not to exterminate through killing. The idea appears to have been to eliminate class enemies through historical processes, which involved killing when necessary but relied also on social and societal evolution. No one ever made a decision to kill all the members of the bourgeoisie, or to kill all the rich peasants.

Still, the idea of killing them all seems to have been in the air—just a step or two away from what was actually happening. When so many people were killed, when such horrors took place, when violence and hysteria were so widespread, it's hard to imagine it could have been even worse. And yet the Soviets may have just missed having an even larger, full-scale holocaust.

How Could Anyone Support This Man?

Stalin's crimes were titanic in scope, intentional, and brutal. I struggle with the idea that I could think of him with anything other than pure revulsion. But many do. So having briefly discussed his major crimes, I'll ask again: how could this man have been, and remain, so popular?

The most basic answer is that tens of millions of people have been willing to balance Stalin's crimes against what they consider to be his strengths and accomplishments.

In his book *All the Kremlin's Men,* Mikhail Zygar quotes Yury Luzhkov, a former mayor of Moscow, as saying, "[Stalin] was responsible for fifty million deaths. The most hideous crime on his black conscience was the murder of twenty million kulaks—the country's strongest economic managers." But in discussing Stalin's role in winning the Second World War, Luzhkov says, "Stalin's role was great. He was one of the most powerful and decisive factors. It was Stalin who managed the country's resources and oversaw its strategy. The first period of the war was his fault, but the second was his triumph."

Similarly, in his interviews with Oliver Stone, Putin puts it this way: "We try to talk about his merits in achieving victory over fascism . . . he turned into a dictator . . . this doesn't mean that he was not capable of bringing together the people of the Soviet Union . . . this doesn't mean . . . that we have to forget all the atrocities Stalin committed—the destruction of millions of our compatriots. These things are not to be forgotten. And he is an ambiguous figure."

Luzhkov and Putin are saying, in their own way, what many Russians have expressed. Stalin had a bad side and a good side. This is a very hard mindset for an American to understand. It involves accepting that someone who killed so many people might have done positive things as well, that they aren't necessarily fully defined by their crimes.

This way of thinking about a brutal leader is not unique to the Soviet Union or Russia. In China, Mao tried to modernize a country with a largely agrarian population. Tens of millions died from policy-induced famine, and perhaps a million or more died in a political terror. Like Stalin, Mao was popular at the time and remains popular among a substantial segment of the Chinese population. This suggests that in the middle of the twentieth century, significant segments of large, heavily agrarian societies were willing to forgive a leader for killing them on an enormous scale, maybe in exchange for rapid economic development.

Of course, how susceptible Soviet and Chinese citizens were to propaganda and lies played a role in Stalin's and Mao's popularity. But even accounting for the ability of state machinery to mislead people, to fool some of the people some of the time, there appears to be some kind of a broad-based willingness, at certain times in certain places, to accept brutality in exchange for economic progress. More than anything else, this may show the degree of misery in the Soviet Union and China, how unbearable life must have been when these were still early industrial societies. If you read about the hardships of peasant life in the Russian countryside before the revolution, or the miseries of early industrial life in the cities, the idea of this trade-off goes from unthinkable to plausible.

But still, Stalin's strengths and accomplishments would have to be enormous for so many people to believe they could even remotely counterbalance his atrocities.

What were they?

Strengths and Accomplishments

Stalin Built the Soviet Union

While Vladimir Lenin is often considered the father of the Soviet Union, and that is true in its own way, he died in early 1924, seven calendar years after the October Revolution, but closer to six actual years. He was ill and largely incapacitated over a year before that.

When Stalin took over, the Soviet Union was a kind of rickety framework for a country more than a functional nation. It was fresh out of a brutal and scarring civil war, and deeply divided by political, ideological, and class conflicts. The countryside—and it was a country of mostly countryside—was barely governed by the central authorities. The economy was in a partial state of recovery due to a limited number of market-oriented concessions Lenin had made as part of his New Economic Policy, but still, the economy was barely functional. In a way, when Stalin took over, the country was almost as much an idea as a reality, and probably more likely to collapse than survive.

By the time Stalin died almost thirty years later, the Soviet Union was a modern, functioning state, and had been for years. It was economically self-sufficient, its republics were fundamentally united, and its federal authority was unquestioned throughout all regions. On top of that, it was a world power.

The hard work, imagination, and suffering of millions of Soviet citizens were central to the growth and development of the state. The Soviet people labored, built, believed in, and invested in the Soviet project, and they paid an enormous price for it. But Stalin's leadership and force of will were undeniably central factors in the tremendous and rapid growth of the state. He was the primary force behind industrialization, collectivization, and the coherence of the country as a group of linked national republics. Put together, these three elements in a sense were the Soviet Union. Stalin was not the ideological or creative father of the Soviet Union—Lenin and Marx filled that role. But he built the country, partly on their design, and partly on the wild improvisation that essentially was Stalinism.

Industrialization may have been Stalin's greatest achievement. Prerevolutionary Russia was industrializing, but was lagging far behind its Western competitors. Stalin led a nationwide effort to catch up at a breakneck pace. The country didn't have the financial resources, capital, technical expertise—really the ability—to accomplish this. But Stalin didn't think the Soviet Union would survive economically if it didn't industrialize quickly. It also wouldn't survive physically—Stalin realized early on that the Second World War was coming at some point, and if the country didn't industrialize, it would be destroyed.

The industrialization of the Soviet Union involved so much waste, failure, bureaucratic stupidity, and most of all, human suffering, that it was a kind of disaster. On the other hand, the country did industrialize, and in time for the German onslaught. That made it an amazing success. Collectivization also transformed the country, but the cost in human misery was much higher than with industrialization, and the end result much more ambiguous.

The rapidity and horrible severity of these transitions in Soviet life gives you a pretty good sense of Stalin. While almost every other leader was willing to compromise on immediately attaining an ideal version of communism in order to make sure the economy, in the short term, produced enough food, Stalin insisted on moving forward toward a stricter, almost purer version of communism—an industrialized state with collective ownership of the means of production—while laying waste to pretty much everything in his way.

Collectivization was a titanic human calamity. But with peasants now living on collective farms, Soviet power finally took hold in the countryside, and the modern Soviet state was rounded out and realized. It would be easy to admire Stalin's will and persistence if millions of people hadn't died as a result of his actions. Some people admire it anyway.

As for cohering the federal state, Stalin inherited a patchwork country of wide-ranging and disparate nationalities. Neither full federal control nor the idea itself of a unified Soviet state had fully taken hold throughout Soviet territory when he came to power. Although his policies toward the nation's diverse nationalities were problematic and changed frequently, there's no doubt that a centralized Soviet state existed and was accepted by most of its citizens within a few years of Stalin taking charge of the country.

There really is no American figure of comparable importance in building the United States. Maybe Washington combined with Adams, Hamilton, and Jefferson? To understand the way many people feel about Stalin's accomplishments, picture those founding fathers as a single person, and imagine that they'd birthed our nation only ninety years ago.

Stalin Led the Soviet Union to Victory in World War II

The Soviet Union's single greatest achievement may have been the defeat of Nazi Germany in World War II. The Soviets faced 80 to 90 percent of Germany's total military strength in the war. They killed many times the number of German soldiers that the Allies did. They probably suffered around 25 million dead, with something like 10 million of them soldiers (the numbers are hard to calculate precisely with such mass casualties, which include people buried in mass graves and soldiers still unaccounted-for, and could actually be much higher). The Soviet Union easily could have been destroyed. Instead, they not only saved themselves, but it's fair to say, considering the nature of the Nazi menace, they saved the world as we knew it.

At the time war broke out, if the Soviets had been a well-fed and strong people, with a well-fed and strong army, it still would have been a phenomenal victory, and a phenomenal act of moral and physical courage, to beat the technologically superior, better-fed, better-equipped German Army. But to have done this in the middle of the extraordinary trauma of Stalin's mass violence against his own people is ten times greater an accomplishment of moral and physical strength, and something for them to be even prouder of.

Stalin's role in this great victory was ambiguous.

On the one hand, without the rapid industrialization he spearheaded, the Soviets would have been run over by Hitler. They wouldn't have had the tanks, planes, artillery, or industrial base to put up a fight. Stalin pushed for this rapid industrialization not just because the Soviet economy needed it but because he knew a second great war was coming, and the country wouldn't survive it without a strong industrial base. Stalin has to receive enormous credit for preparing for war like this, which likely not only avoided an even more calamitous physical destruction of the country, but also prevented the even greater degree of atrocities the Nazis almost certainly would have committed in a longer and broader occupation.

Stalin also played a key role in keeping the country together during the war. He was a popular leader, and most of his people and his soldiers believed in him, trusted him, and followed him. He motivated the Soviet people to survive, and to fight, under the direst possible circumstances. People followed and believed in Stalin in part because of the strength he projected as a leader. But he also acted in ways that inspired devotion. He stayed in Moscow even when the Germans were close to capturing it, steadying the city. Both of his sons fought in the war, and one died.

The nation's willingness to follow Stalin was vital because the Soviets easily could have lost the war. Cohesion and an ability to keep fighting, even in the face of terrible losses and long odds, were in their own way as important for victory as the newly modernized Soviet industry and the great Soviet landmass were. This probably means that what came to be called Stalin's "cult of personality" had some utility beyond control, grandiosity, and the bizarre exercise of power. Stalin's godlike status united the people and helped win the war.

When I first studied Soviet history, Stalin was often derided for poor decision-making in the war, and was considered an incompetent military strategist. Historians have reexamined his wartime role since then, and now some believe that, although he made mistakes, Stalin's decision-making on most matters, including strategy, was good. I'm closely following historian Geoffrey Roberts's analysis here. Stalin appears to have personally managed all aspects of the war effort—political, economic, diplomatic, and military. On the military side, he was heavily involved in tactics, strategy, and supply. This is consistent with who Stalin was and how he ran the Soviet Union, so it rings true. His strengths may have been less in battle tactics than in morale, strategy, mobilization, and logistics. But that's what you'd expect in a civilian leader.

Stalin's most important strategic decision may have been signing a nonaggression pact with Hitler in 1939, a shocking development that allowed Hitler to focus on his western front, and led directly to Soviet invasions of Poland, Lithuania, Latvia, Estonia, and parts of Finland and Romania, as well as the related murder by the Soviets of an estimated 22,000 Polish officers and intellectuals in the Katyn Forest and several other sites, mass deportations, and countless other atrocities. Many in the West, including the Soviet Union's chief supporters there, were horrified that Stalin would make peace with the German fascist regime. And since many of the consequences were so devastating for so many, the pact is often viewed as a nefarious betrayal of the forces fighting Hitler.

It certainly was a betrayal, of both the anti-Hitler forces and everything the Soviet Union stood for too. Still, to understand it fully, it has to be seen as a kind of bitter pill that Stalin swallowed. Stalin believed the greatest danger facing the Soviet Union was actually a coalition of the Germans and the British. This may sound unthinkable to us, but Britain was so hostile toward the Soviet Union—and in Stalin's mind both Germany and Britain were capitalist aggressors—that it made a kind of sense.

Stalin still preferred, and actively sought, a clearer alliance with Britain in an anti-Hitler coalition He reached out to Britain, but the effort was stymied by both his own ideology, which could only see the capitalist countries as determined to destroy the Soviet Union, and by the analogous British assumption that the Soviet Union was intent on destroying the capitalist West. Neither side could see past itself enough to trust the other. Once his efforts to ally with Britain against the Germans failed, Stalin saw allying with Germany as the only remaining option.

As this kind of second or third choice, strategically at least, the pact was arguably a smart effort to buy time for the Soviet Union to prepare for war, regardless of whether Stalin's fears about Britain were going to be realized. By the time Hitler invaded the Soviet Union in 1941, the Soviets had tripled the number of people in their armed forces from what it had been only a few years earlier.

According to Roberts, Stalin was also excellent at managing relations between his generals, which resulted in increasingly well-conceived and agile war plans, particularly in the victory at Stalingrad, which turned the tide of the war. Overall, Stalin's authority and endless energy guided not just his generals but the entire army and the entire country.

But Stalin also committed unspeakable offenses that crippled the Soviet war effort. He had more than three-quarters of the Soviet officer corps purged in the years leading up to the war. This meant that the Red Army was mostly led by inexperienced officers when the war started, a disaster whose cost can't even be estimated.

Stalin also refused to accept warnings that the initial German attack was imminent, so the country was surprised by the German blitzkrieg. This is a little more complicated than it sounds. There were constant warnings of an impending attack, and it was hard to know which one to believe. Stalin also thought Germany would wait to attack the Soviet Union until after it defeated Britain, in order to avoid fighting a two-front war (that's what they should have done). He also held out some hope of a diplomatic solution, and didn't want to provoke Germany with an even bigger mobilization. And finally, Stalin thought Soviet defenses would hold even if there was a German attack. But at the end of the day, Stalin was fooled, and the price was enormously high.

Roberts also describes a number of significant tactical mistakes that Stalin made. He launched a massive counteroffensive right after the initial German attacks instead of waiting and drawing the Nazi army further into the Soviet interior, a costly mistake. He also refused to withdraw from Kiev, even though his generals told him to. Six hundred thousand Red Army soldiers were killed as a result. There were other tactical mistakes as well, though most were made on the advice of his generals.

Finally, through his use of indiscriminate terror before the war, both against the officer ranks and throughout society, Stalin had created an environment where it could be dangerous for people to behave in rational ways. In a broader sense, society was gripped by a series of delusions and even a kind of mania. It's hard to say what this does to a war effort. But a terrified society is probably not the best equipped to face the challenges and make the decisions required in wartime.

Stalin, then, deserves both significant credit for the victory and significant blame for how badly the war went (it would have gone badly no matter what, but wouldn't have gone quite as badly if Stalin had acted differently). Still, at the end of the day, the Soviets won a war for their very existence, and to an undeniable degree the survival of the rest of the world too. Stalin led that war. There is simply no denying him credit for that, and we can't expect most Russians to deny him credit, either.

Apart from what he actually did, figuring out how to feel about Stalin's role in the war is further muddied by his actions immediately after it ended. Stalin sent many returning Soviet soldiers to the Gulag, particularly those who had been German POWs. If you revere Stalin because of what he did during the war, this should create a problem for you. You can't fully appreciate and respect the victory and the victors in the Second World War while also venerating the man who put so many of the great and brave men who fought the war in the Gulag. From this perspective, maybe Russians should have to choose between World War II and Stalin.

Stalin Was a Strong and Highly Intelligent Leader

It's hard to speak generally about a group as broad as the Soviet population, but ethnic Russians often voice a desire to be ruled by strong leaders, who presumably ensure stability. In *The Future Is History*, Gessen points out that one way repressive regimes get support is by providing a predictable way of life, free from the anxiety produced by opportunity and possibility. This is one kind of stability. I am referring here to the more literal stability of a country free from war, revolution, and the physical destruction they cause. Not surprisingly, the more suffering of this type a country endures, the more it craves the stability of their absence.

The United States is (or at least has been) a fundamentally self-supporting structure. The leaders come and go, but the country stays together. The Soviet Union lacked, and Russia lacks, this fundamental sense of stability. Even at its most stable—and for long stretches the Soviet Union was fairly stable—there was always some sense that the leaders of the country were playing a vital role in holding it together.

Fears of the country collapsing were hardly theoretical. When Stalin took over, Russia had recently fallen completely apart, during the revolution and civil war. The population had suffered unimaginably, with death, disease, hunger and sorrow everywhere. Having an overly strong leader could result in even more suffering, and in fact it did. But in a history full of strife, war, the threat of collapse, actual collapse, and the psychic blow to Russians specifically of losing their empire, it makes sense that a political culture developed (or endured) that saw strong leaders as the best hope for lowering the odds of misery.

There was no question that Stalin embodied a kind of strength. He worked incessantly. He had no trouble making decisions. He had principles that he stated clearly and followed (Marxism-Leninism). He made up his mind on massive social and societal transformations and then saw them through (industrialization, collectivization). Stalin's worldview was constrained by his orthodox communism, but that was common in the circles he ran in.

Stalin also had a more archaic kind of strength. He eliminated anyone who caused him trouble, or he worried might cause him trouble in the future. Most people around him who survived readily deferred to him. Kotkin theorizes that despite his murderous ways and the direct threat he posed to them, no one in his circle ever killed him because they all realized no one could replace him. Stalin was understood to be the only member of the top leadership capable of running the country. Murdering those who might replace you and terrorizing everyone else into dependence isn't good or moral leadership, but the results were perceived by many in the Soviet Union as a form of strength.

The strength Stalin projected was backed up by a formidable intelligence. When I first studied Soviet history, my teachers argued that he was simple and small-minded compared to Lenin, his genius predecessor. Sure, he had street smarts, which he adapted to the world of politics, and he was cunning, which allowed him to consolidate power. But unlike Lenin, he wasn't particularly smart or creative. I don't think this vision of Stalin came entirely from my teachers—it formed from my own misunderstandings as well. But in any case, that picture was wrong.

Stalin was extremely smart, to put it mildly. He was a thinker, in every sense of the word. Perhaps he wasn't quite the original theoretician that Lenin was, but he certainly had a well-developed intellect. According to Kotkin, he read voraciously, and was able to understand and synthesize vast amounts of information on any topic, even technical issues, although he didn't have any scientific training or education. When Stalin met with aircraft designers or engineers of virtually any stripe, they were invariably surprised to discover he had actually read and understood the papers they'd sent him. He also wrote thoughtfully, and could come up with his own ideas and theories.

Stalin's organizational skills were also unparalleled. He essentially outorganized Trotsky into the leadership of the Soviet Union. He figured out how to move and structure people and institutions to further his political power, and to make things happen. His organizational abilities were not just self-serving, they were country-serving. Put together, Stalin's skills and abilities in these areas were unique and, in the political sphere, probably on the level of genius.

Stalin Was Synonymous with a System
That Elevated Multitudes out of Poverty

Many Soviet citizens, or their parents, were peasants and impoverished workers who were educated and brought into higher social strata, first by the revolution and then under Stalin. This rapid social ascension happened to a huge number of people in a way that is extremely rare. It fostered a belief and loyalty in the Soviet system and in Stalin.

Economic conditions in the country more generally were also improving under Stalin, even if they remained in many ways quite poor. Although the post-Stalin period brought a more dramatic increase in living standards, industrialization during Stalin's rule brought some noticeable improvement for many, and at the very least a realistic hope for further improvement to come.

Less tangible benefits than economic and social progress also built support for and loyalty to Stalin. Every other word spoken by the leadership and the party/state was about how workers and peasants were the heroes of the new order. These words were sincere, part of the bedrock of Bolshevik belief and ideology. They affected people. Many also found profound meaning in their lives through communist ideology, which filled a void, and for some took the place of religion. Stalin was the undisputed leader of the mass movement that was providing this meaning.

———————

On the simplest level, Stalin's popularity stemmed (and still stems) from his supporters' willingness to consider these strengths and accomplishments when evaluating him, instead of judging him based solely on his crimes. This is a hard mentality for an American to understand, and very unsettling—considering any positive side of a barbaric killer seems immoral, a denial of the severity of the crimes.

But are we as different from Stalin's supporters as we think?

It's useful to look at the terrible things that have been done in our country, too, to see if we've responded to our earlier leaders any differently from how Soviets and Russians responded to theirs.

Slavery, of course, ended in America sixty or seventy years before Stalin's worst crimes (not very long, really), and had gone on for roughly 250 years before that. If we were looking for an era-appropriate analogy to slavery, Russian serfdom might be better, although the differences between serfdom and slavery were as great as the similarities. But the goal here is not to find a precise analogy. It's to find the best way to see ourselves, and to help us understand Soviet and Russian feelings and attitudes.

George Washington (along with other founding fathers) was a slave owner. Many people feel that he, and other leaders throughout history, should be judged in the context of their time, and perhaps that's true. But at least some people in America understood at the time that slavery was a great evil. And Washington was fully participating in one of the greatest crimes against humanity in history. As our first president, he did nothing to stop it.

Washington was, and is, considered by many to have been a good, decent, and honorable man. But he was a monster to other people, in his case the slaves he held in bondage. People who mistreated their slaves in particularly cruel ways were even more monstrous, but holding people in bondage at all is a horrifying act. Washington's beliefs and attitudes changed to some degree during his life, and by the time he died, he arranged for his slaves to be freed after his wife's death. It's fair to say that he became somewhat less monstrous. But still, is this a man we want to name every other street in our country after?

At least for now, the answer is apparently yes, and voices seeking change in our pantheon of heroes are widely considered to be going too far if they include Washington on the list of those we shouldn't be venerating.

Many of the poorest people in Tsarist Russia felt liberated by the Bolshevik revolution, and then raised up by Stalin. He was probably going to be a hero to many of them no matter what else he did. We should be able to understand this, because Washington has been a hero to many of us even though he held slaves. We focus on his strengths and accomplishments, and underplay his moral crimes.

It seems possible, then, that our contrasting feelings about Washington and Stalin may be a case of "when it's our guy, it's okay." We'll forgive our heroes and leaders—we'll forgive ourselves—for all kinds of moral horrors, but we aren't forgiving in the same way when the perpetrators of horrible crimes are foreign leaders.

For both Russia and the United States, judging historical figures ultimately becomes an act of deciding—deciding who we are and who we want to be in relation to those figures. I don't think we should dismiss, ignore, or throw away George Washington because he owned slaves. But we shouldn't turn his great moral failings into a footnote either. And those failings are sufficient to keep him from being a great national hero whom we see only as the father of our country. Alternately, if we can see our country in all its complexity—good and bad, virtuous and evil, and everything in between—then we can see Washington as the father of that country. That, of course, he's perfect for.

To be clear, then, I am not saying Stalin deserved the admiration so many felt, and continue to feel, for him. I am saying I can make sense of it without having to resort to claims that his supporters were or are necessarily immoral or deluded. We are struggling with similar questions in the United States as we argue over how to think about our own founding fathers. I struggle with it. The founding fathers seem brilliant, full of incredible political foresight, and responsible fairly directly for much that is good in my own life. They also had various levels of complicity in slavery. I've worked hard to let admiration and revulsion for the same people coexist in my brain. It isn't easy. It's more comfortable to pick one—revulsion or admiration—and settle on that.

Is Russia's reckoning with Stalin going any worse or more slowly than our reckoning with the horrors of slavery and the Americans who supported it?

Soviet society grappled openly with Stalin's legacy under Khrushchev, then again under Gorbachev. Periods of intense debate and reflection alternated with periods when the issue was censored out of public discourse. Both societal and governmental response to the issue has fluctuated since the collapse of the Soviet Union. Stephen Cohen points out that Moscow currently has two separate monuments to Stalin's victims, both state-sponsored: the Museum of the History of the Gulag, opened in 2015, and a monument to Stalin's victims unveiled in 2017. There are many more memorials in towns and villages across the country. But some have been shut down, and a human-rights group that focuses on remembering Stalin's victims has been attacked by the government. Society remains deeply divided on Stalin and his legacy.

In the United States, over a century and a half after slavery was abolished, we are engaged in a deeply painful and polarizing struggle about its legacy. Many people are trying to confront and remedy structural racism across a broad range of American institutions. Many others don't even see that racism, much less think it has to be addressed. Governments and protesters are taking down Confederate monuments, and correctly identifying southern Civil War generals as traitors, while some still consider them heroes. Although we have a number of historic sites, museums, and plaques related to slavery around the country, we only have a handful of memorials specifically dedicated to its victims and legacy (including a national lynching memorial that opened in Alabama in 2018). There are no such memorials in our capital.

The shrinking but still significant number of Americans sticking by the Confederate flag can help us understand the complexity of Stalin's legacy even better. The Confederacy was responsible for defending one of the most brutal atrocities in human history. But the majority of those who, until recently, were still flying the Confederate flag didn't support slavery. The flag represented something different and more complicated to them, including certain traditional values (their belief that they could separate those values from the colossal racism the flag symbolized is striking).

Likewise, although a small number of extremists in Russia to-day are calling for a return of large-scale, state-sponsored violence, most of Stalin's current supporters, as Stephen Cohen and others have pointed out, don't miss and don't support Stalin's terror, and don't want to bring back his level of mass violence or re-pression. It was the rest of the package they liked. They, too, feel they can separate that side of Stalin and Stalinism from its cruel, murderous legacy.

So where are we, really, in comparison to Russia? Almost a hun-dred and sixty years after the end of the Civil War, the debate over the legacy of slavery is raging all across our country. In Russia, it is less than seventy years since Stalin's death. Is it really that sur-prising that his legacy remains hotly debated and divisive, that not everyone is willing to condemn him?

I've spoken so far in terms of "Stalin" and "Soviet citizens." But it's problematic to focus on a single individual, even one with such enormous power, while lumping everyone else into a broad cate-gory under them. This way of looking at history and politics tends to exaggerate the influence of leaders and diminish or miss entirely the volition of the many other individuals (and groups) that make up any society. Scholars figured out long ago that you get a more profound and realistic sense of a country—of history itself—when you look closely at the everyday lives of ordinary people.

In the Soviet Union, life went on during Stalin's time in power. People didn't just sit in their apartments waiting to be picked up for arrest or execution. It wasn't simply thirty years of unmitigated fear and terror for everyone. Soviets lived, loved, went to work. They built things. There was ordinary life, even though it was a unique Soviet experience of ordinary life.

None of this should be a surprise, but before I specifically con-sidered it, I had only imagined hundreds of millions of people cow-ering in fear throughout the decades of Stalin's rule. I thought life was essentially two-dimensional in a totalitarian society. Hannah Arendt, not the first or only writer to describe totalitarianism but probably the most influential, based her description of this type of system on both Nazi Germany and the Soviet Union, so of course to some degree it accurately describes important aspects of Soviet society: the way all political institutions were replaced with new ones; the destruction of all existing social and legal traditions; the single-minded pursuit of a goal like industrialization regardless of the cost; an all-encompassing ideology; refusal to allow any dissent; the use of arbitrary terror to subjugate the population. All of this is incredibly incisive, and Arendt captured and categorized much about Soviet politics with a singular genius (for a fuller description of Arendt's work on totalitarianism, if you don't want to tackle Arendt herself, see Masha Gessen's *The Future Is History*.)

But I'm more interested in the concept of totalitarianism that filtered into the popular consciousness (and into my own). In the popular imagination, the ideas of Arendt and others were oversimplified and turned into the notion that Soviet rulers were able to exercise so much control over the lives and minds of their citizens that ordinary people were effectively reduced to a near-brainwashed state. Because all information was controlled by the authorities, and nothing but propaganda was fed to the masses, free thinking was killed off, and a population of near robots was created.

This vision of Soviet society was at odds with the simultaneous Western belief that the Soviet populace didn't and couldn't possibly support its wicked government. But either of these ways of perceiving Soviet society was okay for those of us who wanted to see the Soviets as totalitarian—we could go with zombies, or with opponents of the system terrified into silence. Both versions allowed us to dismiss the idea that there was such a thing as genuine support for the Soviet state.

The zombie vision of totalitarianism, and Arendt's more complex take, were both off-base in the post-Stalin years, when all aspects of Soviet life opened up considerably. But they were also wrong during Stalin's time, when people retained significant levels of autonomy and had a far more intricate and complex relationship with the state than they would under a "totalitarian" regime. In fairness, exercising control over what information comes in and out of your country runs the risk of feeding your enemy's wildest fantasies about you. Totalitarianism was the West's wildest fantasy about the Soviet Union.

Although defining the Soviet Union as a totalitarian state misrepresents what life and politics were like there, there was a very strong emotional-political connection between individual and state. Sheila Fitzpatrick uses suicide in Stalin's time to illustrate this point. Sometimes people left suicide notes blaming the state for their death. The state could be blamed for virtually anything, because it was overly involved in all aspects of life, and to a degree claimed dominion over, and thus responsibility for, everything. The state understood suicide in the same way, and investigations often concluded that suicides were political acts, even when there was no evidence of it. The state saw everything in political terms, so naturally it assumed suicides had a political motive and meaning. This wasn't a sign of totalitarianism, but it was evidence of a highly fused relationship between state and subject in the Soviet Union.

Eventually, the totalitarian framework for understanding Soviet society mostly died off among academics. Their exposure to (or academic discovery of) the complexity and richness of life even during Stalin's time showed that the totalitarian model was too rigid and formulaic, and didn't allow for the complexity and diversity of life in the Soviet Union. But somehow what they figured out never made it into the mainstream of Western political and cultural thought. Politicians, journalists, many intellectuals, and ordinary political observers still frequently refer to the Soviet Union as totalitarian. We sometimes jump to this model to understand a country like North Korea too. But we should realize from the Soviet experience that countries, and people, don't work this way. If we start imagining totalitarianism and brainwashing, it means we don't yet know enough about what's really going on in another country.

––––––––––

I've focused in this section on trying to understand Stalin's supporters, and I've gotten to the point where their positions make sense to me. But that doesn't mean I agree with their conclusions. Although it's not my place to say what Russia should do or what Russians should think, I have my own opinion on Stalin as a historical figure.

I believe Stalin was a mass murderer and a horrible human being. He built a nation under extremely difficult circumstances. He played some part in winning a war that helped save the world.

But he failed miserably at his most obvious job, which was leading his country out of its revolutionary phase into a more peaceful and brighter future. Lenin died just a few years after the Russian civil war ended. As the next leader, Stalin should have ratcheted down the violence. He ratcheted it up instead, creating so much terror and trauma that his country never fully recovered. The dream that he pursued, that he believed in, and that so many of his countrymen invested everything in, collapsed in large part as a result of this failure.

How exactly did Stalin and his legacy contribute to the collapse of the Soviet Union?

First, the revolution's already high level of party-government oppression developed into something unique and terrible under Stalin. Even though the practice of violent repression was greatly reduced after his death, it never went away. A significant tension between the authorities and the people in the Soviet Union became a permanent feature of life. It led to surveillance of the people, distrust of the people, a smothering of creativity and growth, brutality, and the suppression of many of the forces that make a society dynamic and successful.

Secondly, as Stephen Cohen points out in *The Victims Return*, the Gulag emptied out after Stalin died, and the conflict between the returning prisoners and those who had taken their places—literally their jobs and sometimes even their apartments—tore at the already frayed fabric of Soviet society. These profound social and psychological fissures persisted through the remaining short life of the USSR.

Thirdly, Khrushchev retreated substantially from Stalin's tyrannical means of governing, but this decent and humane change proved too threatening to most of those in power. Something had gotten calcified in the hearts and minds of the authorities under Stalin. Their own ability to move forward, to grow, to lead their people, was ruined by what they had done and who they became. Their ability to govern, to pursue their own original communist ideals with anything that might have truly pushed the country forward, was destroyed. This is undoubtedly part of why the Soviet economy never became fully viable. The structural deficiencies of socialism/communism are often pointed to as the singular cause of Soviet economic failure, but we don't really know what might have happened with more successful and imaginative leadership. Nobody took on the fundamental structural problems of the Soviet economy until Gorbachev, and by then it was too late.

Finally, Stalin turned the Soviet Union into a nation suffering a collective trauma. Trauma victims need to confront what happened to them in order to heal, and that just didn't happen in the Soviet Union. The process of self-reflection started under Khrushchev, but was reversed under Brezhnev. It started again under Gorbachev, with open debate and discussion about what had happened under Stalin, but then the country collapsed in the middle of this second reckoning. The nation was not yet able, or at least willing, to openly process all the suffering it had gone through. Stalin was the architect of this suffering, and bears great responsibility for it.

Could Stalin, or someone else, have built the Soviet Union without so much cruelty? Although it's easy to imagine some level of state violence going hand in hand with rapid and successful industrialization, or with some of the other Soviet efforts to transform and develop their country, overall it's hard to see how the massive levels of repression under Stalin did any good. Some historians have argued that mass incarceration created the forced labor pool necessary to complete so much work in such a short time at minimal cost, but close studies of this question make a compelling case that forced labor was an inefficient and economically costly way to achieve growth. Prisoner labor probably wasn't the best way to build the country, even if market-based alternatives were ruled out. As for whether the Soviet Union could have been kept in one piece without so much violence, the high level of popular support for Soviet ideals suggest high levels of violence probably weren't necessary to maintain stability. Of course, we'll never know what would have happened to the Soviet Union had there been no Stalin, or much less Stalinist violence—maybe it would have prospered, maybe it would have been wiped out in World War II, maybe it would have developed into something we can't quite imagine.

Had the country survived, Stalin's legacy would be at least somewhat different. He'd be a terrible man who succeeded. As it is, he was too awful, destroyed too many lives, and didn't even build a country that could last.

Of course, it's easy for me to pass these judgments, to reconcile all of these complicated historical events—to try to understand all of this suffering—when it was not my parents or children who died in the terror, not my parents or children who died in the war, and for that matter not my relatives who survived all of it, either, to prosper or not afterward. I can think and rethink and come to my conclusions with just words and ideas. Soviets then, and Russians now, don't have it so easy.

7. THE SOVIET LEGAL SYSTEM WAS NOT A COMPLETE SHAM

I always assumed Soviet law was a charade, a cynical tool used to attack innocent people under Stalin, and to repress citizens who openly opposed the regime after Stalin. In Stalin's time, it was completely Orwellian, but post-Stalin, it was only a little bit better, still used as a tool to make innocent people suffer, just less frequently.

I first started running into facts and stories that didn't fit into this framework through the world of espionage. While I was writing the pilot of *The Americans*, I read a book called *Farewell: The Greatest Spy Story of the Twentieth Century*, written by Sergei Kostin and his colleague Eric Raynaud (Sergei later became our consultant on the show). It told the story of Vladimir Vetrov, a KGB officer who spied for the French in the early 1980s. Vetrov provided intelligence that allowed the West both to understand and thwart Soviet efforts to steal Western technology. One of the strangest things the United States allegedly did in the Cold War was blow up a section of a Trans-Siberian gas pipeline inside the Soviet Union by covertly altering stolen software used to manage the pipeline. This was inspired and made possible by information Vetrov provided. (It also may not have happened, as I'll discuss later.)

The authorities eventually became suspicious of Vetrov. The investigation into his crimes was thorough, painstaking, and required compelling evidence before he could be charged. The system of procurators, investigators, and judges, though significantly different from ours, used procedures and practices designed to get to the truth, not simply to railroad Vetrov at all costs. During searches for evidence and interrogations, Vetrov's family was treated respectfully (although they became isolated because of societal fear and stigma).

All of this surprised me. The process was more legalistic, and fairer, than I ever would have imagined. I'd assumed if you were suspected of being a spy in the Soviet Union, and there was any compelling evidence against you at all, you were arrested, tortured, and probably executed regardless of whether or not the authorities had proof you were guilty.

But it was the method of Vetrov's execution that really challenged not just my views on Soviet criminal justice but also how I thought about the entire Soviet system of power and authority. We re-created this method of execution for a sequence on *The Americans*, copying it straight out of Kostin and Reynaud's book. It isn't clear if every detail of this model was followed in Vetrov's case, but this was probably how the Soviets carried out most executions at the time.

On the date of an execution, a special squad of officers came to a condemned person's cell. The convict had no idea this was an execution squad, or even that special execution squads existed. The officers might tell the prisoner they were being transferred to another location, or some other lie, then bring them to a special facility, sometimes in a basement of the prison they were already in. As soon as the squad and the condemned person arrived, a procurator would inform the prisoner that their final appeal had been rejected and that their sentence would be carried out shortly. At that exact moment, members of the execution squad would shoot the prisoner in the back of the head.

This procedure was specially designed to spare the condemned from mental suffering. Since the prisoner didn't know they were going to be executed, they didn't spend time in their cells terrified they were about to die. Even in the final walk to their execution, they were spared the anxiety of knowing what was about to happen. Within the context of an execution, the goal, and the requirement, was to be as humane as possible. During one execution, the officers made a prisoner kneel over a barrel filled with sand. This team was disbanded for degrading the prisoner.

This method of execution appears to have been the norm at least by the 1980s. According to Kostin and Reynaud, there were five executing prisons in the Soviet Union, each with a six-man team that usually met from two to four times a month. It seems likely this was enough to carry out any executions in the country.

It's worth noting that the focus on humane execution didn't extend to the victim's family. Families were not informed what was happening, and had to work through several layers of bureaucracy just to discover that their relative had been shot. And they were not allowed to know where their family member had been buried (always in a mass grave).

Still, this style of execution compares favorably to our system, where a prisoner spends years contemplating their fate, and once they realize almost all appeals are exhausted, still has quite a bit of time left to think about what's going to happen to them.

The very idea that the Soviets would be concerned about the feelings of someone they were going to execute—that they would want to be humane in these circumstances, and in fact go to great lengths to be humane—was a revelation to me. Along with the high burden of proof in espionage cases, it suggested that my perception of Soviet justice as fully Orwellian was off.

I started to take a closer look at the history of the Soviet legal system (I am referring to the courts, the prisons, and the law itself, and not to police enforcement) to see what I could find. Before relating what I discovered, I want to say that the Soviet legal system is a vast subject, and I haven't spent half my life thinking about it, as I have with some of the other topics I discuss in this book. Still, what I have learned more recently has profoundly challenged the basic assumptions I used to have, and suggests a fundamental reassessment in this area is a valuable part of reconceiving how to think about the Soviet Union in general. I rely very heavily on the work of Peter H. Solomon for this account (almost entirely in the section right below), and on Sheila Fitzpatrick to a lesser degree. They shouldn't be held remotely accountable for my broader interpretations.

Here's some of what I learned.

After the Bolshevik revolution, Marxism was the guiding principle of the new post-revolutionary state (not formally established as the Soviet Union until 1922). It was Marxism that provided fairness and justice, not "the law." It was in fact considered Western and bourgeois to think of the law as the ultimate guarantor of justice. For the Bolsheviks, nothing could sit above Marxism, or have the potential to override it. The law was also suspect because it had been an instrument of Tsarist and bourgeois power before the revolution. (It would not have been wildly off-base to think that the legal system in America at the time was in certain ways a tool of capitalist power.)

Despite this prejudice against legalistic systems, being in power meant administering a country, which required laws. So the Bolsheviks had a problem. The law was suspect, but they needed laws. This dilemma resulted in a complex and uniquely Bolshevik system of justice.

For example, in the early Bolshevik justice system, it wasn't even clear that judges should follow the law. Many argued they should follow, first and foremost, their revolutionary instincts. Judges and interrogators usually weren't even lawyers. It was more important for them to be communists.

The administration of justice was also bifurcated in a problematic way. There was an official system, through the People's Commissariat for Justice and the courts, that tried to deal with criminals through a legal process. But at the same time, the Cheka was, often randomly, terrorizing suspected opponents of the regime, detaining and often killing them in an extrajudicial process. The Cheka even started building its own camps shortly after the revolution, so it had a kind of parallel prison system too.

This complex system had to deal with quite a bit of crime. In a country I always thought had superior social control, it wasn't uncommon for gangs of thugs to attack people on the streets, particularly in the early decades of Soviet rule. But the authorities had a general ambivalence about common criminals that persisted throughout the Soviet era. Robbers, violent criminals, even murderers were considered class-friendly, led astray by oppressive capitalists.

This lenient attitude toward ordinary criminals was, just like the Bolshevik revolution itself, somewhat utopian, and even enlightened. Particularly if they'd committed minor crimes, the state preferred to sentence these working-class criminals to labor without incarceration, believing they should be rehabilitated, not punished.

But violent and petty offenders were only one kind of criminal. The system also dealt with political criminals. In fact, the key to understanding the Soviet justice system is realizing that it considered people who threatened the state to be the most serious and dangerous criminals. Since the Soviet state felt that it was threatened by political dissenters, dissenters were considered criminals. The Soviet state actually felt political dissenters were more of a threat than common criminals, and early in the Soviet era, incarcerated far more of them. These political offenders in particular were subject to unjust and often bitterly cruel abuses.

The two-track system—one following a legal and judicial framework and the other one using extrajudicial means (although the boundaries overlapped)—continued through the 1920s and 1930s. As Stalin's repressions grew and broadened, the OGPU (which succeeded the Cheka) and its successor, the NKVD, started arresting and imprisoning an ever-broadening range of people, from alleged kulaks to party members to a virtually random collection of completely innocent people. When they pulled their victims off the streets, the secret police claimed they had violated actual laws. But they usually didn't move these people through the official courts.

Eventually, filled up by these mass arrests, the camps of the OGPU and then NKVD came to substantially outnumber the prisons run by the mainstream justice system. In 1934, the regular prisons were absorbed by the NKVD into its by now much larger Gulag system. The merging of the two prison systems was a sign that the extralegal system was winning the day. After someone was arrested and tortured, an actual court might now hand down an actual sentence before someone was sent to the camps, but there was no legitimate legal practice left in the process by this point.

This was probably the end of the well-intentioned, utopian-based part of the Soviet Union's legal system. But it had existed.

My initial exposure to the Soviet legal system under Stalin revolved entirely around two singular and brutal human disasters—the show trials and the Gulag system.

The show trials were a series of widely publicized trials between 1936 and 1938 that Stalin used to destroy those he considered dangerous opponents at the top levels of the Communist Party. These trials were bizarre affairs. The evidence was almost entirely fabricated, and also fantastical. Loyal communists who had dedicated their lives to the cause were charged with everything from intentionally sabotaging Soviet infrastructure to spying for multiple foreign governments. The accused were tortured and threatened so severely that they admitted to even the most preposterous accusations in court.

The Gulag was the system of Soviet prison camps where millions of people suffered and died, in particularly huge numbers during Stalin's rule.

I learned about these two terrifying aspects of Soviet history in my college course with Wolfgang Leonhard. As Wolfgang lectured on the show trials and the Gulag, they felt to me like horrific fairy tales coming to life, proof unfolding before my eyes of a weird Orwellian society, one that still existed (kind of).

The show trials and the Gulag were equally appealing to me, in a very dark way. I read transcripts of the trials, and puzzled over how anyone could even pull off such a spectacle, not to mention get some people to believe it was all authentic. As for the Gulag, after Leonhard's lectures, I bought a copy of Solzhenitsyn's *The Gulag Archipelago* (abridged—the unabridged books were thousands of pages long; I didn't need to know about the Gulag that badly). Here I found the same horror, almost magically blended with a literary and artistic style I'd never encountered before (because Solzhenitsyn invented it). Even though *The Gulag Archipelago* was a famous book, none of my friends were reading it, and it felt oddly my own. In some way, I longed to inhabit a world where people thought and wrote like this.

The show trials and the Gulag truly represented the depths of human depravity and cynicism. But in their particulars, as I discovered later, both turned out to be more complex than I realized.

Bizarrely, the show trials had a progressive genesis. According to Solomon, the Bolsheviks felt their early efforts at creating a justice system were too formal and complex, too remote from the people. So they came up with the idea of staging what they called "demonstration trials" in villages and factories around the country. These trials would both bring justice closer to the people and act as a form of political agitation. None of this could be accomplished unless the trials had the desired outcome, which meant the defense had to make a case, but not too strong of a case.

The show trials were an almost natural extension of these demonstration trials, but now targeting political adversaries instead of ordinary criminals. And instead of a mere bias for the prosecution, in the show trials virtually everything was fabricated. But the goal was still similar—to influence and propagandize. The show trials of course had additional aims—to eliminate Stalin's rivals or (imagined) enemies, and to scare the populace into submission and compliance.

The fascinating genesis of the show trials didn't make them any less ugly. But it still surprised me. It had never occurred to me that the show trials grew out of anything. I had learned about them, and intuitively understood them, as a complete aberration, the product of a sick but inventive mind (they were that too). Their roots in a logically consistent set of ideas made them at least somewhat less weird and surreal, more recognizably human.

The Gulag system was also more complex than I realized. I had always seen the Gulag as Soviet-style concentration camps for Stalin's enemies, separate from a mainstream prison system that I assumed also existed for ordinary criminals (even though I knew some ordinary criminals were in the camps). The Gulag was, I thought, another strange aberration like the show trials, a fantastical outgrowth of Stalin's original but psychotic brain.

This wasn't entirely wrong, but it wasn't entirely right either. The Gulag became the Soviet Union's mainstream prison system. It housed, eventually, all of the country's criminals who were arrested and sentenced (there were older Tsarist prisons, not camps, that were used to house prisoners awaiting trials, prisoners under interrogation, and prisoners in transit, but these became part of the Gulag system too). During peak terror, and perhaps through most of Stalin's rule, Anne Applebaum told me she believed common criminals made up a small percentage of the camp population. But they served their time in camp. The rest of the camp population consisted of various stripes of real and imagined political adversaries, as well as people who had done literally nothing or almost literally nothing (in some cases "stealing" a pencil from their workplace).

Because the Gulag was a prison system, meant to protect the state, and not simply a political concentration camp (though again, it was that too), there were laws and rules to protect prisoners, and there were efforts to keep conditions in the camps from being cruel. According to Applebaum, commissions existed to look into prisoners' complaints. There was a Gulag Inspectorate inside the Soviet Procurator's Office charged with investigating abuses. Its inspectors traveled the country trying to make sure regulations, including those that protected prisoners, were followed. The rules weren't meaningless, and the inspectorate did have some power. Anyone from individual guards to camp administrators could receive a criminal sentence for cruelty toward prisoners, and they did with some frequency.

But these larger administrative efforts to control or moderate the Gulag usually failed, and the system as a whole was horribly cruel and full of endless abuse. Prisoners were, as a rule, starved and overworked; put in lice-ridden, overcrowded barracks; and subject to capricious brutality. Sometimes they were shot, though most died as a result of the conditions they lived in, literally starved, worked, and frozen to death. Several million prisoners died this way.

It's hard to understand a system that inflicts so much suffering while simultaneously promulgating and sometimes following rules and regulations meant to prevent abuse. This contradiction played out in various ways. For example, guards received rewards for shooting prisoners who were trying to escape. Sometimes guards who wanted to get this reward encouraged prisoners to try and escape, and then shot them. But the state didn't accept this conduct, and sometimes these guards were tried, convicted, and sent to prison (becoming camp inmates themselves). Were these particular un-ordered murders the state's fault? They were not beneficial to the state. But the state had put guards in an environment with little respect for human life, and then had little control over them.

I wouldn't have been able to make any sense of this strange contradiction back when I saw the Gulag as a conscious instrument for inflicting suffering (and again, it was partly that). But once I understood the Gulag was also the Soviet Union's ordinary prison system, functioning under extremely dark and unusual circumstances, with at least some well-intentioned people involved, it all made more sense. It also helped me see that the U.S. prison system could also be partially described as a system that inflicts enormous suffering while simultaneously promulgating and sometimes following rules and regulations meant to prevent abuse, although this was true to an exponentially greater degree in the Gulag system.

———

The show trials and the Gulag were more complex than I'd always assumed, but just as horrible. Other aspects of the Soviet legal system were less horrific, and probably for that reason I didn't know they existed. For example, Soviet courts handled civil disputes. If your husband wasn't paying child support, you might obtain a court order and bring it to his place of employment, where they could garnish his wages. The civil component of the court system was unreliable, but had higher standards of truth and fairness than I would have expected, even though bribery was rampant.

The legal system also wasn't the only, or even the primary, place where citizens could turn for justice. They could make appeals to a party committee, or send letters to top Soviet officials, or go to the secret police. All of these methods were broadly acceptable, and could lead to investigations and sometimes help. Even the secret police, who might respond to conflicts between citizens by intervening in catastrophic extrajudicial ways, also sometimes responded in an appropriate and helpful manner.

The variety of official or quasi-official methods for handling disputes wasn't necessarily a strength of the system, but it did increase the chances that the state would address a citizen's problems one way or another. And citizens had all kinds of problems, including many that were specific to Soviet life. In the Stalin era, people sometimes made false denunciations against their neighbors because they could get an arrested person's apartment as a reward for turning them in. Either the victim or the perpetrator might request official help under these circumstances. There were innumerable requests for official re-enfranchisement of class aliens—this meant that after kulaks or members of other socially alien classes had been officially disenfranchised (losing their right to vote, to reside in a city, and so on), they could sometimes petition later to have those rights restored. Soviet officials inside and outside the legal system dealt with these and many other types of problems.

———————

Soviet law was handed down from above. But citizens did sometimes have influence over it. The highest law was the Soviet Constitution, and historian Samantha Lomb describes the surprising process used to create a new one in 1936. Just as the terror was heating up, Stalin and the Soviet leadership put out a draft of the new constitution. It was circulated widely around the country, and discussed at meetings in factories and other workplaces. Citizens didn't initially show up to these meetings, at which point the leadership demanded that people become a part of the process. This sounds like a typical Soviet charade—a kind of pretend compliance. That's how I always viewed any kind of forced participation in the Soviet Union.

But Stalin and the leadership were truly interested in knowing what the population thought of the draft constitution. Feedback from these meetings was compiled, summarized, and presented to Stalin and the other leaders. There weren't a lot of changes made in response to the input, in part because many of the opinions challenged central party tenets about the class structure in the country or suggested ideas like creating peasant unions that would have threatened the party's power.

The responses were not uniformly challenging, though, and didn't suggest that citizens were looking for greater freedom. People were apparently not interested in habeas corpus, for example. They likely wanted stability first and foremost, and thought the authorities should have a stronger hand at a time of considerable crime.

Neither the more challenging responses that came out of this process nor the failure to alter the constitution significantly in response to input meant the act of soliciting responses to the constitution was an empty one. As Lomb points out, getting people to participate was how things got done in the Soviet Union. Whether it was the Five-Year Plan or collectivization, the mass projects of the state all depended on mass participation for their success (the same was largely true of the terror).

Of course, this Soviet version of an open process coexisted with the terrible repression taking place at the time. One didn't preclude the other. This was part of how the Soviet Union functioned.

After Stalin's death, even though the judicial system reasserted itself over the extrajudicial system, the state still criminalized most kinds of free political conduct. It imprisoned people who spoke out against the state, and even sent its opponents to psychiatric prisons, where they were tortured with psychotropic medications.

Along with the show trials and the Gulag, this persecution of political opponents from the 1960s through the 1980s became my other primary window into the Soviet justice system. As I studied Soviet history and politics and read the American media, the legal system still seemed like a complete sham to me as it put these dissidents through what looked like mock trials, maybe not quite on the level of Stalin's show trials, but not entirely different. From a procedural standpoint, the main problem was that the verdict was preordained. Not surprisingly then, the proceedings had a scripted quality. But there was one important element of these trials I didn't quite grasp. The authorities did not pluck innocent people out of nowhere, like they did in Stalin's time. The accused had usually taken on the state.

Had they actually committed a crime? Dissidents generally pointed out that their activity did not violate Soviet law. The Soviet Constitution granted citizens fairly broad rights, including the right to assemble and speak freely. Article 50 of the constitution reads:

> In accordance with the interests of the people and in order to strengthen and develop the socialist system, citizens of the USSR are guaranteed freedom of speech, of the press, and of assembly, meetings, street processions and demonstrations.

Maybe what comes before the first comma above invalidates what comes after. It's hard to say, though I can imagine American lawyers arguing endlessly about this.

In 1975, during the Brezhnev era, the Soviets also signed the Helsinki Accords, which stated, among other things:

> The participating States will respect human rights and fundamental freedoms, including the freedom of thought, conscience,

religion or belief, for all without distinction as to race, sex, language or religion.

They will promote and encourage the effective exercise of civil, political, economic, social, cultural and other rights and freedoms all of which derive from the inherent dignity of the human person and are essential for his free and full development.

The Helsinki Accords further bound signatories to act in accordance with the Universal Declaration of Human Rights, which states in Article 19, among other items that didn't match up with Soviet reality:

Everyone has the right to freedom of opinion and expression; this right includes freedom to hold opinions without interference and to seek, receive and impart information and ideas through any media and regardless of frontiers.

Both Soviet and international law provided powerful ammunition for Soviet dissidents. They also argued that the authorities themselves were violating Soviet law, and that their protests were meant to help the Soviet state, not harm it. As discussed earlier, it's hard to know what percentage of dissidents actually wanted to reform the Soviet state and what percentage wanted to get rid of it. But these were all strong and valid arguments, not just intellectually and morally, but through the lens of Soviet and international law.

The authorities' legal case wasn't absurd either, though. As noted above, the Soviet legal system was predicated primarily on the principle of protecting the state. In the post-Stalin era, each republic had its own criminal code, similar to one another but separate from the constitution, as most of our federal and state laws are separate from our Constitution. The Russian Republic criminal code included Article 70, which outlawed

Agitation or propaganda carried on for the purpose of subverting or weakening Soviet authority or of committing particular especially

dangerous crimes against the state, or the [verbal] spreading for
the same purpose of slanderous fabrications which defame the Soviet political and social system, or the circulation or preparation
or keeping, for the same purpose, of literature of such content . . .
    . . . [Violations] shall be punished by deprivation of freedom
for a term of 6 months to 7 years, with or without additional exile
for a term of 2 to 5 years, or by exile for a term of 2 to 5 years.

It wasn't hard to make a case that much of the dissidents' work
violated the first clause—that they were engaging in propaganda
or agitation with the purpose of undermining or weakening Soviet
authority. I'm not saying dissidents were doing that, but rather
that one could reasonably make such a case. There's also a reasonable case to make against the dissidents regarding the final clause,
on circulation or preparation or keeping of literature for the purpose of subverting or weakening Soviet authority. There is no case
to be made that the dissidents engaged in any slanderous fabrications, because what they said was true, not fabricated (invalidat-
ing charges frequently brought under Article 190, which required
fabrication). Likewise, whether dissidents intended grave crimes
against the Soviet state was probably in the eye of the beholder,
but was essentially a baseless claim.

Still, there was enough in Article 70 to reasonably claim the dissidents were breaking the law. Their vocal protests and principled
opposition undermined the international reputation of the Soviet
Union, primarily by bringing to light repressive activities of the
authorities, and as such arguably harmed the Soviet state.

In the Soviet system, guilt or innocence was effectively determined during pretrial investigations, especially in political cases.
This turned the courts into rubber stamps, but real investigations
did take place. Even if, morally speaking, dissidents never should
have been charged, they usually had acted in ways that could be
interpreted as carrying out some of the actions they were charged
with, unlike in Stalin's time when accusations were often fabricated
out of whole cloth (dissidents did also sometimes face fabricated

charges, such as espionage and treason, and were also sometimes threatened with these capital charges to extract confessions and cooperation).

Reading transcripts of the dissidents' trials is an odd experience. First and foremost, it's painful. Good, heroic people are being persecuted. Sometimes it feels like those persecuting them are abominable, a collection of soulless liars and judicial bureaucrats almost happily destroying these honest people. But other times, it feels like the procurators and judges are sincere and even oddly well-meaning in their defense of their state, and aren't factually all wrong about everything. They often make sense, not just in terms of the letter of the law, but in a human way. It's possible to feel how threatened and undermined they feel by opponents of the state, a state that they themselves have fully given themselves over to.

To be clear, I'm not arguing that Soviet law was just or moral. I'm saying it was not a sham, not a false front with everyone involved behaving cynically. The system had enough internal logic to suggest that many of those who made and adjudicated the law believed in it, and were not cynics or hypocrites. The apparent sincerity of many of those involved in the judicial process, top to bottom, is further suggested by the way the leading political authorities were flummoxed by the dissidents, unsure exactly how to think about or deal with them. KGB documents show Andropov and his colleagues puzzling over how dissidents could feel the way they did. They even met several times with the more prominent dissidents and tried to convince them they were misunderstanding the country and its leadership. Misunderstanding the dissidents completely themselves, they sometimes thought these meetings had gone well, and that they'd convinced the dissidents of the error of their ways.

The British philosopher and social scientist Rom Harré wrote, "Our personal being is created by our coming to believe a theory of self based on our society's working conception of a person." In other words, our entire identity—who we are—comes into being when we accept what our culture says a person is. Soviet culture said a person was group-oriented, and much less individualistic than in Western culture. Andropov and his kind had fully incorporated this conception of a person into their identities. They literally couldn't understand the dissidents, whose identities hadn't been formed around this Soviet cultural idea. But the authorities expected and demanded that this self-concept take hold in everyone. Those in power didn't doubt they were following the right path in demanding the cultural norm be followed. They tried persuasion and threats first—as a matter of course, dissidents were given a chance to stop their activities and recant instead of going to trial and then, unavoidably, prison. When persuasion and threats didn't work, they turned to the law to force compliance.

I have, as stated previously, been trying to determine here if the Soviet legal system was different from how I'd always imagined it to be. Was it on any level a system of law and justice or was it simply a cynical tool? Did it exist on a continuum of legal systems—with successes and failures at providing justice—or was it something entirely different, a legal system in name only?

I have not, then, been trying to judge the system's morality. There is no question that even in the post-Stalin period components of the legal system actively participated in gross miscarriages of justice and deeply immoral activity, and failed to check such activity by the state. At its worst, when courts ordered psychiatric evaluations for obviously healthy people, the legal system played an active role in sending some dissidents to psychiatric institutions, where they were imprisoned under false diagnoses and tortured with psychotropic drugs (sometimes the KGB did this without involving the courts, but not always).

Even here, at least some, and perhaps many, participants in these grotesque abuses were likely true believers who thought any deviation from Soviet norms constituted an actual mental illness, and believed they were doing the right thing by treating dissidents accordingly. Ibram X. Kendi, in his study of American racism *Stamped from the Beginning*, quotes Louisiana doctor Samuel A. Cartwright as writing in the 1850s that enslaved people needed someone to take care of them, and those who wanted to run away were mentally ill with a condition called drapetomania. Likewise, Kendi writes that after Black rebellions in cities across America in 1967, racist American psychiatrists diagnosed rioters as having schizophrenia, defined in this case as a "Black disease" manifesting in rage. In the Soviet Union, dissenters sent to mental hospitals were diagnosed as having "sluggish schizophrenia." The willingness of oppressors at such different times in such different places to diagnose someone as mentally ill who was simply resisting the oppressor's system is an indication that these diagnoses were not mere lies, but at least in some cases the sincere beliefs of people who literally could not imagine their own worldview was not shared by others.

I had a version of this same limitation, an assumption that my worldview had to be shared by others. It revealed itself in my certainty that Soviet leaders were cynical instead of sincere, that the Soviet population could not possibly have supported its government, that Soviet procurators and judges were all aware, even in the post-Stalin era, that they were participating in a bizarre and sick charade, but did it anyway out of self-interest. This certainty that people couldn't be that different from me was a failure in my understanding of the breadth and complexity of human nature, a misunderstanding about other people and about myself.

8. THE SOVIETS WERE NOT THAT DEDICATED TO THE IDEA OF WORLD COMMUNIST DOMINATION

I grew up believing that the Soviet Union was determined to spread communism around the world. I got this idea mostly from American media and culture, but I think my father believed it too.

It's not hard to see where this idea came from. The goal of spreading communism worldwide had deep roots in Marxist ideology, and the Bolshevik revolution was centered on the simple notion that workers and oppressed people everywhere deserved a better fate, and needed to rise up and grab it. For years the Soviet Union used the Comintern, an organization of international communists that it sponsored and controlled, to spread communism (it was disbanded in 1943). Eastern Europe was forcibly turned communist after the war, and the Soviet Union financially and militarily supported radical left-wing governments around the world almost until its demise.

But already by 1924, when Stalin proposed the Soviet Union pursue "Socialism in One Country" (their own), the imperative of spreading communism was actually losing its central importance in Soviet ideology and practice. By the end of the Second World War, world communist domination was no longer a real long-term strategic objective for the Soviets. Most of the efforts to spread communism after the war were more about competing with the United States and defending itself against the West than any fervent ideological belief in the eventual worldwide triumph of communism.

My own fervent belief that the Soviets wanted to take over the world was firmly in place by college, when the movie *Red Dawn* came out. It told the story of a Soviet invasion of America, and a group of high school students who turned themselves into partisans and fought back. The movie was widely criticized for being inflammatory and unrealistic, but I told anyone who would listen to me (a fairly small group) that this criticism was absurd, because the Soviets had invaded and taken over the countries of Eastern Europe in the same way they took over America in the movie. They did this kind of thing. That didn't mean the Soviets would do it in America, but it meant thinking about it was perfectly reasonable. It meant that making sure they couldn't do it was a good idea.

Nowadays, I don't see how the mindset behind either the early Soviet resolve to spread communism or the much milder efforts to do so after the war were that different from how we thought in America about spreading democracy. I was raised to believe that democracy was special, was the birthright of oppressed peoples, and should be spread worldwide. For many Soviets immediately after the revolution, and still some later on, their commitment to communism, their belief that it made them special, and that all peoples deserved these same privileges, were a mirror image of how we felt about democracy. They thought that having a more just system gave them the right, as we thought having a more just system gave us the right, to interfere in other countries' affairs.

The first Cold War is over, and in its aftermath we've seen the frequently devastating results of trying to spread democracy. The notion that this is a decent or responsible goal has lost its luster. But in America, the idea that there is something inherently special about our country remains, along with the idea that this specialness grants certain privileges in foreign policy. The same holds true in Russia, primarily among segments of its leadership, where a desire remains to spread more authoritarian types of government. In both cases, the belief that our systems of governance should be spread seems less ideologically based now than it used to be. So why does it persist? Most likely, for the same reason these proselytizing instincts were so strong during the Cold War. Spreading communism and democracy was never truly about helping other countries, but stemmed from a parallel Soviet and American need to feel superior to one another.

SOCIETY AND ME

How did I misunderstand the Soviet Union so badly, or understand it so minimally? I've already described how my own psychology and family background pushed me toward a binary way of seeing the world, and in particular the Soviet Union. And I've now detailed many of the specific misunderstandings I had. But there was also a way in which these factors were aided and made more powerful by cultural forces in our society that also encouraged absolutist politics. There was a mechanism in use, a system that doled out and controlled the information I took in.

To a significant degree—more significant if you are a thinker over a feeler, and even more if you are a reader/thinker—culture transmits its values and rules through information. The information I got about the Soviet Union came from many places. I read the work of journalists, politicians, spies, émigrés, dissidents. I read newspapers and magazines, and watched television. Up until the collapse of the Soviet Union, I was (or thought I was) familiar with the major Sovietologists of the time. These sources all confirmed the same image of the Soviet Union—it was a one-dimensional, ruthless totalitarian state. And this interpretation seemed obvious to me. It seemed less like an interpretation than a fact.

It turns out there was a more nuanced strain in academia. Quite a few books were available in the 1980s, when I was starting to study the Soviet Union seriously, that had a rich and complex view of the country. In *Red Flag Unfurled: History, Historians, and the Russian Revolution*, Ronald G. Suny explains that, by the 1980s, revisionist social historians looking at the lives of factory workers and peasants challenged the whole picture of totalitarianism even under Stalin, questioning the idea that there was total dominance from above going hand in hand with complete atomization of the individual below.

But these ideas didn't gain traction outside of academia, either in the public sphere or in government. Our cultural system of collecting information and processing it for consumption essentially ignored them. Most of what I read about the Soviet Union was selected by people who understood and believed in the central premises of our culture. Editors gave out assignments, reporters chose to follow leads, publishers picked book topics, translators who either came from our culture or embraced our culture enough to learn our language picked what they were going to translate, on and on and on. The information that made it through this selection process was chosen first and foremost because it had a point of view that was deeply negative about the Soviet Union.

This information was largely selected, influenced, and produced by the groups I mentioned above—academics, journalists, spies, politicians, Soviet dissidents, and Soviet émigrés. But Soviet émigrés played a particularly significant role in shaping America's perception of the Soviet Union, or at least in shaping my perception. Émigrés spoke loudly, convincingly, expertly, and it seemed with almost one voice about the clear rottenness of their former country.

Who would think to doubt them? They had lived there. They had suffered. They knew! And they were speaking to a huge audience (including me) who already agreed with them. No wonder they were more widely heard than the few voices proposing we had the Soviet Union wrong.

Of course, if an American in prison (for the sake of analogy, let's say someone who was wrongfully convicted) gets out and says our country sucks in every possible way, what can you say? They have one perspective. It isn't right or wrong.

The problem wasn't really with the émigrés, who had lived their lives, were entitled to their opinions, and had many valid points. The problem was there weren't any countervailing views that made their way into the mainstream of public discourse. This isn't to say there weren't countervailing views, in particular from the academics who swam against the tide of mainstream Sovietology in the United States. But alternate views just weren't going to get very far. They had to make it through too many layers, a gauntlet of societal self-censorship.

The émigrés' views, on the other hand, were embraced because they confirmed what so many of us already thought—America was superior; a repressive society could only be fully evil; everything had to be wrong with the Soviet Union and nothing could be good about it.

This suggests that the way people think in societies may come first, followed then by government censorship or self-censorship, rather than the more common belief that government censorship of information successfully manipulates and heavily influences people. In other words, maybe censorship and state control of information only push people in the direction they already want to go, only confirm the way they already think.

I formed my beliefs in a society with more or less complete freedom to find and access any information I wanted. But in addition to a powerful cultural censorship, a profound self-censorship also kept unorthodox views invisible to me. I chose what information I was going to take in about the Soviet Union, and weeded out what I didn't already agree with. This kind of self-censorship can be as powerful and even dangerous as the type of state censorship we've long feared and decried (though it's not as obviously unpleasant).

Even with no state pressure to limit my understanding, only cultural, psychological, and peer pressure, I failed to gain a level of insight or understanding about the Soviet Union any deeper than what the average semi-imaginary propagandized Soviet citizen on the other side of the world had about the United States.

The information I needed in order to see the Soviet Union more fully was there, right in front of me. In fact, I did actually see some of it, sort of. While trying to turn myself into a kind of junior Sovietologist in college, I read bits and pieces by the most famous Soviet experts, such as E. H. Carr, Isaac Deutscher, Moshe Lewin, Alexander Dallin, and Robert Tucker, who offered more complex views of Soviet history and politics. But I didn't delve deeply into their work. I glanced at books by these historians more to create the pretense that I'd read them than in an effort to actually absorb anything. This pretense was mostly for myself. I wanted to track these books down in the library stacks, I wanted to hold them, carry them in my bag, as if being in temporary possession of them would magically transfer their contents into my brain. Because most of all, I wanted to feel that I knew things. But I was too blocked to actually learn. (I'm actually concerned about carrying on this pretense even now, and need to make clear that I still haven't really read these historians since then, I've mostly read about them. Likewise, I haven't finished every book in my bibliography, although I have not included books that I only scanned or read tiny parts of.)

The one book about the Soviet Union by a Western historian that I did read cover to cover outside of any class in college, Stephen Cohen's *Rethinking the Soviet Experience*, which I mentioned previously, still didn't get through to me. I can actually remember seeing this book on the table at the bookstore the day I bought it. It was appealingly thin. Rereading it recently, I see that Cohen laid out pretty clearly that the Soviet Union was complex, was not a totalitarian state, and that the population was not united against the party and government. I remember telling a friend (both of us still in college) that Cohen was "naïve." Still, the fact that I remember actually buying this book over thirty years ago is strong evidence that something got through, and it's interesting to see how similar many of my thoughts now are to his.

I've detailed how a self-inflicted and society-inflicted myopia caused me to misunderstand how Soviet society functioned on almost every level. But most of what I misunderstood—most of what I could not see—adds up to a single, fundamental truth: The Soviet Union was a complete society. Just like ours, or any other society. It was a full and complex country, with people leading their lives there. It was not a simple place full of cardboard cutouts, which was what my imagination had turned it into to suit my psychological and political purposes.

To understand this rudimentary and elusive truth about the Soviet Union, I had to open up enough to see things from a different perspective. Years of therapy loosened the grip of binary perspectives, first in my inner world, and then in how I related to the outer world. Too much certainty lost its appeal, and was revealed as a crutch. Then Cherkashin's *Spy Handler* and its sympathetic, human portrayal of KGB officers led me to think back on my experiences with the refusenik in Leningrad. And rethinking what I'd experienced in the Soviet Union all those years earlier led me to reconsider many of my thoughts and assumptions about the country, including my core belief that it was an evil empire.

When I created *The Americans*, I'd already figured out that the Soviet Union, and even the KGB, weren't as bad as I'd always thought. I understood that I, and often we, stopped seeing the humanity in others once we defined them as an enemy. I was going to make a TV show that showed the KGB as something other than an evil organization, and more importantly, showed KGB officers as sympathetic, fully human people.

I thought I'd already reached the place I was going. But there was a whole world, quite literally, still to discover, and doing research for the show allowed me to see the country much more fully. I found all kinds of new information that opened up Soviet reality (as noted previously, I couldn't find information that contradicted what I thought until I went looking for it—once I already agreed with it).

As I read and thought, I saw that people were living a rich, diverse life in the Soviet Union, even during Stalin's reign. All the death and destruction I'd always known about was a major part of life, but there was more. I let go of the stereotype of the "gray" Soviet Union. I saw what was right in front of me, which was a country with good sides and bad sides. A country with citizens who had a wide range of feelings about it. And I saw all kinds of institutions, not just a Communist Party riding herd over an obedient population, a Komsomol (communist youth league) full of slavish members, and newspapers whose only role was to spew out propaganda. In the real Soviet Union, Komsomol members, who were in their teens and twenties, felt some ability to act independently, and didn't always do what they were told. Citizens wrote letters to newspapers complaining about everything, and were often taken seriously. People found all kinds of ways to get by, and ways to push back. This was a country with a future, which might get better or worse. Just like our country.

At least, that's how I think it happened. None of this was a fully linear process. When, exactly, did I reassess everything I'd ever thought and believed about the Soviet Union and Russia? I'd say it started unconsciously when I first met the refusenik in Leningrad, blossomed into a conscious process when I read *Spy Handler*, developed into a coherent idea when I created *The Americans*, and gathered more and more supporting ideas—a firm structure— while we were making the show. But that's more of a guess—a need to have a story—than a definitive timeline.

Most of this process took place in my head, and involved books, experiences, travel, conversations, endless thinking and considering. It also took place inside a broader culture, which had not only kept alternate views about the Soviet Union on a near-invisible fringe when I was younger but had also bombarded me from childhood on with sinister and untrustworthy Soviets (Boris and Natasha from *The Rocky and Bullwinkle Show*); a dangerous Soviet Union bent on our destruction (*Red Dawn*); Soviets who were vicious and lethal and controlled by their government *even when they were athletes* (*Rocky IV*). Boris and Natasha were allegedly from "Pottsylvania," but with Russian names and accents, so you couldn't miss the point. This all died down after the Cold War ended, but its effect on me remained.

There was one particular movie that helped nudge me in a different direction. Shortly after I read *Spy Handler*, I watched Vladimir Menshov's 1979 film *Moscow Does Not Believe in Tears*, the story of a group of young women making their way in Moscow. In this film, I felt like I was actually seeing a full country open up before me, actually seeing it visually. I've seen a lot of Soviet films, and many are great, and many are challenging in all sorts of ways. But this one is uniquely good at showing someone with a narrow view of the Soviet Union that people lived regular lives there, that the constraints and even brutalities of the system weren't the defining characteristics of every person's life all the time.

———

There are still more risk factors for having a shallow, black-and-white view of another society—not spending much time there, not speaking the language, not knowing enough people from there. I had all of these problems to varying degrees.

So did Reagan and Gorbachev. But both men may have gone through something similar to what I did, a reassessment of their basic beliefs and attitudes about the country they were fighting against in the Cold War. When Gorbachev met Reagan face-to-face for the first time at the Geneva Summit in 1985, the encounter changed his political viewpoint enough that he actually stopped using the language of communist propaganda that he'd relied on his entire life when talking about the United States. Reagan had proved to be a genuine person he could talk to and understand, not the stereotypical evil imperialist he'd expected. As Gorbachev's view broadened, the old language didn't fit anymore. To understand this, you have to realize just how sheltered most Soviet leaders were, having been brought up with limited exposure to noncommunist ideas, and often having traveled little outside the country. For that matter, political leaders in general aren't necessarily more worldly or better informed than the average citizen of their country, which is easy to forget in light of their power and prestige.

As for Reagan, his hardline stance against the Soviet Union softened considerably in his second term. In 1988, he even publicly stated that the Soviet Union was no longer an evil empire. Although Reagan's views were complicated and don't fit neatly into a narrative where he went from thinking the Soviet Union was bad to thinking it was less bad, there's little doubt that his views did alter to a degree in response to the changes Gorbachev was making in the Soviet Union.

It's also possible Reagan was influenced by *Moscow Does Not Believe in Tears*. Before his first meeting with Gorbachev in 1985, Reagan watched the movie, which his briefers thought might give him a window into the Russian soul. It's often claimed that Reagan was heavily influenced by movies. After seeing *The Day After*, a TV miniseries that offered a stark and realistic portrayal of the aftermath of a nuclear exchange with the Soviets, Reagan was deeply affected, but felt the movie showed why his policy of nuclear deterrence was right. His diaries don't support a popular version of this story that has him rethinking his position on nuclear arms after seeing the film.

But could *Moscow Does Not Believe in Tears* have had a major impact on how Reagan viewed the Soviet Union? The film's portrait of day to day life in Moscow is profoundly different from anything you'd ever imagine if you had a one-dimensional view of the Soviet Union. I like to think of Reagan's fairy-tale notion of an evil empire colliding with the picture of real Soviet life in Menshov's film, and not fully surviving the encounter. (The film is a romance, and I don't want to suggest it's a full or literal portrait of Soviet reality.)

Of course, even though Reagan's views on the Soviet Union softened, neither Menshov's movie nor anything else got him over the idea that the United States should destroy the Soviet Union. Or more accurately, destroy the Soviet system.

This twisted idea, which animated me for many years too, was so awful and absurd, so wrongheaded, yet it seemed so obvious at the time. I don't know what to call it except a horrible delusion, almost a product of a mental illness. But I wasn't mentally ill, was I? It doesn't matter that the Soviets were halfheartedly trying to destroy us, too, which was also sick and awful.

The idea that we had the right—that I had the duty—to destroy other nations, other inferior systems, was enabled (and to some degree caused) by my sense of the United States as the greatest nation on Earth. We were a light unto the nations, a country that behaved better than other countries. But the way we treated Native Americans, our participation in slavery, how we treated African Americans post-slavery—in international relations, in our actions in Latin America, Vietnam, everything that has happened recently in Iraq, in so many countries and regions of the world where we've taken unjustified military action—much of this is comparable to or worse than the most closely analogous Soviet behavior. And there are ways in which Soviet behavior was worse. They had their flaws, we had ours.

As rethinking the Soviet Union led me to rethink our own country, to some degree my sense of America came more in line with how other nations see us (or at least I stopped assuming their views were always based on blind anti-American prejudice). Except for a brief period when some citizens of nations that were oppressed by the Soviets in Eastern Europe lionized us (which helped us cling to an idealized version of ourselves), other countries have often clearly expressed how they see and experience us. Sometimes these views are purely negative, but often they're complex and ambivalent, taking into account our positive and negative sides. We are rarely perceived by outsiders as being the greatest nation on Earth. I should have taken note earlier, and now I do.

In part to understand my own country, and myself, and in part for its own sake, I have tried to reassess the Soviet Union, to look more evenly at what it was. This would have been a difficult task in the middle of a bitter conflict like the Cold War. But thirty years after the collapse of the Soviet Union, it's easier. For me, this is partly because I've changed, and partly because my enemy disappeared. But it's also easier to see the Soviet Union now because there is more information available. As opposed to a small number of historians fighting a mainstream consensus, there are now all kinds of historians digging into the complexity of Soviet life and society, and they themselves have access to an unprecedented amount of information from a greatly expanded number of sources. Their work is more readily available, less subject to societal self-censorship (and my personal self-censorship). They are turning the black-and-white picture gray.

The popular imagination in the West is still lagging behind these historians in its assessment of the Soviet Union, in part because a second cold war continues to thrive on the same absolutist thinking that nurtured the first conflict. But here's one stab at how to look back at the Soviet Union, free from the blinders of the Cold War. This is, if anything, an experiment in reordering the various facts and interpretations of Soviet society. It is how things are starting to look to me, and also a guess at how history might remember the Soviet Union in time.

Number one, a brave experiment to try a new form of egalitarianism in the midst of the great inequalities of the early industrialized world. Number two, a place that produced the horrible suffering, deprivations, and mass murders of the Stalin era. Number three, the country whose army beat Hitler and the Nazis. Number four, a failed experiment in communism, which largely discredited it as a viable economic system.

Two of those four things are positive. Of course, one could easily put together a very different list, focused more on Soviet crimes and failures. But the fact that the state, and the experiment, ultimately failed, and that the state was repressive, may not loom as large one day when we look back at the Soviet Union. States often fail. Many states are repressive.

ENEMIES, AND REPEAT

FIVE THINGS TO RECONSIDER
ABOUT MODERN-DAY RUSSIA

I believe we are making the same mistakes with Russia today that we made in the Soviet era. We see only what's bad in Russia and its leadership, then compare their flaws with our virtues. We see Russia and Putin one-dimensionally. We act aggressively, while convinced we're only defending ourselves from Russia.

In an effort to break out of this pattern, I'm going to challenge some of the misconceptions about Russia and Putin I hear most frequently. I will challenge the notion of Putin as a ruthless dictator, and the idea that modern-day Russia is best seen as a highly repressive, deeply corrupt state. This is not to say that Putin is not at times ruthless, or that Russia is not repressive. It is likely that Putin sometimes has his enemies murdered, and the Russian state employs widespread repressive tactics, sometimes violent, even lethal, against its citizens. Repression is used to frighten, marginalize, and silence people, which is indefensible. But when we focus solely on this repression, we fail to see both its true dimensions as well as the level of freedom that exists in Russia today.

Because so much of what I am about to discuss is a life-and-death matter for many inside Russia, I want to be clear that my goal is not to defend or absolve Putin or the Russian authorities, or any political leader, or any political system. I am trying to expand our understanding of a vilified enemy. I believe a more complex, less black-and-white view of Russia is the single most important key to breaking the habit of mutual hostility that's led us into a new cold war.

1. IS PUTIN A RUTHLESS DICTATOR?

Putin is generally portrayed in the West as a cold, murderous, highly autocratic leader. It's easy to see where this reputation came from. Putin likes to play the tough guy (cold), has probably ordered people killed (murderous), and has more or less installed himself as the lifetime leader of a state that isn't a liberal democracy (highly autocratic).

But this vision of Putin is also one-dimensional, and misses a lot about him and his role in Russian society and government. We need a more complex view of Putin so that we can determine if a positive relationship with him, and Russia while he leads it, is possible.

As I've said, my intent is not to defend Putin but to see him more clearly. I will look at his strengths and accomplishments, take issue with false or exaggerated accusations against him, and enumerate and describe his flaws.

Putin Saved Russia

I don't think it's an exaggeration to say that Putin saved Russia. When he became president, the degree of lawlessness—the degree to which the state had lost control, or had been so thoroughly compromised by criminal actors that it had in effect lost control—is hard to overstate. Violent crime had skyrocketed during Russia's transition from the centralized Soviet economy to a free market. Trying to run any kind of business, or really make money at all, was dangerous. The police were heavily corrupted. Criminal gangs became so powerful in the 1990s that Russia was literally in danger of becoming a mafia-controlled state.

Putin wrested control of the country back from criminal elements and reasserted government authority. Russia became fundamentally safer. The sense of pervasive chaos was replaced by a general feeling that the government was back in charge. Organized crime remained a potent force in society, and even maintained some connections with state security (including the ability to bribe corrupt security officials). But it no longer threatened to take de facto control of the country. This early success of Putin's was indescribably important to Russia. It was also a huge favor to the world, considering the obvious dangers of a nuclear armed state run by criminals.

It's rare for Putin to get credit for any of this in the West. People focus on the criminality that remains, or point to ways in which Russian oligarchs are above the law. And in fairness, even in Russia, some seem to consider Putin's reassertion of government control important, but something he did a long time ago. Still, it's probably among the reasons Putin is popular at home. And it's part and parcel with another source of his popularity—he's kept Russia fundamentally stable throughout his time in power. This stability has come with significant repression and restrictions on personal and political freedoms, but its benefits shouldn't be denied.

Is Putin a Killer?

Putin is frequently referred to in America, both by the media and individual politicians, as "a killer." This is a tricky word to use in describing a head of state. Leaders are often responsible for people being killed, and this alone doesn't necessarily earn them the title "killer." But Putin is widely believed to be directly responsible for multiple assassinations of Russians at home and abroad, and many believe he was also behind a specific instance of terrorism inside Russia that killed hundreds. When American politicians and journalists call him a killer, it is often in a context and with a tone that implies this is the primary way he should be seen and understood, that he is fundamentally less a legitimate head of state than a tyrant who regularly uses state assassination against his enemies.

So let's look at who Putin has and hasn't killed. It's important to note that we are dealing with the available facts in an area of secrecy and cover-up. It is rarely possible to come to definitive conclusions. What follows are, instead, best guesses.

Putin is commonly blamed for killing people in the following four categories (others would organize this differently):

Domestic terrorists
Former spies/traitors
Journalists
Political opponents

Domestic Terrorists

Did Putin order his security services to blow up an apartment building full of Russian citizens in an effort to boost his popularity?

My Guess: Probably not.

A number of American journalists, politicians, academics and other experts (there are dissenters) have suggested that Putin was behind the "apartment bombings"—a series of four attacks on residential apartment buildings in Russia in September 1999 that killed almost three hundred people. The contention is that Putin, together with the security services, orchestrated the attacks so that he could take a firm hand in combating the invented terrorists they blamed for the bombings (Putin was prime minister at the time, and had recently been director of the Federal Security Service [FSB] and secretary of the Security Council). According to this theory, Putin believed that his strong and decisive response to the bombings (especially his prosecution of the recently launched Second Chechen War—the terrorists were allegedly Chechen) would boost his popularity and help him win the presidency in the upcoming election (he did win).

There are some facts that suggest this story is true. Most damn-ingly, about a week after what turned out to be the last bombing, an alleged explosive device was found and defused at another build-ing in Russia, in the city of Ryazan. Local police arrested three FSB officers who were seen planting it. (The FSB claimed their officers had planted bags of sugar in the building as part of an anti-terror training exercise.)

Also troubling is the claim that Gennadiy Seleznyov, the speaker of the Russian legislative assembly, the Duma, stated in session that he had received a report of an apartment building being blown up in Volgodonsk. In fact, an apartment building had been blown up the morning he made his statement, but in Moscow, not Vol-godonsk. Then, another building was blown up three days later, this time in Volgodonsk. This suggested to some that the security services had accidentally tipped off Seleznyov to their next planned bombing.

Finally, a string of people independently investigating the apart-ment bombings were killed, which suggests the authorities might have been covering up what they did.

The story about Seleznyov in the Duma is confusing and hard to evaluate, though. And many of those killed while investigat-ing the bombings had a range of enemies who might have wanted them dead for other reasons (I'll discuss some of these killings in more detail later in this section). The only really compelling piece of evidence that points to official complicity in the bombings is that FSB officers were seen planting an alleged bomb in an apart-ment building during the period these attacks were taking place. In fact, isn't that alone sufficient proof that the authorities—or at least some element of the authorities—were behind the bombings?

There are other ways to explain why officers of the Federal Se-curity Service might have planted a bomb—real or fake—in an apartment building, though. One possibility is that it was, in fact, part of a training exercise, as officials claimed. Another possibility is that the FSB planted it with the intention of "discovering" it, ei-ther to show that the state was in control, or to portray themselves as heroes who saved the day after the previous apartment bombings made them look ineffective.

A motive along these lines is particularly plausible in the context of the multiple terror attacks carried out in Russia by Chechen militants over the preceding years in response to the first war in Chechnya. In 1995, Chechen militants seized a hospital in the city of Budyonnovsk. More than a hundred people died in the attack and subsequent assault by Russian security forces. In 1996, Chechen militants took hostages at a hospital in Dagestan, where again many were killed in the rescue attempt. Between the end of the first war in Chechnya in 1996 and the apartment bombings, attacks continued. Several people were killed by a bomb on a train between Moscow and Saint Petersburg in 1997. More than fifty people were killed in a bombing at a market in Vladikavkaz in early 1999. This is only a partial list.

Unable to respond effectively to the terror sweeping Russia, officials high up or lower down could well have conceived of planting and "discovering" a bomb to burnish their reputation and/or send the message that the situation was under control. Taking advantage of real terror attacks to get credit for foiling a false one, while also reassuring the population that the authorities were in control, would be the kind of craven, clumsy, often partially successful deceit that was in the bones of the Russian state bureaucracy. The Soviet Union had functioned in part through party and state officials engaging in dishonest and careerist actions, sometimes with good intentions.

This is, of course, all speculation. The real bombings could have been carried out by FSB officers, even ones operating under Putin's orders. But the case that Putin and the FSB carried out the bombings has many of the hallmarks of a conspiracy theory. Conspiracy theories often explain events as plots carried out by powerful people or organizations working together in secret to carry out sinister goals, often with the aim of controlling a nation (Putin and the FSB working to ensure his election). They are usually built not on single facts but by associating a range of disparate facts with each other, some of which may be true, some of which may be false, and still others of which are true or partly true but potentially misleading (arrest of FSB officers for planting a bomb, a hard-to-explain mistake by the speaker of the Duma, shutting down of investigations, suspicious deaths of investigators). And conspiracy theories usually require believing that a large number of people are able to keep their sinister actions secret (carrying out the bombings would have required the cooperation of multiple FSB officers and officials, all of whom would have had to keep it a secret).

Conspiracy theories that suggest the White House, CIA and FBI were behind 9/11 often begin with the catastrophic failure of the CIA and FBI to share information about the attackers. Conspiracy theorists leap from there to the assessment that this failure can only be understood as part of a coordinated plan to perpetrate the attack (the real explanation was bureaucratic suspicion and incompetence). But perhaps most important, conspiracy theorists lack even the most basic faith in our leaders and bureaucrats, and believe President Bush, along with a range of people at the CIA and FBI, would commit mass murder against American citizens.

Of course, all sensible people know that Bush, the CIA, and FBI were not behind 9/11. And most Americans aren't vulnerable to invented facts and wild interpretations about 9/11 because we understand our leaders and our government officials would never carry out a mass attack against their own people.

But some who understand that basic fact about our own leaders and government officials don't understand it's also true about Putin and people who work at the FSB. They instead believe that Putin and his security services would blow up an apartment building full of innocent Russians. I believe this is a fundamental misunderstanding of who these people are. Putin and most of his security service officers are patriots. They are genuinely dedicated to protecting and defending their country. There is nothing in their history or way of looking at the world that suggests they would ever carry out a mass murder of innocent Russians, a full-on act of domestic terrorism. Yes, sometimes they kill and poison people they consider enemies, as I'll detail below. But there is no reason to believe that they are more likely to carry out a mass slaughter of their own citizens than our officials in the CIA, FBI, and White House would be.

Even in Stalin's time, the secret police didn't blow up scores of people in their homes. Innocent people were usually arrested and often run through a veneer of a judicial process so that neither the population nor the authorities themselves would start to think of the party and state as terrorists or killers. This was vitally important for the regime's self-concept.

The randomness and degree of state terror decreased enormously after Stalin. There were ups and downs in the scale of official repression in both the post-Stalin and the post-Soviet era, but there hasn't been any outright mass terrorism by the state or its security forces against Russian citizens. There has been extrajudicial arrest, even torture, and brutal state warfare in Chechnya, but these are the frequent mechanisms of many states that don't engage in mass bombings of their own citizens.

The idea that Putin and the FSB were behind the apartment bombings has been repeated over and over in the West, and rarely challenged as a conspiracy theory. Why is this?

Research has demonstrated that people are more likely to believe conspiracy theories about opponents and people they're in conflict with. The general anti-Russian/anti-Putin sentiment in the U.S. media and among American political elites likely predisposed some otherwise careful journalists and others to look less critically at the facts in this case. Because many (not all) of the experts on Russia that the media relies on repeated the theory that Putin may have been behind the bombings, it was even easier for reporters to skip their usual more thorough investigation.

Who did perpetrate the bombings?

The official investigation blamed Chechen separatists. This is certainly plausible, as Russia had been (and was again) in a brutal war with Chechnya, and violent separatist and anti-Russian feeling there was strong. Likewise, the string of terror attacks in Russia that preceded the bombings had been openly and clearly carried out by Chechen separatists.

But at least for now, we don't know who did it.

I doubt it was Putin and his security services, though. Still, since Russian political elites generally eschew careful and honest investigations when the government is accused of malfeasance, we won't have a definitive answer for some time, if ever. This hostility toward investigation is complex—sometimes it serves to cover up criminal activity, large-scale and small, but it is also just a different form of politics, where the authorities insist on being above scrutiny. This may have some advantages for them, but it also leaves them particularly vulnerable to conspiracy theorists, since the government doesn't do the basic work of uncovering the truth.

Former Spies/Traitors

Does Putin order his security services to kill former spies he believes are traitors?

My Guess: Probably.

The most famous example here is Alexander Litvinenko. Litvinenko was a former FSB officer who, when Putin was still head of the security service, began accusing it of widespread corruption. Litvinenko later wrote a book claiming that Putin and the FSB were behind the Russian apartment bombings. He also accused the Russian president of being a pedophile.

Litvinenko moved to Britain in 2000, and was killed there by a dose of radioactive polonium in 2006. The route of two former KGB officers carrying polonium from Russia to Britain and then to a meeting with Litvinenko has been convincingly reconstructed. Although I argue elsewhere that Putin isn't responsible for everything that happens in Russia, which also might mean that he isn't responsible for everything that happens in the security services, it seems likely that no one would distribute polonium or order an assassination using polonium without Putin's approval.

Putin's own comments about traitors, made several years later, strongly suggest a motive for killing Litvinenko. "Traitors will kick the bucket, believe me. Those other folks betrayed their friends, their brothers in arms. Whatever they got in exchange for it, those thirty pieces of silver they were given, they will choke on them."

A final piece of evidence of Russian state responsibility for the murder is that Andrei Lugovoi, one of the two men (along with Dmitri Kovtun) who traveled to Britain and appear to have poisoned Litvinenko, was elected to the Russian Duma the following year. Candidates for the Duma are elected based on a party list. Lugovoi was the second name on the list of the Liberal Democratic Party of Russia, a nationalist and socially conservative party, despite its name. It's interesting to note that he wasn't elected as a candidate of United Russia, the party most closely associated with Putin. Was the Liberal Democratic Party of Russia just acting as a proxy for Putin and the security services? Or did Lugovoi's actions square with the Liberal Democratic Party's own worldview and desires, so they put him on their ballot?

Regardless, Putin probably ordered the killing of Litvinenko. I do not say definitely because the inner workings of the Kremlin on security matters are obviously opaque—maybe officials take clues from Putin and do what they think he wants, and maybe they are right sometimes and wrong other times. I do not mention these possibilities in any way to absolve Putin of responsibility even if he did not directly order the killing, but rather to be precise about what we do and don't know.

Putin is likely also directly responsible for the more recent poisoning of Sergei Skripal and his daughter Yulia (both of whom recovered), though it's likely the daughter was an unintended victim, as neither the post-Stalin Soviet Union nor Russia have a history of attacking their enemies' family members. Dawn Sturgess, a British woman, died after coming in contact with the poison used against Skripal. The evidence in the Skripal case consisted of another distinctive and tightly controlled weapon (Novichok nerve agent); a clear trail left by the assailants; the identification of the assailants (in this case) as members of Soviet military intelligence; and Putin's own comments confirming the motive. Speaking in Moscow several months after the poisoning, Putin said, "I see that some of your colleagues are pushing the theory that Mr. Skripal was almost some kind of human-rights activist. He was simply a spy. A traitor to the Motherland. There is such a concept—a traitor to the Motherland. He was one of those. . . . He's simply a scumbag, that's all."

The assailants were interviewed on Russian television, and their denials were unconvincing and borderline absurd. Putin publicly denied the accusations as well, as he did with Litvinenko. But what else could he do? These were assassinations or attempted assassinations with little effort to keep the perpetrators' identities secret, and the denials came with a wink.

One theory to explain the use of traceable Russian weapons in these attacks is that Putin and the security services want potential traitors inside Russia to know what will happen to them if they act against the Russian state. This seems plausible.

These cases demonstrate Putin's likely willingness to murder people he considers traitors. We don't know if Litvinenko was killed because his accusations against Putin and the FSB were considered damaging, or because they were personally embarrassing to Putin, or if Litvinenko consulted with foreign intelligence services, which Putin and others in the security services could have considered crossing a line. The Russian leadership may also have some entirely different way of thinking about it. The motive in the Skripal poisoning is even more complicated, since he ended up in Britain in the first place after being traded in a spy swap, which should have guaranteed his safety. Some have speculated that the Russian authorities felt Skripal betrayed the unwritten terms of a spy swap by continuing to work for foreign intelligence agencies against Russia after the trade (work that may have gone beyond consulting). I never heard of these unwritten rules of the spy swap, but one of the problems with unwritten rules is you may not agree on what they are.

Whatever the exact motive, these murders suggest that Putin, while having in some ways moved on successfully from his career in espionage to the much wider stage of leading an entire country, at least in part remains stuck back in that old world, with its heavy focus on loyalty and traitors and its toolkit of esoteric weapons.

Journalists

Does Putin order his security services to murder journalists?

My Guess: I doubt it.

As of this writing, approximately twenty-eight journalists have been killed in Russia since Putin came to power, and several more have been killed outside of Russia. These murdered journalists were reporting on various problems in Russia—corruption, organized crime, the war in Chechnya, et cetera.

I urge everyone to learn more about each of the murdered journalists. They all worked at great risk to improve their society, and were killed for it.

The murder of Anna Politkovskaya in 2006 received the most attention in the West. Politkovskaya was a crusading journalist who wrote extensively on Chechnya. After she was killed, Putin said

> With regards to the murder of the journalist Anna Politkovskaya, then I have already said and I can say once again that this is a disgusting crime. To kill not only a journalist but also a woman and a mother. And the experts know well . . . that perhaps because Ms. Politkovskaya held very radical views she did not have a serious influence on the political mood in our country. But she was very well known in journalistic circles and in human rights circles. And in my opinion murdering such a person certainly does much greater damage from the authorities' point of view, authorities that she strongly criticized, than her publications ever did. Moreover, we have reliable, consistent information that many people who are hiding from Russian justice have been harboring the idea that

they will use somebody as a victim to create a wave of anti-Russian sentiment in the world. I do not know who has carried out this crime. But whoever they were and whatever their motives, they are criminals. They must be found, brought to justice and punished. The Russian authorities will do everything they can to ensure that this takes place.

This is a complicated statement, and may hint at Putin's position on the killing of journalists in general. He sounds somewhat sympathetic to the victim, though less deeply engaged with the human tragedy than with its political repercussions. He says that killing Politkovskaya did not serve the interests of the authorities, which he likely believes, and which makes sense—Putin and the Kremlin thrive on stability, and they look like they aren't in control when journalists are murdered. Killing journalists also is not the way they usually handle the ones they can't control. They isolate them and have them fired, and sometimes take over their newspapers and TV stations. They also exercise control of the mass media in a way that makes independent reporting less of a threat to the authorities in general. These methods have been quite successful in isolating opposition journalists and limiting their overall influence.

Putin also points out in his statement that killing journalists could create anti-Russian sentiment abroad. This isn't the primary consideration for the Kremlin, but it certainly carries at least some weight.

Overall, Putin's public response to Politkovskaya's murder was logical, consistent, and in step with how his government has often functioned. This all suggests an attitude and policy inconsistent with carrying out murders of journalists.

Politkovskaya's killers, mostly members of a single Chechen family, were caught, tried and sentenced, unlike those of most other murdered journalists. But whoever ordered the hit was never brought to justice. It's reasonable to think it may have been powerful Chechens who wanted to silence her or punish her for her reporting on Chechnya (although she had other enemies as well). Chechen leader Ramzan Kadyrov may well have been behind the killing, something I'll discuss in more detail while reviewing the murder of Boris Nemtsov.

It's worth noting that I have seen and heard Putin quoted about Politkovskaya's killing many times over the years, but all that's usually repeated or reprinted is this portion of what he said:

> . . . perhaps because Ms. Politkovskaya held very radical views she did not have a serious influence on the political mood in our country. But she was very well known in journalistic circles and in human rights circles. And in my opinion murdering such a person certainly does much greater damage from the authorities' point of view, authorities that she strongly criticized, than her publications ever did.

Separated from the earlier part of the statement where Putin condemns the crime, this comes across as if he's exclusively concerned with the damage her murder did to the state. He sounds remarkably callous, even twisted. I have also occasionally seen Putin quoted as saying her murder was disgusting. But in these cases, the next line is often left out: "To kill not only a journalist but also a woman and a mother." This is the part that makes him sound somewhat sincere (although he certainly shows no sign of appreciating Politkovskaya for the hero that she was).

In other cases where Russian journalists were killed, accusations that Putin and his security services were involved lack concrete evidence. Obviously, that doesn't prove anything—people can be killed and the evidence successfully concealed. As I stated previously, I am making guesses. But I am skeptical about these accusations against Putin and the security services, and suspect they rest in part on questionable assumptions about their motives and strategies.

In most instances where journalists were murdered, people threatened by their reporting who were not closely connected to the office of the president or the security services may well have been responsible. There is a long list in Russia of people who don't want to be exposed, and who these journalists bravely went after: corrupt businessmen, corrupt politicians, corrupt military leaders, members of criminal organizations. Ultranationalists offended by negative coverage may also have been behind some of the killings.

If a businessman or politician wants to kill a journalist in Russia, they often hire someone from a Russian criminal group to do it. Since there are some ties in Russia between criminal groups and state security, it's possible personnel or resources of state security have been used in some of these killings. A former Moscow police officer was one of those convicted in Politkovskaya's murder. This leads some to suspect the state is behind the killings, when in fact the involvement of state officials may instead be a sign of poor state control over its bureaucracy.

Either way, the consequences—powerful people in Russia killing those who try to expose them or work against them, generally with impunity—predates Putin, and was already a systemic problem in the 1990s, before he took over.

Political Opponents

Does Putin order his security services to murder his political opponents?

My Guess: Unclear, although he is at the very least complicit in poisoning some of them.

There can be a fuzzy line between journalists and political opposition figures in Russia. Some active politicians also work as journalists. Some journalists see part of their job as challenging the regime. Here, though, I'm referring specifically to people like Alexei Navalny and Mikhail Khodorkovsky who have directly challenged Putin in the political arena. The Kremlin has worked against these opponents in much the same way they've dealt with journalists—isolating them, disrupting their activities, and at times arresting and imprisoning them. Has Putin also had some of his political opponents murdered, or poisoned?

Boris Nemtsov was one of the most prominent of these opposition figures, both inside and outside of Russia. Originally a supporter of Putin, Nemtsov became a leading proponent of democracy and civil rights in Russia, and later an outspoken critic of the war in Ukraine. In 2015, shortly after threatening to release a trove of documents about the government's involvement in that war, he was shot and killed while walking across a bridge close to the Kremlin.

Five men were convicted of Nemtsov's murder (although the trial was procedurally problematic). Several of the men had links to military officials in Chechnya, and thus arguably to Ramzan Kadyrov, head of the Chechen Republic. This suggests the possibility that Kadyrov ordered Nemtsov's murder. For some, that implies Putin was behind the murder, because of his relationship with Kadyrov. But that relationship is extremely complicated. Kadyrov keeps order in Chechnya, and in particular keeps Muslim extremists there under control. This is invaluable to Putin, who can't risk another war in Chechnya. Putin's side of the bargain is providing Kadyrov with money and a free hand to handle his internal affairs as brutally as he wants to. But there is no evidence Putin uses Kadyrov to kill his own opponents.

It also seems unclear whether Putin would have ordered the killing when he wasn't especially threatened by Nemtsov, and given that he'd generally been able to control opposition leaders fairly effectively without violence up to that point. Of course, it's possible that the documents Nemtsov was planning to release on Ukraine contained some sort of bombshell that would have prompted Putin to have him killed. But killing someone is hardly a surefire way to keep any documents they have from being released.

There have been reports that Putin was furious about Nemtsov's murder. This seems plausible. The killing made Putin look bad and made Russia look out of control, just like the killing of Politkovskaya did. But the Nemtsov case is muddy and unclear, and it's difficult to make a confident guess about who was behind his murder.

Like Nemtsov, Sergei Yushenkov and Yuri Shchekochikhin were prominent opposition figures. They died within a few months of each other in 2003. Yushenkov was shot, and Shchekochikhin died suddenly in what many considered suspicious circumstances that could not be adequately investigated because authorities wouldn't release his medical reports. Both were members of the Russian Parliament, and also served on an independent public commission that tried to investigate the apartment bombings. They were also involved in or linked to independent journalistic investigations of the bombings. This leads some to charge they were killed as part of a cover-up. Because so much about the apartment bombings was indeed covered up, this is quite possible. But so far there's no way to establish a conclusive connection between the killing of Yushenkov and possible killing of Shchekochikhin and their work investigating the bombings.

Yushenkov and Shchekochikhin were both outspoken and active. Yushenkov formed a liberal political party that was highly critical of the government. He also investigated possible FSB involvement in a later terrorist attack at a Moscow theater. Shchekochikhin was a journalist as well as a politician, and was a critic of organized crime and the security services. Both men had a long list of enemies from investigating and speaking out about a range of corrupt and criminal activities in Russia. It's possible they each ran afoul of powerful people they'd challenged or exposed. Their antagonists definitely included people in the FSB.

But I am not a trained investigator. And there is limited public information available on these cases. Or perhaps more to the point, there were never thorough, trustworthy investigations. I can't really guess at who killed Yushenkov and possibly Shchekochikhin. There's certainly a possibility of state/government involvement, and I can't rule out Putin, although there's no evidence linking him to their deaths.

What about opposition figures inside Russia who were poisoned, even if the victims didn't die? In other words, is Putin a poisoner? In recent years, opposition activists Pyotr Verzilov, Vladimir

Kara-Murza (twice), and most recently as of this writing Alexei Navalny have all been poisoned. Navalny is currently the most prominent opposition leader in Russia. The poison used on him has been
confirmed as a Novichok agent, a class of toxins developed in the
Soviet Union in the 1970s and 1980s (and also used against Skripal
in Britain).

The evidence we have so far strongly supports a conclusion that
the Russian security services poisoned Navalny, and not rogue elements of the security services, but the full-bore apparatus. The investigative website Bellingcat tracked several Russian FSB officers
to the general area of Navalny's poisoning and tied them to elements of the security service that develop and use poisons. Navalny
himself tricked an FSB officer into confirming that the poisoning
was intentional. In a taped phone call, Navalny pretended to be an
aide to a former FSB chief/current secretary of the Security Council of Russia, and the officer willingly reported to him. It seems
close to certain the Russian security services poisoned Navalny.

The Navalny case is a turning point—there is now direct evidence of the Russian security services poisoning political opposition figures inside Russia. Previous to this, only cases of former
spies and traitors abroad like Litvinenko and Skripal had a clear
link to the Russian state apparatus. It now appears increasingly
likely the authorities are behind all or many of the poisonings of
political opposition figures—Kara-Murza, for example.

Now that we have compelling evidence of this direct link to the
authorities, the primary remaining question becomes whether the
security services are acting in Putin's interests without getting his
explicit approval (perhaps for deniability), or whether he is directly
ordering these attacks. This question can't currently be answered,
although it seems unlikely such a large and highly coordinated effort as the attack on Navalny, almost by definition ordered by the
top echelons of the security services, would take place without Putin's direct approval.

Whatever the case may be, Putin's denial of any state involvement in the Navalny poisoning, and smarmy counteraccusations

that Navalny is in league with Western intelligence agencies in a plot to discredit Russia, make him an accomplice regardless of whether he ordered the attack. If chemical-weapon attacks are taking place in your country against your citizens, and you refuse to investigate them while leading or participating in the process of fabricating counteraccusations, you take on significant responsibility for the attacks.

It's worth parsing this specific accusation that Navalny and other regime opponents are in league with Western intelligence agencies. Is this a literal claim? It may well be. Putin and others in the Russian leadership have at times demonstrated paranoia about Western intelligence agencies acting against them, and it is certainly possible they believe these agencies are working with the state's political opponents. There may also be a less paranoid version of this particular accusation: in their heads, Putin and his cohorts may look at Western support, financial and propagandistic, for the Russian opposition, and consider all of it a part of the work of Western intelligence agencies, with the details somewhat unimportant. In this sense, although I'm loath to discount the literal interpretation—political leaders very often do say what they think—these accusations against political opponents may instead have a more complicated meaning. Putin thinks the liberal opposition in particular acts as a kind of fifth column for a system of Western liberal democracy that seeks to overthrow the Russian political system. He believes this "fifth column" has the same aim as Western intelligence agencies, so they are in league.

Still, even if this worldview has a certain internal logic to it, when Putin and his allies accuse their opponents of espionage and treason, they are losing some contact with reality. Again, I mean this less as a criticism than an observation I would make about people operating in many political systems in different contexts, including our own.

Finally, it's curious that the former spy Skripal abroad, and Navalny and the other poisoned opposition figures inside Russia, survived. These weapons may not be easy to use, and incompetence can't be ruled out as a possible explanation either. But there is also a possibility the poisoners are not always trying to kill their victims, or care more about sending a message of intimidation than having their victims die. It's an odd part of a puzzle that cannot yet be solved.

———————

Whatever Putin's involvement is in some of the killings and poisonings he's often accused of, has he created a culture where this type of political violence is possible, with or without his approval? This is a more complicated question. Putin came to power at a time when Russia was overwhelmed with violence, including murders that were financially motivated, murders that were politically motivated, and murders where you couldn't even draw a clear line showing where the political elements began and ended. Putin restored order and the level of killing was reduced. So should we focus on how the problem has gotten better under Putin, or on how serious of a problem remains after thirty years of his leadership? In their totality, are the murders that continue to take place more like remnants of the earlier violence, or do they represent a new form of political violence actually encouraged by his various stripes of intolerance, his failure to do more to stop them, and of course his active use of violent and brutal methods like poisoning and perhaps murder against some of his opponents?

After Nemtsov was killed, Putin said: "The most serious attention should be paid to high-profile crimes, including those with political motives. We need to finally rid Russia of disgraces and tragedies like the one that we have recently endured and seen, I mean the murder, the provocative murder, of Boris Nemtsov right in the centre of the capital."

Does Putin really believe this? If so, does it apply to all political murders? Putin dodges a lot when speaking with the Western media, so little that he says can be taken at face value. But his response to Nemtsov's murder could well have been sincere. A few years later, in 2018, in response to questions about political killings in Russia from Fox News journalist Chris Wallace, Putin defended himself by saying that America has had political killings, too, like the murders of John F. Kennedy and Martin Luther King Jr.

Putin's analogy is not exact—many of those getting killed in Russia are opponents of Putin (I say many because there are also political killings in Russia more closely connected to regional than federal politics), whereas opponents of American presidents have not wound up dead. But Putin still makes a reasonable point: leaders are not necessarily able to control political murder in their countries. Putin himself may well be behind some of the acts of political violence in Russia and opposed to some of the others.

In any case, Putin is certainly not doing much to make Russia safe for people who disagree with him, or those who want to take on various societal ills like crime and corruption. He has not thrown his considerable weight behind focusing societal outrage on political killings, and he hasn't made strong and specific efforts to counteract them.

Everyone will have to make their own decision about whether or not to call Putin a killer, or think of him as one. He has almost certainly had people murdered and poisoned. But for me, if my guesses about his behavior are correct, using the word "killer" as a primary way of labeling or understanding him is misleading. It suggests that Putin uses killing as a political weapon more broadly and consistently than he probably does, and reduces the man to only his worst instincts and behaviors (somewhat like labeling George W. Bush "a torturer"). In the pages ahead, I will consider other sides of Putin, and try to flesh out a more complex and balanced view.

What Motivates Putin?

In the American media, Putin is often presented as having several primary motivations—making Russia a great power again, enriching himself and his friends, and maintaining his personal power.

The idea that Putin might be primarily motivated by a desire to help his people and his country is rarely considered.

We're always guessing when we try to figure out what motivates someone. Motives are inevitably mixed and you can't prove what's in a person's heart. But the American media's guesses about Putin are narrow and stem to some degree from our own fears and negative attitudes. Putin probably does want to make Russia a great power again, or at least increase its power and influence substantially. Why wouldn't he? He may even want to enrich himself and his friends. And there can be little doubt that he has gone to great lengths to maintain his personal power. The problem is trying to explain everything he does through these lenses, and failing to consider that these motivations could be secondary instead of primary.

The American media largely assumed it was just a power play when Putin got rid of direct elections for governor in Russia's federal regions in 2004. Putin began nominating all regional governors himself, and these nominations were generally rubber stamped by the relevant regional legislatures. Because direct elections were being replaced with presidential nominations, it's easy to see why this looked like a simple antidemocratic power grab. If Putin is seen only as an autocrat who consistently seeks more power, it fits his usual pattern. (In 2012, then President Medvedev reinstituted direct elections for governors following national protests against electoral fraud, although the Kremlin still maintained control over who was allowed to run.)

Putin himself claimed that ending direct elections of governors was necessary to keep the country together. Stephen Kotkin, and I'm sure others, explain the measure in a way that suggests Putin may have had a point. After the collapse of the Soviet Union, Russia's federal regions were in many ways like disconnected fiefs. They had a high degree of independence from Moscow, with budgetary policies and treaties with the center that often contradicted the federal constitution. They had significant power over federal officers—police, tax collectors—since they supplied them with offices, housing, and salary supplements. The regions could, and did, flout federal law almost at will. So Putin's primary aim in making sure he could control who held regional governorships may well have been to reassert central authority, to preserve a strong federal structure, and to keep it intact at a time when the state was fragile and threatened (arguably by both the refusal of the regions' political leaders to submit to federal authority and a series of terror attacks the previous summer). This explanation does not exclude Putin wanting to increase his power, but it suggests a more nuanced reason than a thirst for power itself.

To a certain degree, Putin was taking a position that many federal leaders in nondemocratic states would be likely to take if federal authority in their country were threatened. I'm not saying it was right or wrong, and I'm not saying Putin's assessment of the threat to central authority was right or wrong. And I'm certainly not denying that Putin and his allies want to move Russia in a less democratic direction, since they find democracy threatening to stability, and stability may be their foremost concern (in recent years, a desire to cement traditional conservative values in Russia and spread them abroad has also become a primary goal of the state). I am only saying that ending the free election of governors was likely motivated at least in part by something more complex, and more reasonable, than Putin's desire to grab power or enrich himself.

Putin's motivations were seen in the same narrow, exclusively negative way when Russia began a military intervention in Syria in 2015. Russia's military action was widely and almost invariably reported as yet another attempt by Putin to reassert Russian power and regain the influence and prestige the Soviet Union once had. In this case, he was thought to be accomplishing this by protecting an authoritarian leader in Syria from the West, in the interests of authoritarian rulers everywhere. He was fighting for Russia's preferred style of government, doing what he could to thwart American efforts to foster a democratic system.

All of this is probably true to a degree. But it fails to recognize the most likely reason Putin sent troops to Syria—because he believed Russia would be safer if the Assad regime didn't fall to ISIS.

Russia has a large and growing Muslim population—currently 10 percent or more of the total—as well as Muslim-majority states along and below its southern border. A destabilized and radicalized Middle East is a particular threat to Russia. Putin may also have been taking an opportunity to reassert Russian influence and power, but most likely his primary concern involved the security of his country.

Can we be sure that Putin is in fact motivated first and foremost by a desire to protect his state, that any lust for power or money is actually secondary? No. But it's telling that Putin, from a young age, wanted to be in the KGB. One of his earliest ambitions revolved around protecting his state. It seems unlikely that his motives have shifted so much that they've become primarily selfish.

Of course, Putin's past in the KGB is generally regarded in the West, and by some in Russia, as proof that he's crooked, dishonest, conspiracy-minded, and willing to use dirty tricks to achieve his goals (the last two are clearly true, to a degree). But working in the intelligence services does not disqualify someone from caring about their country and its future. On the contrary, people often go into intelligence work because they care deeply about their country. Serving in an intelligence service is also consistent with being particularly concerned about a country's stability, especially in Russia, with its recent history of revolution and civil war, national collapse, and its problems of demographic integrity.

With time, some intelligence-service officers become corrupted, or their idealistic motivations wane. But this isn't a rule. It's even possible to become corrupted and still care about your country and its future. None of this is unique to Russia's intelligence services, or even to intelligence services themselves. Many of these issues of power, corruption, and the way politicians' early idealism can fade are powerful forces in our country too.

I am personally sympathetic to those looking for a democratic transformation in Russia, but I don't assume Putin and other opponents of liberalism and democracy are necessarily corrupt or simply looking to remain in power. I believe they have a different set of goals and a different set of fears than I do, and as they pursue these goals and confront these fears, their complex motivations include basic patriotism and a desire to protect and take care of the citizens they lead.

"Bad Putin"—Russia's Nasty, Lying President

Putin can be extremely defensive. He is also, at times, boorish, even immature. Shortly after he became president, as he was launching the second war in Chechnya, Putin told a TV reporter, "We will chase terrorists everywhere. If in an airport, then in the airport. So if we find them in the toilet, excuse me, we'll rub them out in the outhouse. And that's it, case closed."

In his interviews with Oliver Stone, when asked if he'd shower next to a gay man in a submarine, Putin said, "Well, I prefer not to go to the shower with him. Why provoke him? But you know, I'm a judo master."

In addition to its homophobia and childishness, this joke highlights something troubling about Putin's way of expressing himself. He doesn't always speak the way we expect a world leader to. And since he speaks intelligently and does sound like a statesman much of the time, it's especially jarring when he doesn't.

An extremely unscientific sample based on interviews and public statements I've seen indicates Putin has become smoother and more statesmanlike as he's gotten older and more experienced as a leader. His boorish side hasn't gone away, but it has moderated. In 2011, looking back on his famous quote about killing Chechen terrorists in the outhouse, Putin said, "I had blurted something unpleasant, out of place. Too bad. I should not have been wagging my tongue like that being a high-level person."

What about Putin's frequent lying? Although many politicians lie and distort to some degree, Putin is particularly confounding in the way he alternates between lying smoothly and convincingly, lying in a self-satisfied, smug way, lying in a sneering and aggressive way, and lying in a defensive manner when he seems to suggest that he, and Russia, are perennial victims.

Dawn Sturgess, the British woman killed by the nerve agent used in the poisoning of Sergei Skripal, appears to have died after putting some of the chemical weapon on her skin after finding it in a discarded perfume bottle presumably used to transport it. Putin's response: "If we're talking about the Skripals being poisoned there, are you trying to say that we also poisoned some homeless person? Sometimes I look at what's going on around this case, and it just surprises me. Some guys came and started to poison bums in your country? What's this nonsense? Are they working to clean up the city or something?"

In a meeting with Angela Merkel in 2012, when she confronted Putin about the prison sentences handed out to members of the performance-art band Pussy Riot, he said: "Does she (Merkel) know that one of them had hanged a Jew in effigy and said that Moscow should be rid of such people? Neither we, nor you, can support people who assume an anti-Semitic position. I ask you to keep that in mind."

Several members of Pussy Riot had participated years earlier in a piece of political theatre where they'd conducted mock hangings of migrant workers, homosexuals, and a Jew, in order to protest mistreatment of those groups.

The lies begin to mount: Putin's denial that Russia invaded Crimea, his denial that Russia or Russian-backed fighters had anything to do with the shootdown of a Malaysian Airlines passenger flight over Ukraine in 2014, his denial of official Russian involvement in the interference with the 2016 U.S. presidential election. Putin lies frequently and brazenly.

Of course, sometimes a head of state has to lie, even when everyone knows they're lying. American leaders lied about our covert action supporting the Mujahideen in Afghanistan. According to Rory Cormac, Professor of International Relations at the University of Nottingham, and Richard J. Aldrich, Professor of International

Security at the University of Warwick, this lie arguably served the United States and the Soviet Union, as it helped prevent direct escalation between the two countries. Denying our involvement in the war also made it possible to maintain the position that we were opposed to nations interfering in each other's affairs. We interfered in other nations' affairs all the time, but denying it was somewhat helpful in the battle of perception that played an important part in the Cold War.

Do Putin's lies serve any of these functions? Some do. Again according to Cormac and Aldrich, refusing to acknowledge Russian interference in Ukraine, or in U.S. elections, allows Russia to claim that it's a responsible state following international norms and standards. Lying about Skripal served this same function. And of course, world leaders rarely admit their covert espionage activities abroad.

But lying about Pussy Riot engaging in an anti-Semitic act is little more than an outright attempt by Putin to deceive his listeners. What purpose does this serve? In general, when Putin lies, it feels like he's reaching back to his past as an intelligence officer, conducting a kind of one-man disinformation campaign. It's also possible he doesn't even expect to be believed, and is just thumbing his nose at his enemies. Or maybe he's speaking primarily to his domestic constituency even when he's abroad, whipping up anti-liberal sentiment and an us-versus-them mentality at home.

Political activist and former chess champion Garry Kasparov argues that Putin is part of a modern propaganda system that is trying to "annihilate" the truth, to throw so much information, true, false, whatever at the wall that people can no longer distinguish truth from lies, and stop even trying. (I think it's important to separate effect from intent here. This is happening to a degree, as I will discuss in greater detail in my section on the Russian press, but it seems unlikely that political and media leaders in Russia ever made a decision to try to wipe out or manipulate truth in this way.)

Timothy Snyder suggests that when Putin lied about sending troops into Ukraine his aim "was not to fool Ukrainians, but to create a bond of willing ignorance with Russians, who were meant to understand that Putin was lying, but to believe him anyway." Snyder goes on to quote reporter Charles Clover from his study of historian Lev Gumilev, "Putin has correctly surmised that lies unite, rather than divide, Russia's political class. The greater and the more obvious the lie, the more its subjects demonstrate their loyalty by accepting it, and the more they participate in the great sacral mystery of Kremlin power."

There is even the possibility that Putin believes some of what appear to be obvious lies and distortions. We don't know what his sources of information are, or what his own people are telling him.

Kotkin quotes a former high-ranking KGB officer and analyst as writing that lying was the overarching factor in the failure of the Soviet Union—"Lies struck at all aspects of our existence, becoming a fatal disease in our blood, destroying our soul." Whatever Putin's intentions are, so much lying is risky in a country where political deceit has such a dangerous history. It also makes him a less credible and effective leader.

———

Putin expresses himself most thoughtfully, and generally comes off better, in situations where he doesn't feel challenged. He's more impressive and more likeable when speaking to a sympathetic interviewer (who isn't?). People who don't like Putin may consider interviews he gives to the Western media a con job, but why? Certainly Putin is trying to influence his Western audience in a specific way. But much of what he says in these interviews makes sense. It should be taken, and debated, on its merits.

It's worth watching his interviews with Charlie Rose, as well as Oliver Stone's *The Putin Interviews*. Stone's series was widely derided in the American press, but it shows a thoughtful and interesting side of Putin. He tells several outrageous lies in these interviews, at one point claiming Russia has "hundreds of TV and radio companies and the state doesn't control them in any fashion." But in one of the interview's most revealing (and funniest) moments, he also pulls Stone back from his own over-the-top conspiracy theories about America.

It's also possible to watch Putin talk to the Russian people in his yearly call-in show *Direct Line*, and to see him address his nation in more formal speeches (with English subtitles). These are chances to see Putin communicating with Russians and compare it to how he speaks to a Western audience. A complex Putin emerges. He is mostly strict, somber, and low-affect when addressing Russians. But sometimes on the call-in show he turns defensive and nasty if someone asks a critical question. The Western media usually presents such moments as breakdowns in a highly stage-managed event, but there is also a possibility that these unscripted questions from the audience suggest the events aren't quite as stage-managed as we've assumed.

The All-Powerful Putin

In the West, Putin is often held responsible for every problem in Russia. But Russia is an enormous country, nearly twice as big as ours in landmass (a little less than half as large in population), with eighty-five federal "subjects" (if you count the two incorporated after the annexation of Crimea). These subjects are somewhat similar to states, each with their own parliament, ministers, and so on. But they are not as structurally uniform as our states—some are oblasts, some are republics, some are krais, and there are other designations as well—each with its own attendant authorities and power bases, too, local governments and local officials all doing the countless things bureaucrats and politicians do. A Russian president can't exert full control over this vast country any more than an American president can exert control over every state, city, county, town, and neighborhood in the United States.

In the Soviet Union, Russia's most recent model for governance, significant power rested in the enormous bureaucracy, and general secretaries post-Stalin shared power with the Politburo, where collaboration and joint leadership were emphasized. Putin

may embrace collective rule less than post-Stalin Soviet general secretaries did, or he may be working collaboratively in ways that are
harder to see (as we tended not to see them in the Soviet Union).
But either way, Putin does not hold absolute power. As one of
many examples, he does not exercise complete control of the security services, even though people often assume this is his main
power base, one he's drawn from to fill many government positions. But the security services are large, and people working in
them at all levels sometimes act based on their personal interests.
This was true in the Soviet Union, and in Russia before that.

This does not absolve Putin of responsibility for what happens
in Russia. Politics itself, obviously, requires that leaders take on significant responsibility for their countries. Of course they should be
held accountable. But there are severe limits on what a leader can
accomplish, and holding them too broadly responsible for everything in their country is disconnected from the real world of limits
and possibilities.

Rather than everything deriving from an all-powerful Putin,
Russia's behavior and policies originate in multiple places, are often
uncoordinated, and don't necessarily make perfect sense. As one of
countless examples, take the Russian government's treatment of
the Levada Center, an independent polling organization. It may
be surprising to those who consider Russia fully authoritarian that
free and honest polling takes place there. Levada polls on the limits
of Putin's popularity, people's apathy about politics, and reasons
people don't like Putin, among other issues. In other words, it asks
about many supposedly taboo topics.

Levada has been targeted by the government. The original
state-controlled polling organization where its namesake Yuri Levada worked was fully taken over by the state. The true independent pollsters from the original organization opened a new polling
organization, which was later labeled as a foreign agent. Nevertheless, it has carried on its work, and so far has been successful in
preserving its independence and integrity.

So why doesn't the government just shut down the reconsti-tuted Levada pollsters? How can we understand a government pol-icy that tolerated them for so long, then started to harass them, but stopped short of destroying them?

There's no one to tell us what actually happened inside the gov-ernment, but there's a lot of speculation. Some believe the growing concern in official Russian circles over foreign funding of NGOs and interference in Russia's internal affairs explains why Levada was targeted. Some suggest the Levada pollsters' new organization was eventually labeled a foreign agent because it threatened the leadership's hegemonic control over information. Some grasp at the well-worn theory that the government is consciously allowing the populace to blow off steam by permitting a limited degree of freedom. Others suggest government leniency stems only from a concern about foreign reactions. And there is also reasonable spec-ulation that Levada wasn't fully shut down simply because it was easier to let it survive while successfully undermining it. All of these explanations make some sense and may well have had a bearing on events.

But the possibility that a state bureaucracy implemented par-tially thought-out and partially considered policies, backtracked a bit for any number of reasons, and then left Levada to its work in a more constricted environment, also fits with what we know about how bureaucracies often function. How a government makes pol-icy, how it launches into action—whether it's the United States or Russia—often lacks coherence. Governments and systems fre-quently don't know exactly what they're doing. Maybe this is ob-vious, but it's easily ignored in the heat of politics. We impose coherence on what we do at home, but even more on what foreign governments do. For example, we see Russia limiting the freedom of its citizens, and we say that the Russian government is deter-mined to repress all of its critics. The way we understand the world, this is what authoritarian states do. We throw out everything that doesn't fit that explanation, and then we can tell ourselves we know what's happening, which feels more important than getting at the messy truth.

Like all states, Russia has its problems. And we have ours. Here, tens of millions of Americans live below the poverty line, some in neighborhoods rife with so much violence that children are shot to death walking to school. Innocent people are killed by the police. America has tackled its epidemic of drugs and violence by incarcerating millions of people, including perhaps half a million black men in state and federal prison right now (and a significant number in local jails as well) whose representation in the prison population is far disproportionate to their numbers in society. These prisoners are often incarcerated for years, some for crimes they didn't commit, some for crimes where the sentence is not commensurate with the infraction, and some for terrible crimes, but committed by minors or young people who grew up in heartbreaking circumstances and were never given the choices and opportunities so many people in this country get.

I have sometimes thought that there isn't much we can do about these terrible injustices. We can't wave a wand and solve such deep-rooted problems, even with financial resources that Russia can only dream of having. But couldn't Putin wave a wand and stop all of the violence carried out against his opponents? Couldn't he stop the rampant corruption? The answer to both of those questions is most likely no.

He could, however, play a different, more constructive role in facing his country's problems. And in cases where he exacerbates problems, he could stop. To become a leader I could actually embrace, Putin would have to reverse course and fight against state-sponsored repression and injustice in Russia. He would have to stop persecuting his opponents—stop killing people he sees as traitors and stop either ordering or passively supporting attacks against opposition figures using poison (or any physical attacks for that matter). He would have to stop telling bald-faced lies.

I wish he would.

Most of the American media, most of our political leaders, and a significant part of our foreign-policy establishment see Putin in black-and-white terms. He has to be bad or good, and of those two choices, they've decided he's bad. But this black-and-white over-simplification works in reverse when our own leaders are involved. George W. Bush prosecuted a brutal war in Iraq that likely killed hundreds of thousands, and he ordered drone strikes in Pakistan that killed not just their targets but many innocents, including children. He authorized the United States to use torture as part of the war on terror. But he's widely considered to be caring, likeable, and funny. Although some Americans condemn him, most people I know, even if they disagree with his policies, have little doubt that he's a fundamentally decent person. Putin prosecuted a brutal war in Chechnya, he is widely believed to have ordered assassinations of people he considers enemies and traitors, and he likely ordered or passively approved the poisoning of a number of opposition figures. He has presided over a crackdown on civil liberties in Russia. Sometimes he lies, and he can be defensive and boorish. But in his case, Americans ignore anything about him that's positive, likeable, or charming. They fail to give him credit for pulling Russia from the brink after the Yeltsin years, for having instituted at least some sound economic policies, and for keeping the country in many ways stable. They see his intelligence as cunning rather than recognizing a leader who thinks and sometimes talks clearly and convincingly about international affairs. Putin is, simply, bad.

"Bad" people, especially if they are powerful, transform into an enemy. Then the exaggerations, one-sided view, and demonization of this enemy creates a false character and a trumped-up villain.

This can easily become a self-fulfilling prophecy. A look at the historical record makes it clear that Putin has become both more anti-Western and more illiberal at home over time. Had we behaved differently, and built a more positive relationship with him, would that have resulted in a more liberal Putin at home, or a less aggressive Putin abroad? Although it's generally a mistake to assume the West has that much influence on internal Russian politics, there does appear to be a link between Putin's fears and anxieties about Western interference in Russian affairs and some of his policies that roll back civil liberties. Either way, there can be little doubt that our own actions and attitudes have been a major factor in shifting Putin's attitude toward the West. At the beginning of his presidency, he was fairly open to us.

We have been so unrelentingly negative about Putin that when Russia interfered with our 2016 presidential election, it just seemed like "Bad Putin" had done something even worse than usual. A bad man had attacked us, and we couldn't really understand why. Was Putin responding to what he perceived as American interference in Russia's 2012 presidential elections? Was he motivated by hatred of Hillary Clinton (stemming from what he saw as her efforts to discredit him and interfere in Russia's 2011 parliamentary elections)? Maybe Putin was retaliating against us because he thought the United States was responsible for the release of the Panama Papers, a trove of leaked documents that exposed, among other things, financial corruption in Putin's inner circle? The American media subtly hinted or outright claimed that Putin's concern about these various issues was paranoid—that he had an almost crazy belief that the West was out to get him, or out to get Russia.

Although Putin may have been motivated to interfere in our elections by any or all of the above factors (not to mention wanting someone friendlier to Russia in the White House), few mentioned that his fears about the United States, even if they included some paranoid elements, were largely justified. Any reasonable person looking at the totality of our actions would conclude that we have been trying to isolate, dominate, and destabilize Russia, and that we hope to get rid of Putin too. In the next chapter, I'll detail our most aggressive actions, but here are just a few.

We've brought many of Russia's neighbors into NATO, a military alliance formed to oppose the Soviet Union. We funded groups in Russia that fight for democracy and transparency in elections—certainly we hoped to create a different kind of political system there (doesn't this count as interference in their elections?). Our support for liberal democratic groups in Russia also strongly suggests the American political establishment hopes the country will adopt a more democratic system, without Putin. (And don't you think most in the American political establishment want Putin out and Russia democratized?)

And then there are sanctions. Our regime of economic sanctions against Russia is a broad-based attack on the Russian economy. It may be intended as a response to Putin or Putinism, or an effort to respond to aggressive Russian actions abroad or specific human-rights violations inside Russia. But there's no question that sanctions undermine Russia as a whole. That's what an economic attack does. Whatever the intentions behind sanctions, it's reasonable and accurate to view them as an effort to grievously harm Russia.

Let's also remember that there was a concerted effort to bring down the Soviet Union, spelled out in Reagan's secret National Security Decision Directive (NSDD) 75. NSDD 75 set out specific "tasks" for the United States, including: "To promote, within the narrow limits available to us, the process of change in the Soviet Union toward a more pluralistic political and economic system in which the power of the privileged ruling elite is gradually reduced."

Putin, of course, grew up in and loyally served the Soviet party/state, and he knows all about NSDD 75 as well as the many times when Reagan was publicly open about American efforts to spread democracy to the Soviet Union (or, as Putin would reasonably see it, to undermine and destroy the Soviet Union). Why wouldn't Putin assume the United States is trying to bring down the current Russian system in the same way, and him with it?

We've certainly interfered in Russian politics, and many Americans feel this is justified because we're trying to subvert an autocracy. Many of us, in fact, believe it is a moral duty for America to democratize foreign countries. But a majority of Russians support Putin, want him as their leader, and traditionally want a strong leader. Notably, when Russia actually ran a serious and lengthy experiment with liberal democracy in the 1990s, it failed. It is hard to justify any interference.

And yet when Putin fights back (meaning Russian attacks on American society or American democracy), or even when he just talks about being attacked in various ways by the West, the American media and political leadership respond as if he's a paranoid aggressor. We would do better to imagine how we would feel, and how we would respond, if a country richer and more powerful than us—probably the closest we can get is to imagine China sometime in a possible future—felt our system of government was inferior to theirs and used their power to "do us the favor" of trying to change it.

2. HOW REPRESSIVE IS RUSSIA?

I'll leave Putin behind (to the degree that's possible—I won't get far) and focus now on a few other general aspects of Russian politics and society.

I think most Americans would be surprised by the level of freedom in Russia today. Because our press mostly focuses on political violence, protesters being arrested, and media outlets being shut down, it's easy to think that Russia is a heavily repressive, authoritarian state where citizens have virtually no freedom at all. But a significant level of personal and political freedom does exist alongside the repression. This remains true even though Putin has presided over a far-reaching rollback in civil rights for the Russian people in recent years.

This is not to say that Russia is a fundamentally free country, just that it's different from what many of us imagine. To get the clearest possible picture of how freedom and repression exist side by side in Russia, I'll examine several specific areas of Russian political and societal life.

Freedom of Expression and Freedom of the Press

I once ignored what I saw with my own eyes about a refusenik's life in Leningrad so that I could keep believing the Soviet Union was a totalitarian, brutally anti-Semitic state. I tried not to repeat this pattern more recently as I struggled to reconcile the many articles and books written and published in Russia that were extremely critical of various aspects of society, and specifically the state apparatus, with what I read and saw in the American media, which insisted Russia was heavily authoritarian and brooked little dissent. This American view isn't concocted out of thin air. Russian journalists are repressed by the state—interrogated by police, threatened, fired from their jobs. People are routinely jailed for expressing their views or standing up to the state. Protests are controlled and limited. This is all horrible, morally and politically wrong, and causes great suffering.

The situation is also more nuanced than the American media usually suggests. Russians today actually have significant though circumscribed latitude to say what they think. Not just in the privacy of their apartments, where even in the post-Stalin Soviet Union many people felt relatively free to speak openly (not everyone, and not always), but also in print, on the Internet, and occasionally even on television.

There is a relatively free-flowing public debate in Russia. The American media and many experts often minimize this open debate by claiming that, despite some narrow open discussion, there is "a line that can't be crossed." Russians can say what they want as long as they don't criticize Putin and the government. That uncrossable line is reportedly so wide that it effectively suppresses free political speech in Russia.

And yet I read Russian journalists and writers criticizing Putin and the government all the time, not just in Western media outlets but in translation from a variety of Russian newspapers and websites.

I asked Larry Bogoslaw, a translator, editor, and expert on the Russian media, to help me sort out what was really going on. Larry's analysis matches up with what I actually see in Russia. Here are some of his thoughts on freedom of the press in Russia, often in more or less his own words, hopelessly mixed up with information from other sources and my own ideas.

Before the 2014 invasion of Crimea, Putin and his allies still cared about what the West thought. They worked hard to stifle any internal criticism, afraid it made them look bad. But after the intense international reaction to the invasion of Crimea, Putin gave up on the West. He no longer felt he had anything to lose from bad press. Ironically, for a while, this led to more freedom and latitude for journalists, writers, and really everyone (several friends of mine from Russia disagree, saying conditions for journalists there have only gotten worse each year).

None of this meant the Russian press was suddenly free. And the state soon changed its tactics toward public information anyway—instead of intimidating and firing noncompliant journalists, and closing media outlets they couldn't successfully take over or co-opt, the authorities greatly expanded the use of two old methods of control: legislation and propaganda. First, they tightened anti-extremism laws. Now virtually any criticism of the authorities, even in social media posts, could be labeled as "hate speech" or blamed for "inciting mass disturbances." Second, the state started overwhelming the population with the information it wanted them to have. Because they'd been half-threatening and half-bribing

journalists into compliance for years, and because quite a few genuinely agreed with the government's positions anyway, it was easy
to get the mass media in Russia to function in lockstep. This may
have been less of a master plan and more of a strategy the Russian
leadership stumbled into, and as I suggested before, it may not
have been conscious. Either way, it worked so well that it didn't
matter if a small group of oppositionists said and wrote what they
wanted. They were drowned out, at least for most Russians.

The linchpin to this strategy is television. Polls suggest over 70
percent of Russians get their news from TV, so if the state wants to
control what information most Russians are exposed to, it has to
control television. Putin's government shut down or took over the
country's independent TV stations, which are now either owned
by the state or by people obedient to the state. A member of Putin's
administration, often his deputy chief of staff, manages all state-run
media, and meets regularly with people running the day-to-day operations of the TV stations to make sure they know what they can
and can't say (these dictates are insinuated by the leadership and
intuited by the media managers rather than stated directly). This
is why Russians who watch their morning news shows on different
channels see the same talking points.

How effective is this strategy? I think we have to ask if people
like Putin because they watch state-controlled TV, or if they choose
state-controlled TV over other sources of news because they like
Putin. If people like a conservative president in America, is that
because they watch Fox News, or do they watch Fox News because
they like the conservative president? In our society, it's obvious this
isn't a simple question with a simple answer. It isn't in Russia either.

One way or another, Russians overwhelmingly make the choice
to watch state-controlled television stations (as opposed to getting
their news exclusively from independent parts of the print media
or the Internet). This choice counts as freedom too. Other sources
of information are available to the 70 percent-plus who get their
news through television. We may not like their choice, but they are

free enough to choose something else, and they don't. (Notably the number of Russians relying exclusively on television for their news has been trending downward.)

State-controlled television is largely one-sided, propagandistic, and frequently full of lies. But it isn't completely monolithic. There are talk shows where a range of opinions are expressed. Anyone questioning the official line on these shows is usually outnumbered and shouted down, and some think allowing these dissenting opinions is just a method to keep them from festering, while also discrediting them. I'm not so sure. We misunderstood some of the ways in which the Soviet press was serving a positive function, because it was so different from how the press worked in our society. The Soviet press did provide some voice to the people, acting at times as a kind of middleman for reporting problems to the authorities. Alternate viewpoints are being voiced on Russian TV. This might be a good thing.

Still, real press freedom exists mainly in parts of the print media and online. Most print media is state-run or state-controlled in less direct ways, but there are a number of independent newspapers and magazines with marginal audiences. The regional press is sometimes more independent. The Internet is fairly free, although that freedom is frequently under attack, more and more using the legislative maneuvers described above.

But print and online journalists can mostly write what they want, if a bit warily. Of course, there are plenty of reasons for them not to be too critical of Putin or the government, and this leads to a fair amount of self-censorship. Journalists, pundits, and academics know they will have more and better job opportunities, and make more money, if they don't openly criticize Putin. They'll also do better if they can keep from running afoul of repressive laws targeting extremism and gay rights, as well as laws regulating political movements and protests.

A friend who used to work in TV news in Russia said he was free to attack any minister or governor, any bureaucrat, and even any event or situation—only Putin and Medvedev were off-limits.

Bogoslaw agrees there is a "line that can't be crossed." In his view, writers can even criticize Putin and the government as much as they want as long as they're essentially speculating. If they start digging for proof to support their theories, they are going too far— they could face legal reprisals and, although it's unclear if it's sanctioned from the top, violence.

Recent events have highlighted some other potentially profound changes in how journalism and the dissemination and acquisition of information work in Russia. I emphasize again how temporary any of this could be in the rapidly changing Russian political and media landscape. But at least as of this writing, according to Ben Smith of the *New York Times*, pervasive corruption in Russia has made it possible for journalists and political activists (which he describes as overlapping categories in Russia) to buy digital records of anyone they're investigating. For example, Navalny was able to obtain travel and phone records of his suspected poisoners. This has been a boon to investigative journalists. It has led to the exposure of corrupt and illegal practices, and has spawned both new media outlets and a wide online audience for their work.

Some of these new media enterprises are headquartered abroad, but much of the work is done inside Russia, and in any case, it is about Russia. This type of journalism benefits from a kind of Internet lawlessness that is ethically complex, and arguably wreaking havoc in the United States (spreading disinformation, promoting conspiracy theories) while also expanding access to information and truth in Russia.

During the Cold War, we felt Soviet citizens were helpless victims of propaganda. Most of us didn't realize Soviets just had to look around to see how their society really functioned. There was an obvious discrepancy between what they saw and what their media told them was going on. Not everyone looked and compared in this way, but many did.

Russian media today is miles from its Soviet past. It is not fully free by a long shot, but it is free in some ways. A lively debate goes on about almost everything, including politics, and this debate is available to those who want to participate in it. Restrictions, state control, and societal practices make it difficult, or perhaps impossible, to expose the broadest possible public to this debate. And it is especially difficult or perhaps impossible to turn these debates into political action. But the debate is taking place, in public.

All of this could be different by the time you read this. Journalism in Russia is full of dynamism, by which I mean it's dynamic in both directions. It is alternately, and arguably even simultaneously, getting better and worse, freer and less free.

Treatment of the Opposition

I argued earlier that Putin and the Russian state use a range of tools to deal with their opponents, from murder and poisoning (rarely) to firing and marginalizing them (frequently). Let's look more closely at a few examples of how the state deals in particular with the liberal opposition.

There have always been Russians who want a more open, democratic country. Generally called the liberal intelligentsia, they get a lot of attention in the West because they share our political values. But they're an almost negligible political minority in Russia.

Experts disagree on whether it was primarily the liberal intelligentsia, the larger urban middle class (including the liberal intelligentsia), or a broader cross-section of society that protested against Putin from 2011 to 2013. Whoever the protesters were, they demanded free and fair elections, an end to election fraud, and that Putin not return as president again after Dmitry Medvedev's term ended.

Many observers agree that Putin likely felt betrayed by these protesters. He had saved the country from Yeltsin and the mafia, and then put in place an economic program that had literally made it possible for the urban middle class to grow. In other words, he had created the very people who he felt were turning on him now (if the experts who believe it was primarily the liberal intelligentsia who were protesting were right, Putin's sense of betrayal was off, since he certainly didn't create this group).

Regardless, after the protests, Putin turned away from the urban middle class, and sought political support in Russia's rural areas, villages, and smaller cities, where the majority of the population lives. (A somewhat similar demographic political divide exists in America.) Since this change, one primary government pattern is to employ a level of repressive measures against any effort by liberalizing forces to speak out or gain followers that the authorities consider significant or threatening. Protests are frequently met with force, and their leaders are frequently arrested and sometimes beaten. Ordinary protesters are arrested as well—anyone who goes to a political rally runs the risk of getting sent to jail for anywhere from several days to several years. These sentences are enough to make protesting dangerous, while also keeping the government from appearing too brutal (or, arguably, while also keeping the government from being too brutal). Individual opposition leaders, as discussed, are also sometimes poisoned, and it has become increasingly apparent that the state is behind some or all of these poisonings.

Navalny's long struggle with the government is probably the best example of how the authorities respond when they feel increasingly threatened. Navalny is complicated, and not exactly a Western-style liberal, but he has many followers in the liberal intelligentsia (and beyond). Navalny has been arrested on trumped-up charges and jailed more than ten times since the anti-Putin protests that began in 2011. He has received both short and several-years-long sentences, but the longer sentences have not been carried out. He's been in jail over two hundred days (and counting) in that ten-year period. His brother Oleg, arrested along with Alexei in 2014 on trumped-up charges, was held for three and a half years, fairly clearly as a lever to use against Navalny. Finally, Navalny was poisoned, arguably as his charges of corruption against the authorities gained wider traction. After receiving medical treatment in Germany, he returned to Russia and was immediately arrested and imprisoned again, then sentenced to serve more than two years in a penal colony. His circumstances may have changed by the time you read this, and there is no way to even predict if he'll still be alive.

Another case that received widespread attention in the west involved Pussy Riot. In 2012, five members of this group went into Moscow's Cathedral of Christ the Savior, wearing balaclavas, and danced in a sacred part of the church where only clerics are allowed while singing a song harshly critical of Putin and the Russian Orthodox Church. Three of the five band members were later brought to trial and sentenced to two years in prison (one group member's sentence was later suspended). In the West, many condemned the Pussy Riot members' arrest and imprisonment.

But Pussy Riot received a good deal less sympathy from the broader public in Russia. Singing a politically and socially provocative song while dancing around in a church isn't going to be popular there. Pussy Riot claimed they were protesting church leaders' support for Putin, and the fusing of state and church in Russia, but the location they chose for this protest was particularly inflammatory. Should the authorities have dealt with them more leniently? Of course. Two years in prison is a serious, devastating punishment for what they did. But it's arguably also a relatively moderate sentence, compared to what they could have received. I don't feel entirely comfortable labeling someone else's prison sentence moderate. But the fact that the state easily could have handed down a much more severe sentence seems important. I'm not quite sure how a roughly analogous situation in the United States would have been resolved.

The treatment of Pussy Riot is somewhat similar to the treatment of Navalny before the state felt more threatened by him. This is, of course, just a fairly logical guess about the state's motivation and decision-making, and may be imparting too much logic to a process that, like most political processes, also functions based on whim, coincidence, and an endless number of nonrational factors.

There is another singular tactic some Russian authorities have used to repress opposition figures that harkens back to the worst abuses of the post-Stalin era. The Federation Global Initiative on Psychiatry has documented over thirty cases since 2012 of punitive psychiatry being used against journalists and opposition figures. As in Soviet times, victims have been falsely diagnosed, imprisoned in psychiatric hospitals, and forced to take psychotropic medications. This method has been primarily used against Crimean Tatars and other Ukrainian opponents who protested the annexation of Crimea. But it has also been used against regime opponents more broadly (and sometimes as a tool of personal revenge by powerful private citizens with state connections).

According to the federation's chief executive, Robert van Voren, there has not been a return of the systemic abuse of psychiatry practiced in the Soviet era—current incarcerations have been for weeks or months, not years, and represent individual abuses by local authorities trying to silence opponents. At the same time, the echoes of the past are disturbing. While the diagnosis used in cases now has changed from the Soviet-era "sluggish schizophrenia" to the more modern "personality disorder," the alleged symptoms are the same: obstinacy, struggle for the truth, and overvaluation of one's own importance. And systemic or not, any reemergence of punitive psychiatry should be very troubling to everyone in Russia, including those directly involved in practicing it and those allowing it to happen. As much as our views of what happened in the Soviet Union were often one-sided and exaggerated, the Soviet party/state was highly repressive, and did terrible damage to itself, as well as its victims, through the use of psychiatry as a tool against political opponents.

Laws About Homosexuality

In 2013, the Russian Duma passed a law making it illegal to disseminate "propaganda of non-traditional sexual relationships," especially to minors. The law's supporters believed information given to minors about LGBTQ issues encouraged them to be gay. Breaking the law was punishable by a fine, or for foreigners, arrest and deportation.

There was substantial concern that this law would lead to increased violence against LGBTQ Russians, and in fact, protesters against the law were beaten in front of the Duma by counterprotesters and then arrested.

Around the same time this federal law was passed, Russia passed a law preventing same-sex couples from adopting children. In 2014, Russia banned same-sex couples and single people in countries that allow gay marriage from adopting Russian children. There was also talk in the Duma about drafting laws that would remove children from same-sex homes in Russia (thankfully this hasn't happened yet).

As is often the case in Russia, enforcement of these laws has been lax. The politicians and activists behind them may have been more interested in making a political point than in actually carrying them out. But that doesn't make the laws themselves, or the direction in which they point Russian society, less troublesome.

Russia's anti-gay laws both reflect and encourage widespread homophobic attitudes, leading to marginalization, harassment, and violence against the LGBTQ community in Russia. Instead of protecting members of this vulnerable group, the state has made their lives considerably harder and more dangerous.

Problems with Civil Society

I have no personal experience with civil-society organizations in Russia, and less exposure to this issue than most of what I write about in this book. I've had to rely more than usual on research, including several reports from the Carnegie Institute, in particular a detailed study by Saskia Brechenmacher, "Civil Society Under Assault," which provides the bulk of the facts, figures, and sometimes language below about civil society in Russia. The general framework for looking at civil society in Russia, and the emphasis on its positive side, should not be attributed to Carnegie or Brechenmacher. Because much of this is new to me, my interpretations, guesses, and ideas probably have a greater chance of missing the mark.

A country's "civil society" comprises all of the organizations that look out for the interests of its citizens but are not part of the government. This includes charities, advocacy groups, even certain organizations with a primarily social function (if their goal is the betterment of people's lives). Civil society supplements the efforts of the government to care for a nation's people, or sometimes works against the government when there is a difference of opinion about how best to serve society.

Civil society can also be defined more broadly to encompass the overall relations between citizens and all the institutions of their country and their government, such as the press, the judiciary, and so on. I'll stick to the narrower definition here so that I can focus on what's been happening with nongovernmental organizations in Russia, which gets a lot of attention in the West.

It's always helpful to start with the Soviet structures that influence, for better or worse, modern day Russia. The Soviet Union, in a sense, had no civil society. The country was conceptually designed for the party/state to provide everything, and was threatened by the idea of any individual or independent organization taking on any of its functions.

But the Soviet state did carry out many civil society–type activities. It initiated massive campaigns to get citizens to educate themselves more, and to drink less. It created and supported society-wide youth groups, cultural clubs, sports clubs, and profession-based societies for writers, scientists, and many others. While heavily politicized and existing in large part to serve the interests of the party/state, these groups also served some of the functions of civil-society organizations. Among other things, they provided an outlet for pushback against the state and the airing of individual and group needs. In the Komsomol and the Writers' Union, for example, doing whatever the party said may have been the norm, but following blindly wasn't as constant or consistent as we tended to imagine. Members of these organizations, at times, resisted party directives, and spoke up against various official policies, without even remotely crossing the line into dissent.

Considering all the civil-society functions it tried to serve, the Soviet Union was in many ways a giant effort to combine civil society and party/government. Or perhaps it was a different way of forming a society based on an awareness of the same problems that civil society seeks to address. In a country conceived to redress capitalist exploitation, one way to accomplish this goal was to try and build a system that created equality by taking care of an incredibly broad range of people's needs.

In the post-Soviet era, citizens have created more traditional forms of civil society in Russia. They've formed organizations that promote the environment, democracy, human rights, women's rights, soldiers' rights, prisoners' rights, rights for the disabled, a range of public-health issues, and more. But from early on in his presidency, Putin thought the independence of these organizations was problematic, a foreign import that didn't fit Russia's political culture. He became even more eager to take control of these groups after the color revolutions in Ukraine and several other former Soviet states in the mid-2000s, which he saw as U.S.-sponsored regime change directed at keeping Russia down, often using civil-society organizations as a tool.

Putin's antipathy toward independent civil society probably reached its peak around the time of the 2011–2013 protests in Russia. He claimed the United States was funding the opposition and using election monitors and other civil-society groups to influence the outcome of Russian elections. Considering the strong antipathy toward Putin in Washington, and the fact that we were funding election monitoring and human-rights groups that were active and vocal during the protests surrounding his return to office after Medvedev's term, was it unreasonable that Putin and the Russian leadership saw organizations that received American funding as tools of our government? They believed groups promoting democracy in Russia while receiving Western funding were interfering in Russia's internal affairs and essentially trying to overthrow the government with help from the West. On a certain level, this is correct. It doesn't account for the fact that these were grassroots organizations with a valid Russian viewpoint. But it's not surprising that our involvement created a problem, as well as a pretext for silencing certain groups.

Putin and the state passed new laws in 2012 and 2015 that restricted what civil-society organizations could do. Organizations that promoted democracy, or challenged the government politically, could now be labeled "foreign agents," and hit with so many rules and restrictions that it became difficult for them to operate (disabling oppositional forces in this way is a kind of Russian bureaucratic specialty). These laws also made it possible to kick foreign funders of Russian civil society out of the country. The National Endowment for Democracy, the National Democratic Institute, the International Republican Institute (all private groups funded at least in part by the U.S. government), as well as USAID (an independent agency of the U.S. government) were prohibited from continuing their work (don't have "democracy" in your name if you want to survive as an NGO in Russia). A meaningful level of civil-society funding by the EU was able to continue.

But what happened overall was complicated and surprising. In America, reading the press, it seemed like Putin shut down almost all civil-society organizations, both because he was paranoid about Western interference in Russia and because civil-society organizations threatened the government by interacting directly with the population. This may or may not be an accurate representation of Putin's feelings, but it doesn't capture what actually happened.

There were, by some counts, several hundred thousand NGOs in Russia in the early/mid-2000s (bet you weren't expecting that many!). A hundred and two of these, often the best-run and most well-known, were labeled foreign agents. These included the Human Rights Center Memorial, the Public Verdict Foundation, and election monitor Golos. Organizations specifically promoting democracy, human rights, and election monitoring were at greatest risk.

But most of the organizations labeled as foreign agents refused to accept it. Both the Presidential Council for Civil Society and Human Rights and Russia's Public Chamber—essentially consultative bodies to the president and state, created by Putin, which many feared would simply rubber stamp his policies (and sometimes did)—challenged parts of the law. Even the justice minister questioned whether the law allowed him to unilaterally register organizations as foreign agents.

Because the new laws were vague, members of civil-society organizations didn't know exactly what they were supposed to do, or how the courts would ultimately interpret elements of the law. Even the state officials carrying out the legally sanctioned harassment of NGOs weren't sure what they were supposed to do, exactly. The inspections they carried out and the fines they levied were haphazard and varied by region. Groups received different types of fines and violations, then went to court to challenge them in cases that were slow to resolve. Fines tended to run around the equivalent of several thousand dollars, an extremely difficult amount for resource-starved organizations to pay.

According to Brechenmacher, as of November 2016, Russian authorities had started judicial proceedings against 235 NGOs. In another 98 cases, NGOs themselves had fought back by taking legal action against the government. In a number of cases, civil-society activists prevailed—for example, in February 2017, the Russian Supreme Court annulled a 300,000 ruble penalty imposed on the Women of the Don (a human- and civil-rights organization). But fighting in court required both resources and advanced organizational abilities. Smaller organizations often couldn't manage it. Many avoided legal proceedings by self-censoring, dropping initiatives that Russian officials might consider political.

According to Human Rights Watch, more than thirty civil-society organizations closed under the pressure of inspections, fines, and requirements to submit all kinds of paperwork. But most organizations didn't disappear. Some changed their names, and/or dropped their official registration, but continued to work.

Organizations that weren't registered were not allowed to work with the government (important for some groups focused on public health or social issues), and they couldn't publish anything, but they could carry on parts of their previous work. Some organizations opened for-profit subsidiaries, which actually allowed them to continue receiving foreign funding, since for-profit organizations weren't covered by the new laws. In other words, there were loopholes (arguably a sign of a less strictly authoritarian and more legalistic system, or possibly more indicative of the power and intricacy of bureaucracy).

Meanwhile, according to Brechenmacher, as Putin tried to bring civil society under state control, organizations that steered clear of politics and worked only on education, health, and social welfare began to receive state financing (many felt these organizations were being corrupted, since a condition of the aid was support for the government). New groups formed, with close ties to local politicians and governments, as well as businesses. For example, the oil company Lukoil funded a number of organizations in the Russian federal subject of Perm, which dealt with everything from promoting indigenous artisans to healthcare. Because these organizations in a sense replaced the groups driven out of existence, the number of civil-society organizations in Russia didn't actually go down. But the model of civil society in Russia was shifting.

Over the last few years, although all the previous problems remain, the situation for civil society in Russia may be improving in some ways. NGOs are proving resilient in the face of the many challenges they face. Many organizations have remained independent, and they seem to be expanding their reach. Private donations and volunteering are both up.

Grassroots, local activism, which threatens the government less than efforts with a national political agenda, has grown substantially. Russia expert Mark Galeotti argues this type of activism, often revolving around environmental movements or local efforts to save a building or a park, constitute a significant civil society in Russia, although participants have to pretend these aren't political movements to avoid crossing the artificial line imposed by the authorities. Engagement and civic consciousness are coalescing around these allegedly "nonpolitical" conflicts as citizens fight against the unwelcome development of public spaces or the closing of hospitals, and work to influence and improve the environment, education, and even garbage transport. People are becoming active in these issues outside of NGOs, which allows a level of engagement and action without the troubles that come with the creation and registration of an official group.

We don't know what form of civil society will prevail in Russia, or how it will ultimately balance its functions with those of the government. But these are natural problems for any country building a new kind of government, as Russia is in the post-Soviet era. The goals of some civil-society advocates may be familiar to those of us in the West, and require a high level of independence. But other groups have been and will be more prone to cooperate with the authorities, which is natural for those who understand and seek a strong government with a powerful leader. These forces are colliding, and the process is another reminder of the vastness and complexity of Russian society.

The changes and upheaval in Russian civil society are part of a painful process, one in which many good people have been harassed and hurt. It's a process in a state where people are unsure of their place, but have rights and recourse, and can push back to some degree against a government trying to force them into line. It has not been a process of a monolithic authoritarian state definitively pouncing on its enemies.

Elections

Elections don't fit perfectly in a section titled "How Repressive Is Russia?" The issue belongs under a heading like "How Democratic Is Russia?" or "How Free Is Russia?" But in America, Russia's elections are often seen as another sign that Russia's government is wholly authoritarian and corrupt, just another tool used to keep the authorities in power.

Elections in Russia are in fact heavily manipulated, with strong government control exercised over who is allowed to run in the first place, and various methods of barely disguised fraud used to determine the outcome. The strong and enduring popularity of Putin (even if it is slipping recently) suggests the presidential elections are not exactly stolen, or at least have mostly reflected the will of the Russian people. But the president currently gets to determine who is allowed to run in gubernatorial elections. Of the two houses of the Russian legislature, only one is elected, and those elections are heavily manipulated. And direct election of mayors, which used to be the norm in Russia, has almost completely disappeared. In all but a handful of Russian cities, regional legislatures now pick the mayor, or sometimes a city manager in place of a mayor.

Some claim this less-than-democratic process is what most Russians want—they're less interested in democracy and more in getting things done. This is probably true to some degree. The word "democracy" itself doesn't have the same unadulterated positive connotation in Russia that it has here. If most Russians actually wanted something that different, it seems unlikely that Putin would be so popular. (Although polling on Putin is somewhat contradictory—it can show high percentages that approve of him, alongside low percentages that trust him—his popularity is almost certainly slipping recently, going back to his decision in 2018 to raise the age at which Russians can receive their pension, and more recently in response to his efforts to end presidential term limits, inadequate state action on Covid, increasing popular support for Navalny/concern about corruption, and a slumping economy.)

Even elections that don't represent the popular will aren't fully symbolic affairs. How can elections with candidates picked or approved by the government, with rampant voter fraud, be anything other than a complete sham? Since the collapse of the Soviet Union, both ordinary citizens and regional politicians have used elections as a vehicle to express their will. For example, candidates who are sanctioned to run in an election but aren't part of the ruling party often receive a significant number of votes. This is a way for the electorate to let the ruling party know they're dissatisfied. I am not suggesting the authorities hold elections for the purpose of hearing the electorate, but rather that even elections with significant fraud can still serve as a partial vehicle to express dissatisfaction and the popular will.

It's also useful to look at Russian elections in their historical context. Fairness in elections may have regressed in recent years, but they are more democratic than they were in Soviet times. Elections aren't fair or unfair, they exist on a spectrum. In the United States, to name two of many examples, we have a serious problem with gerrymandering, and with the outsize influence of wealthy campaign contributors. That makes our elections less fair. There's no reason for us to criticize or look down on Russia's elections simply because they're currently at a different place on the spectrum than we are. That doesn't mean their elections shouldn't be evaluated clearly and honestly. It means our evaluation is again somewhat tainted by our sense of superiority. Instead of judging, we should hope for Russia's continued progress in electoral fairness, and they should hope for ours.

––––––––

In the post-Yeltsin years, the Russian state has increasingly restricted the rights of the population. The state has gone after political opponents using both violent and legal means, it has deprived liberals of a voice, passed anti-gay laws, and harassed civil-society groups. Although society is politically much freer than in the Soviet era, it is less free than during the Yeltsin era.

Some of the old Soviet cancers are returning too—misuse of psychiatric prisons, a dangerous culture of lying, social and political disenfranchisement, and repression of those who want greater individual rights. This isn't necessarily surprising. Russia is not a liberal society, and never has been. In the Soviet era, dissidents never had broad support, and neither do liberals in Russia today. The crackdown on civil rights, the movement toward a more socially controlled and conservative society, are not taking place just because the authorities want it that way.

It's again useful to look at ourselves in order to check our tendency to judge Russia. The civil-rights movement in America seemed to have achieved many of its goals in the 1960s and 1970s. And yet it has hardly been a straight shot forward from there. Our country incarcerates a massive and disproportionate number of minorities. Racially motivated killings are common, sometimes even carried out by agents of the state. Racially motivated mass shootings have taken place recently at churches and synagogues. These are not exact analogies to what's happening in Russia, because our problems aren't the same as theirs. But our old cancers aren't cured either. And our insistence that we hold the moral high ground on all matters of social and political freedom misses many of the hard truths about our own country.

3. RUSSIA IS NOT PRIMARILY A KLEPTOCRACY OR AN OLIGARCHY

When the Soviet Union collapsed, there was widespread agreement that the wealth of the state should be divided up among its former citizens. In a communist country, it legally and ethically belonged to them. But this was a tricky project. The state's wealth consisted mostly of an enormous number of failing industries, an indescribable amount of real estate, and abundant natural resources. It's not easy to split that up between a few hundred million people.

Yeltsin and his advisers, led by Anatoly Chubais, devised a voucher system meant to give each citizen the opportunity to buy shares in newly privatized companies that would presumably end up owning the country's industries and natural resources. But because the Soviet Union had never had any private businesses, the plan barely made sense to a lot of people. The vouchers seemed essentially worthless, and many desperate and near-starving former

Soviet citizens sold them to speculators. At the same time, the state auctioned off certain industries, and buyers with powerful connections bought enterprises for much less than they were worth. Banks also gained control of industries in exchange for loaning the government money, transactions that were also grossly unfair.

Almost before you knew it, a small number of shrewd businessmen owned most of the country's natural resources. These became the original "oligarchs." Some of the country's giant failing industries ended up owned or controlled by the people who had run them in the Soviet era. The state kept much of the real estate connected to the business of government—party and government headquarters and offices, et cetera. Most ordinary citizens ended up with one thing—they became eligible to buy the apartments they lived in (although the process of actually privatizing individual apartments has been long and complicated).

This vast transfer of wealth was created, marshaled along, and legitimized by a Russian government that wanted to create a strong capitalist economy as quickly and efficiently as possible. But their plan was a sickening failure.

Was it also corrupt? Some of it was. But that isn't the only way to understand what happened. A society was making a huge transition. There was no generally accepted model for how to transform a country from socialist to capitalist. When the road taken in Russia robbed almost everyone of what was rightfully theirs as the heirs of a country built in part on the principle of collective ownership, a tiny few benefitted enormously. And when those few then colluded with the government to keep and expand their wealth and power, endemic corruption flourished.

The system that sprouted up after the great sell-off is often referred to as a kleptocracy or an oligarchy. Powerful officials in government use their positions to steal (kleptocracy). Most of the country's wealth is in the hands of a small number of powerful people (oligarchs).

But I'm not so sure we should see Russia as a kleptocracy or an oligarchy. Let's look at kleptocracy first. Different societies have different levels of corruption, correlated to how developed their economies and legal systems are. In the United States, we're at a different place on the corruption spectrum from Russia, just like we're on a different place on the election spectrum. In the United States, former government officials join defense contractors, former politicians join corporate boards, former presidents and their wives write books that earn them millions of dollars. We've found a way for our public servants to get rich, our system just requires they do it after their public service is over (or even between stints of public service).

Every country has its elite, and the political elite usually makes money. If your country is politically and culturally more tolerant of corruption, and lacks sophisticated legal safeguards to fight against it, the political elite will generally be more corrupt in order to make that money. If your country is less politically and culturally tolerant of corruption, and has more legal safeguards to fight against it, they'll be less corrupt—it won't be necessary to be as corrupt. Systems may evolve in part specifically to help political elites make their money in less corrupt ways.

It would be nice if, over time, both governments and individuals reliably became more honest. Certainly this can happen. But it's unreasonable to consider ourselves superior to people in more corrupt countries who are doing what people inevitably do in all political and financial systems, including our own, just because at a particular moment in time their form and level of corruption is different from ours.

Has Putin personally crossed some kind of line, taking corruption to an unprecedented level? I don't know. Many of his friends have gotten extremely wealthy, clearly as a result of their connection to Putin, and these friends along with other Putin associates appear in turn to have helped his ex-wife and children in business and financial matters, leading to considerable accumulation of wealth. Maybe Putin has also amassed great personal wealth himself. There is circumstantial evidence to suggest this. But I have not yet seen conclusive proof.

Russia, then, has elements of kleptocracy, as do we. But corruption and the accumulation of vast wealth and power exist on a continuum, and I do not see some clear line that Russia has crossed that turns them into a kleptocracy. I think it's reductive as a description of the country.

Is Russia better described as an oligarchy? Putin argues, with some justification, that the real danger of oligarchy is when rich people amass too much political power (arguably a notion with Marxist roots). This threatens the state itself, which can be turned into a vehicle for making money. Putin claims that he has prevented this by making sure the richest Russians stay out of the political arena.

There is little doubt that Putin has in fact limited the political influence of Russia's billionaires. Surely this is in part because they could threaten his own power—if Putin had fought the oligarchs, then helped distribute power in Russia in a more balanced or democratic way, it would be a different matter. And regardless of Putin's efforts, the richest Russians do of course have a level of political power and influence. Still, Putin is right that keeping the nation's billionaires from actually running the political system is probably a good idea. We can look at our own country to see the damage done when billionaires wield enormous political influence.

Our eagerness to attack Russia as an oligarchy raises the question of why we don't call our billionaires in the United States oligarchs. It's true that Russia's richest men came into their money in an unusual, brutally unfair way. It would be a stretch to say they earned it. But are they that different from Western billionaires, individuals with vast wealth, many multiples of what any person could ever need even for a life of incredible luxury, who often work against the common interest to keep and expand that wealth?

When we go on about Russian oligarchs, we are really just complaining about capitalism. An earlier stage than ours, but still. We watch the upsetting and ugly things happening in Russia as a vast gap in wealth grows between rich and poor, and whether we acknowledge it or not, we see a reflection of the upsetting and ugly disparity here too.

4. THE RT NETWORK ISN'T JUST PROPAGANDA

RT (which used to be called Russia Today, but changed its name to something less openly Russia-centric) is an international television station broadcasting in multiple languages around the world. In the West, the RT network is generally dismissed as a propaganda arm of the Russian government aimed at non-Russian speakers. This is an understandable position. Although the network claims to be independent, the Russian government and private concerns beholden to the government finance and control the station.

Still, RT is something more complicated than a simple propaganda tool. It's true that RT's mission, on one level, is propagandistic—the Russian government uses the channel to spread information that it hopes will influence people. But in the West, especially in relation to anything Soviet or Russian, the term "propaganda" also implies lies, cynicism, and disingenuousness. RT America, the network's station in the United States that I'm discussing here and will from now on refer to just as RT, certainly has a share of those traits, but also seems to represent how the Russian government, and perhaps a significant segment of the Russian population, view the world. Many and likely most of RT's employees are politically in sync with the Russian government, so the station's reporting probably expresses official Russian views somewhat organically.

The programming itself is an odd mix. Most of the reporting is about the West, not Russia. The station often features guests from the fringe ends of the American political spectrum. It frequently backs up its reporting by trotting out "experts" who have little claim to actual expertise. Although some of the hosts on the more news-oriented programs are more balanced than the pundits on their other shows (and lacking the slickness of a CNN or Fox News host, oddly more relatable), the individual programs are a mix of good and bad, some thoughtful and some highly conspiratorial.

RT's better reporting often focuses on America's social problems, such as poverty and homelessness. Some of this reporting is good enough to be on a mainstream American news channel, but there is so much of it on RT that it appears to be part of an effort to make America look bad. Other reporting highlights extremist groups and political divisions in the country, and is often more ham-fisted than the reporting on the dysfunctions of the American economic system.

On the day of the 2020 American presidential election, all the lead stories on RT were about fears of mayhem, such as businesses and apartment buildings boarding up in preparation for civil unrest. RT was clearly reporting here with a slant that American democracy was in bad shape, and repeatedly suggested that the election was fraudulent (largely by giving voice to Americans who made this claim, rather than saying it directly themselves). Rudy Giuliani was on a lot, sometimes challenged, sometimes not. Again, some of the claims and criticisms leveled at American democracy on that day were valid, but repeated over and over on a Russian network, it was impossible to avoid the sense that they were actually rooting for the civil unrest and explosions of violence they were constantly talking about.

RT also at times broadcasts outrageous lies. It gave air time to conspiracy theories about 9/11 and the Boston Marathon bombing, to name a few. RT apologized later for spreading 9/11 conspiracy theories. On the other hand, it's hard to know how to take this apology, since the channel's editor in chief, Margarita Simonyan, hasn't stopped spreading lies and disinformation—her interview of the two Russian military intelligence officers charged by British authorities with the attempted murder of the Skripals, for example, was a shameless and embarrassing propaganda affair (this was on a state-controlled channel inside Russia, not on RT). She also tweeted baseless and propagandistic claims that the 2020 American election was "neither free nor fair."

RT has gotten slicker over the years—both better at creating watchable and sometimes interesting programming, and better at putting forward an understandable vision of itself. The station's promotional commercials for itself suggest it's the place to go for both sides of the story, a solution to the problem of America's divided and highly partisan media, which they dismiss as fake news. At other times, such as in one ad featuring an animated rap video about the station, its efforts are as awkward and tone-deaf as the worst KGB propaganda.

Some have suggested RT's overall goal is to spread the message that the West is in decline. Others think the grand plan is to bombard people with so much information of so many different kinds that they don't know what to think, confusing people and making the truth harder to grasp (which some experts theorize is the leadership's method inside Russia, too).

This may be right. But I have doubts about most of the theories that explain RT as a finely honed propaganda tool with a clear mission. Maybe Russia's leaders sat in a room and planned to undermine the West with a television station that would mix truth and falsehood, and subtly but constantly make the West look bad. But it seems just as likely that the Russian leadership wanted to spread their views in an international media landscape that seemed biased against them. The mix of human beings, ideas, and journalism that followed became RT.

As for RT's Russian journalists and programmers (the hosts are often American, as are some other employees), I suspect they are mostly mirroring elements of Russia's own media, doing what they know how to do here. This is probably just a group of patriotic Russian journalists showing us how they really see the world, and perhaps at the same time revealing how many non-Americans look at us. They are programming their truth. Most of them likely believe they have created a channel that is above the other news outlets, less partisan, more fair.

Why would they even want to do this in America? Maybe just for the stupendous irony of it all—that after all our two countries have been through together, Russia will now provide the United States with a more balanced and less crazed source of news. If they were actually doing that, maybe they'd be beating us at our own game.

In 2017, RT registered as a foreign agent in America, under pressure from the Justice Department that was partly motivated by the station's role in Russia's interference in the 2016 U.S. election. This was appropriate; RT is a foreign agent—in this case, a tool and to a degree an arm of a foreign government. How to treat and think about a foreign-agent media outlet in a free society is complicated, though. During the Cold War, the United States beamed Radio Liberty and the Voice of America into the Soviet Union. Certainly these were foreign agents too (I am using the literal sense of the term here, not the precise American legal definition). Like RT, Radio Liberty and Voice of America were (and are) funded by the U.S. government, and like RT they claim to be autonomous. But Radio Liberty was created to provide Soviet citizens with an alternate source of news about the Soviet Union, news that was naturally in line with mainstream American political views, and therefore the U.S. government's views. Employees of that station believed what they were saying, so naturally they didn't feel that they were taking direction from the American government. Radio Liberty and Voice of America served a propagandistic function, but most Americans never would have agreed that the information they reported was itself propaganda. Of course, unlike RT, Radio Liberty and Voice of America didn't propagate outright falsehoods. But this is not the main thrust of RT's content. Mostly it chooses news, information, and ideas to present that conform to an anti-American worldview. Radio Liberty and Voice of America did the same, but the worldview was anti-Soviet.

Is RT, then, similar to Radio Liberty and Voice of America, which were weapons we used in the Cold War? Or is it like the pundit side of Fox News? There, too, a worldview is presented, and sometimes false information is reported. To us, of course, there's a

major difference between Radio Liberty and Fox News. One was
state-financed and used as a weapon against another country. The
other is private, and an important part of our media ecosystem.
But the lines don't have to be so distinct. RT may be a little bit
Radio Liberty and a little bit Fox News.

Radio Liberty and Voice of America still broadcast in Russian
today, carrying radio programs and video programs on satellite and
on the Internet. Should we be doing this? Should RT be doing
this? Maybe trying to broadcast your worldview inside a country
you have a contentious relationship with is a bad idea. It seems
more likely to sow distrust and anger than to win hearts and minds.

A few years ago, I became friendly with a man who worked at
RT in the United States (a young, idealistic American might well go
to work for Radio Free Europe/Radio Liberty or Voice of America
or Fox News). We went out to dinner one night, and at one point,
he told me about a woman he used to date in Russia whose father
was a well-known spy (I assumed a Soviet who had spied for the
United States). My friend said that he would never choose that life.
As soon as he said this, I thought he was probably sending me a
message. He thought it was possible I still worked for the CIA, and
he wanted to let me know that no one should try to recruit him to
spy on Russia. I didn't still work for the CIA, and in fact would have
hated to see someone I liked as much as him sucked into the world
of espionage. His comment was an odd but simple transaction, and
in a way I felt pleased that we'd been able to quietly work through
this invisible anxiety between us. Of course, it's also possible I was
imagining this subtext. (I had wondered myself if he was a possible
Russian intelligence officer. I didn't think so. But you never know.)

With that out of the way, we talked more about RT, and it became clear that my friend thought his job was spreading the truth
and fighting lies. He certainly didn't think he worked at a propaganda outlet. He felt the American media was feeding its viewers and listeners constant false information about Russia, and he
wanted to correct it. I agree with him that the American media

often distorts events in Russia, and I have no problem seeing why a Russian would feel that way even more strongly than I do. My friend put a human face to the arguments about RT, and although he was a mid-level journalist, and did not represent those in charge of the station, he believed in his work, and was neither a liar nor a propagandist.

5. RUSSIA'S WARS HAVE BEEN BRUTAL, DEVASTATING MISTAKES—BUT NO WORSE THAN OURS

Since the collapse of the Soviet Union, Russia and America have both engaged in numerous armed conflicts. The following are partial lists. I'm not including Russian military actions that followed immediately after and were a direct consequence of the collapse of the Soviet Union itself, or various smaller Russian and American military actions, including a significant number of U.S. raids, training operations, disaster relief missions, and efforts to evacuate our citizens from countries in crisis. The dates below are sometimes approximate, especially end dates of conflicts, which can at times be hard to determine.

The main difference between what I'm calling a war and what I'm calling a military action is the size and length of the conflict, although the distinction is fairly muddy.

Russia has been involved in the following wars and military actions since the collapse of the Soviet Union:

Wars

Chechnya—1994–1996
Chechnya (including early fighting in Dagestan)—1999–2009
Georgia—2008
Ukraine—the extent of direct Russian military involvement in Ukraine is disputed, but Russian separatist forces there likely have included: local Russians (from Ukraine), civilian

Russian volunteers who've come over from Russia, and members of the Russian military broken off from their regular units in an effort to hide direct Russian military involvement. There is also significant direct state/military logistics and weapons support for the separatist forces. 2014–present

Military Actions

Crimea—2014
Syria—2015–present

The United States has been involved in the following wars and military actions over roughly the same period (since the collapse of the Soviet Union):

Wars

Iraq—1991 (Kuwait)
Afghanistan—2001–2021 (if scheduled withdrawal completed)
Iraq—2003–2011 (limited troops redeployed 2014–present)

Military Actions

Somalia—1992–1995, 2007–2021
Haiti—1994–1995
Bosnia–1995 (NATO involvement began 1992)
Kosovo–1999 (NATO)
Libya–2011, 2015–2019
Syria—2014–present
Yemen—2015–2021

Is Russia doing more damage in the world than we are? Looking through these lists, that would be a very hard case to make. Chechnya was devastated in both the first and second Russian wars there—it's complicated to compare levels of devastation, but the physical damage done to Chechnya bears some resemblance to the destruction caused by our wars in Afghanistan and Iraq. The death toll in Chechnya is many times lower.

Ukraine has been destabilized in a way that makes it hard for the state to move forward, and Crimea has been annexed. Many U.S. wars and military actions have left countries destabilized. There's really nothing to compare Crimea to.

Few of these wars or actions on either country's part seem particularly defensible. Although there were reasons for every conflict, in most cases they probably didn't justify armed intervention. Both countries have behaved brutally and inexcusably.

It's hard to say which country was more incompetent in its use of force. At the moment, Putin seems to have derived some benefit from the second war in Chechnya, a harder case to make with the American wars in Iraq and Afghanistan.

OUR PART

U sing the perspective (hopefully) gained from our reexamination of the Soviet Union and Russia, let's take a brief look at some (a sample) of the ways in which we wronged the Soviets and later the Russians. Americans have largely understood these aggressive acts as justifiable parts of a policy designed to defeat an enemy. Let's see how they look when they're compiled into a long-running string of actions and choices.

HOSTILE AMERICAN ACTIONS TOWARD THE SOVIET UNION AND RUSSIA

Spy flights and harassment over and around Soviet territory

Around 1950, the United States began sending aircraft over the Soviet Union to take photographs of what was going on below. We generally associate these missions with the U2 flights (which began a few years later), and usually focus on Francis Gary Powers getting shot down in 1960. But how often do Americans stop to think about what we were actually doing? With the full knowledge of the Soviet Union, who could see the flights on radar, we were sending spy planes into their airspace, over many years, even though we were not at war with them. Since Soviet planes and antiaircraft couldn't reach our planes initially, there was nothing they could do about it (later, their ability to fight back improved somewhat). But this wasn't all. We also sent spy planes on missions around the periphery of the Soviet Union, and sometimes these flights also crossed into Soviet territory—maybe by mistake.

Later, the mission expanded beyond spying. According to author Peter Schweizer, who learned about it from high-level sources in the Defense and State Departments, throughout the 1980s U.S. military aircraft buzzed Soviet borders, but now the goal was at times to confuse and intimidate the Soviet leadership. The Reagan administration thought this would put them on the defensive and make it less likely they'd take risks. This was a somewhat abstract goal, but these harassing flights were also sometimes used to send more specific messages. In 1981 we tried to deter an aggressive Soviet military move into Poland in part by buzzing Soviet borders, which we again thought would create uncertainty and make Soviet leaders more timid. Remember this harassment next time Russian jets are buzzing U.S. ships, planes, and territory, and we complain that it's unthinkably stupid and that the Russian military is acting unprofessionally (to be clear, it is unspeakably stupid and unprofessional, it's just important to note we're not above it ourselves).

Between 1950 and 1991, around a hundred U.S. airmen were shot down and killed on surveillance flights near and over Soviet, Chinese, and North Korean territory (I believe most of these took place near and over the Soviet Union). Having read and thought about the Soviet Union more or less my whole life, I never heard that our spy flights were so extensive, or that we were buzzing their borders in a harassing manner, and I certainly had no idea we'd lost numerous pilots and airmen in this way. Then I saw a small reference to these flights in a book by Dmitri Volkogonov, the historian and retired Soviet general, and confirmed some of the details in a book by a former air force general, Christopher S. Adams Jr. I think the details of this history are fairly obscure. But it's instructive to know that every generation of post-Stalin Soviet leadership lived with American aircraft overflying and sometimes buzzing their nation on a regular basis.

Imagine if, from the 1950s through 1991, Soviet aircraft regularly overflew the United States and buzzed its borders. And we were powerless to defend ourselves against it, until we improved our air-defense capabilities, and started regularly shooting down what Soviet aircraft we could.

(I have pieced together this analysis of surveillance and harassing flights from several Soviet and American sources. It looks, sounds, and feels right to me, but it has not been studied sufficiently by historians to establish all of it as fact. My source for the harassing intention of some flights in the 1980s is *Victory* by Peter Schweizer, and comes from high-level participants in White House decision-making. The claim is so specific, and so disconnected from any public discourse, that it seems likely to be true or partially true.)

Stationing nuclear missiles in Turkey

In 1959, the United States deployed nuclear weapons in Turkey. Turkey, of course, bordered the Soviet Union. Think of the USSR stationing nuclear missiles in Mexico. One of the reasons the Soviets put missiles in Cuba was to counteract the threat from the U.S. missiles in Turkey. There were other complex geopolitical forces at work, some centered on the ongoing conflict over Berlin. These forces combined to instigate the Cuban Missile Crisis.

Imposing a grain embargo

At the beginning of 1980, we imposed a grain embargo on the Soviet Union to protest their invasion of Afghanistan. Although the Soviet Union had an enormous amount of fertile land, weaknesses in most areas of cultivation, harvesting, and transport left them perennially unable to produce enough grain for their population. They used precious hard currency to buy grain from other countries in complex, multiyear deals. The United States was one of their chief suppliers. A grain embargo was a dubious proposition, since the Soviets were easily able to buy all the grain they needed from other countries, although some think the American plan was mostly to make that a more costly proposition. In any case, the grain embargo was certainly a strong political statement, and at least some in the KGB felt the United States was using food as a weapon against them.

Arming Mujahideen who fought and killed Soviet soldiers in Afghanistan

Almost as soon as the Soviets invaded Afghanistan, the CIA started supplying weapons to the Mujahideen. This effort grew substantially over time, as the United States helped the Afghan rebels become a force that mounted a devastating resistance to the Soviet Army. Ultimately, we provided the Mujahideen with Stinger antiaircraft missiles, which many credit with turning the tide of the war, although some more recent analyses question whether the Stingers played such a significant role.

In the Cold War, arming an enemy of your enemy was a standard tactic, even if the results were tragic and caused tremendous loss of life. But what about this:

Supporting Mujahideen attacks against Soviet territory

In the mid-1980s, again according to Schweizer, the Mujahideen started crossing the border into the Soviet Union. They staged a number of attacks on airfields, border posts, and hydroelectric stations in Soviet Central Asia. It seems possible these attacks were conceived by, and likely they were supported with special weapons and training from, the United States. To make sure this sinks in, I'll state it differently—we supported and specially armed rebels when they attacked the Soviet Union, and may have come up with or helped come up with the whole idea for these attacks. Was this an act of war by us against the Soviet Union? I'm not sure, but I'd say maybe. It's certainly reckless aggression virtually without precedent in the Cold War, except maybe for this:

Blowing up a Trans-Siberian natural gas pipeline

In 1982, an alleged covert operation ordered by President Reagan may have blown up a section of a Trans-Siberian pipeline in the Urengoy gas field in Siberia. This has been labeled the largest man-made non-nuclear explosion in history. To clarify, this was *inside* the Soviet Union. The Soviets had stolen the software necessary to run the pipeline from a Canadian firm, and through our contacts with that firm, we were allegedly able to manipulate the software and cause the explosion. It's worth noting that the Soviets tried to buy the software they needed legally from the United States, but we turned them down, since we prohibited technology transfer that might benefit their military. (We also prohibited technology transfer more broadly. This embargo had its ups and downs over the years, but generally also targeted the entire Soviet economy, since the whole country was considered a security threat.)

Would blowing up a gas pipeline inside the Soviet Union have been an act of war? An act of terrorism? I've seen at least one claim that the actual plan was for the pipeline to spring a massive series of leaks rather than explode . . . does this make a difference? Likewise, I've heard another claim from a source who was close to the events (if they happened) that we blew the pipeline up more than once, though I haven't been able to verify this. The operation was part of a broader covert program aimed at turning Soviet commercial and technological theft against them—when the Soviets stole computer chips and software, the CIA sometimes knew ahead of time what they were going to steal, and modified the hardware or software to wreak havoc in the Soviet military-industrial complex. But of course, producing and transporting natural gas was not a part of the military-industrial complex (unless you really wanted it to be—likely some went to the military too—but that's not what the vast majority of the natural gas moving through the pipeline was for). Can we even come up with an analogy for what we may have done here? How about the obvious one—the Soviets sabotaging a gas pipeline on American soil. Can you imagine our reaction?

I am not sure this event actually took place, though. Several Russians have claimed the whole thing is a hoax, and that the pipeline was never attacked. I don't have enough information to determine if this is a serious possibility or a kind of reverse conspiracy theory. Even stretching my imagination, I cannot come up with a motive for pretending to have blown up the pipeline (especially since the operation didn't leak until after the Cold War). But I have seen an increasing number of experts who are skeptical it happened.

My main interest in looking at conspiracy theories is trying to understand when I or someone else is trapped in one. One thing I believe happens is that somebody like me uncovers a few discordant facts, often in an area like science they don't really understand, and thinks they've stumbled onto the truth, but in fact they are buying into a conspiracy theory. Or even originating a conspiracy theory. Of course, there are much more malicious people involved at times. In any case, I find the contradictory claims and currents of information about the pipeline explosion fascinating, but I cannot determine what did or did not happen. In part because alleged acts like this one begin with a covert intelligence operation that is by nature conspiratorial, they are particularly difficult to untangle.

*Trying to spread democracy around the world
and overthrow communist systems*

Throughout the Soviet era and beyond, we have tried to spread a liberal, democratic order around the world. We fought wars, spent vast amounts of money, and worked hard to roll back communism, including inside the Soviet Union.

*Withdrawing from the ABM Treaty and deploying
a missile shield around Russia*

In May 1972, the United States and the Soviet Union signed the Anti-Ballistic Missile Treaty, which strictly limited how many anti-missile systems each country could deploy. Since defensive systems undermine deterrence (it's important to know you can retaliate after being attacked without your missiles being intercepted), this treaty was always considered a major arms-control success. In June 2002, the United States unilaterally withdrew from the ABM Treaty, with President George W. Bush claiming it was a relic of the Cold War, and that we needed a national missile defense to deal with growing missile threats. The United States then planned a missile shield for NATO and Europe. The first antimissile system was put in place in Romania in 2016 with another section currently being built in Poland (completion now projected for 2022). This system is designed to protect Europe from nuclear missiles launched from Iran and possibly other states, but the United States claims it is neither intended to nor designed to counter a Russian nuclear threat. Russia, on the other hand, sees it as a defensive missile shield on its border, presenting a clear security threat.

*Bringing former Warsaw Pact states and
Soviet republics into NATO*

In 1999, eight years after the collapse of the Soviet Union, three former members of the Warsaw Pact were admitted to NATO: Poland, Hungary, and the Czech Republic (the Czech Republic was a part of Warsaw Pact member Czechoslovakia). In 2004, three former Soviet republics were admitted to NATO: Latvia, Lithuania, and Estonia, along with more former members of the Warsaw Pact: Bulgaria, Romania, and Slovakia (Slovakia had been the other part of Czechoslovakia). Albania and Croatia joined in 2009. Of these countries, Estonia and Latvia have borders with Russia.

Lithuania and Poland share a border with the Russian enclave of Kaliningrad. The rest of these countries are nearby. It's no surprise that many in Russia felt they were being encircled.

This expansion of our military alliance was an inherently aggressive and destabilizing act. It's easy to understand former Soviet republics and satellites wanting to be under the NATO umbrella to protect themselves from possible Russian aggression—why wouldn't they be afraid, given their history? But it's important to note that fear of Russian aggression was just a fear, justified or not. Bringing these countries into NATO was an actual aggressive act against Russia.

Russia also feels they were given clear guarantees that NATO would never expand eastward if the Soviet Union allowed a unified Germany to join NATO. Some of the U.S. politicians and diplomats involved in the negotiations on German reunification after the Berlin Wall came down agree these promises were made, while others dispute it. Nothing was put in writing. Since the Warsaw Pact still existed in 1990 when these negotiations were taking place, talking and even thinking clearly about those countries ever joining NATO was a complicated matter, and a perfect recipe for bitter misunderstandings later. That being said, the most compelling personal accounts and most comprehensive historical analysis suggest that the spirit of the negotiations was clear—a mutual understanding that NATO would not expand farther to the east, ever.

Carrying out cyberattacks on Russian infrastructure

Press reports on intelligence activities are often wrong, so it's difficult to confirm the exact nature of American cyberattacks against Russia, and on Russian critical infrastructure in particular. But American news reports based on off-the-record sources in the intelligence community suggest such attacks have taken place, including against extremely provocative targets like the Russian power grid. These appear to be intrusions to install malware that could be used at a later date during a conflict to, for example, shut down the power grid.

Imposing current economic sanctions

We have imposed more than seventy rounds of sanctions on Russian individuals, companies, and government agencies since 2012. It's been hard to keep track of them all. Sanctions have come in response to the Russian military action in Ukraine, the annexation of Crimea, election interference, cyberattacks, human-rights abuses, the use of a chemical weapon in the attack on Sergei Skripal, weapons proliferation, illicit trade with North Korea related to their nuclear program, the Russian role in Syria, and oligarchs profiting from a corrupt system.

Sanctions often originate as executive orders that are then codified by Congress. They can make it illegal for U.S. persons to work with Russia in key sectors of their economy, notably finance, defense, and oil. Sanctions can block trade, procurement contracts, and export licenses. When specific individuals are sanctioned, their assets can be blocked, they lose access to U.S. financial institutions, and they aren't allowed to travel to the U.S.

According to Cyrus Newlin, an associate fellow at the Center for Strategic and International Studies, and Jeffrey Mankoff, a distinguished research fellow at National Defense University, Institute for National Strategic Studies, sanctions have acquired a somewhat arbitrary nature (they are used so broadly that it's hard to tell what part of Russian policy or society we're going to target next). They're also legally complex in a way that makes them hard to lift. And they can hurt private businesses in response to the foreign policy decisions of the Russian government. As such, it's easy to understand why Russian leaders think sanctions are an effort to weaken Russia and punish the country for pursuing its national interests. Some Russians also believe sanctions are part of an effort to force a leadership change.

Do sanctions actually work? Some seek to directly change Russia's behavior, while others are intended to simply punish Russia for what it's already done. It's hard to make a case that they've been successful in either way. They have definitely done damage. Russia's GDP has contracted as a result of sanctions, and the loans available to them now, primarily from China, are a fraction of what they could get before. But there has been no discernible change in Russian policy as a result. Some feel there is value simply in using sanctions to draw a red line, saying if Russia crosses it, there will be consequences.

Although sanctions may seem at times like a reasonable and measured response to troubling events, they have become so numerous and broad that they constitute a real attack on the Russian economy. Such an aggressive tactic mostly serves to escalate tensions without providing a tangible benefit.

———————

Many will object to every item on this list by saying, "They started it." We imposed sanctions because they invaded Ukraine and annexed Crimea. We (maybe) blew up a Trans-Siberian gas pipeline because they stole our technology (it was actually Canada's technology they allegedly stole, but let's not split hairs). We imposed the grain embargo because they invaded Afghanistan; we helped the Mujahideen attack the Soviet Union because they invaded Afghanistan.

How far back should we go? We fought against them from the beginning, sending American troops to Russia on the side of the Whites fighting the Bolsheviks during their civil war. Was that their fault for having a revolution? Maybe it all started there.

Or maybe it was before that, when communists first said the proletariat would overthrow the bourgeoisie and destroy world capitalism. So we tried to destroy the Soviet Union because . . . they were communists who wanted to destroy capitalism and take over the world.

Like most games of "who started it," it's impossible to say where this conflict really began. And like all long-lasting feuds, after a while, it hardly matters.

THEIR PART

Looking at the list of our hostile actions, it's easy to see how Russia could feel provoked by us, and how they could believe they're just defending themselves when they retaliate. But now, in fairness, let's look at a (partial) list of things the Soviets and Russians have done to us.

HOSTILE SOVIET/RUSSIAN ACTIONS TOWARD THE UNITED STATES

Planting deep-cover spies inside our country

Soviet (and later Russian) intelligence services sent deep-cover spies to live in the United States, posing as ordinary citizens. Early on, these spies helped steal plans for how to build an atomic bomb. Later, their value was questionable. But this particular and somewhat rare type of espionage was especially weird and aggressive, and sowed fear and distrust.

Attacking our social fabric with propaganda

Soviet intelligence services launched numerous and bizarre propaganda efforts on American soil. They used false documents and rumors to try to enflame racial tensions with the hope of sparking a race war. For example, in the early 1970s, they forged and distributed a fake pamphlet to Black militant groups purportedly written by the Jewish Defense League that was full of racist plots and insults. They fabricated a presidential memorandum during the Carter years that suggested the president was purposefully trying to pit Black and white Americans against each other. I'll take up this ongoing attack on our politics and social fabric a bit later in this list.

Stealing our technology

Soviet intelligence agencies, particularly in the postwar period, went to great lengths to steal Western technology. In general, their espionage activities were targeted as much at helping their economy by stealing our know-how as they were at gathering political intelligence. This fostered a feeling in the United States that the Soviets were immoral thieves and couldn't be dealt with in a businesslike manner.

Starting the Korean War

In early 1950, Stalin gave North Korean leader Kim Il Sung permission to invade South Korea. There are also schools of thought that he masterminded the entire conflict in order to achieve some or all of the following goals: harm the U.S. reputation, bog down its troops, radicalize Asia, create an even deeper split between the United States and China, and distract America from its interests in Europe, where Stalin hoped to further build socialism in preparation for an expected Third World War. Stalin's ability to so successfully forecast events and implement a plan like this is debatable, and there are limits to how much we can blame the Soviets for our own bad decisions. But there is no doubt that the Soviets were—

Arming North Korean soldiers, who fought
and killed American soldiers in Korea

The Soviet Union provided arms to North Korea and China during the war, and Soviet pilots flew missions against us. Stalin may also have played a role in preventing the United States and North Korea from ending the war much earlier, as the above Soviet interests were further served by a protracted conflict.

Putting nuclear missiles in Cuba

The Soviet Union stationed nuclear weapons less than a hundred miles from the U.S. mainland, creating widespread fear and almost starting a nuclear war.

Blaming the AIDS virus on us

Probably the most successful KGB disinformation campaign of all time involved starting a rumor that the United States created and intentionally spread the AIDS virus. This lie was and still is believed in many parts of the world, and has done significant damage to our international reputation.

Illegally assembling a vast trove of biological weapons

The Soviets employed tens of thousands of people in a secret program to build a vast stockpile of biological weapons. This was in direct contravention of the Biological Weapons Convention that it signed in 1972.

Arming North Vietnamese soldiers, who fought
and killed American soldiers in Vietnam

The Soviet Union provided arms and advisers to North Vietnam. In a long and cataclysmic war, the Soviet Union bore at least some responsibility for tens of thousands of American casualties.

Riddling our new embassy in Moscow
with listening devices

In the late 1970s and early 1980s, the Soviets provided us with precast concrete to use in the construction of our new embassy building in Moscow. After the building was partially completed, we discovered the Soviets had planted sophisticated, almost undetectable listening devices in the concrete (including steel reinforcing rods designed to act as antennas).

Shooting down KAL 007

In 1983, the Soviets shot down a civilian airliner that had strayed into their airspace, killing 269 people. I hesitate to include this on the list, because it was not an American plane, and because it was in some ways an accident, in the sense that they thought they were shooting down a plane on a spy mission, and most likely did not know there were civilians on board. Our long history of spy flights around and directly over the Soviet Union helped pave the way for this tragedy, and we share some responsibility for it.

Trying to spread communism around the world
and overthrow liberal democratic systems

The Soviets thought communism was special in the same way we felt democracy was special, and they tried to spread it around the world. Although these efforts eventually lost some of their early intensity, the Soviets interfered in many nations' internal affairs, including ours. The current effort to undermine liberal democracies and replace them with systems more like Russia's is in a sense a return to these previous goals, minus the communism.

Harassing U.S. diplomats

In the mid-2000s, the Russians allegedly harassed U.S. diplomats and spies in the Soviet Union in unusual and threatening ways—breaking into their apartments, in one case defecating on a man's carpet, in another case poisoning a family's dog.

Buzzing our military planes and ships

Over the last few years, Russian combat aircraft have buzzed our naval vessels in international waters and flown dangerously close to our air force planes in international airspace.

Interfering in our 2016 presidential election

I argue at the end of this section that this was a somewhat understandable response to the full range of U.S. actions against the Soviet Union and Russia, and that it fits a pattern of mutually reinforcing hostile activity. But it was still an egregious act, and certain to increase animosity.

Carrying out cyberattacks on American infrastructure

As noted above, press reports on intelligence activities are often wrong, so it's also difficult to confirm the exact nature of Russian cyberattacks against America. The attack on our 2016 election appears to have included multiple penetrations of state voting systems, such as registration databases, although none that directly compromised vote tallying. Reports suggest that Russian attacks on our critical infrastructure, like ours on their power grid, focus on compromising the systems for future more serious attacks. After the 2020 election, a massive penetration of multiple American government agencies, likely carried out by Russia, was detected.

Using social media to attack and undermine American society

Russia is using propaganda and disinformation to sow chaos and divide our society. They are manipulating everything from racial tensions to pandemics in an effort to undermine and delegitimize liberal democracy, and the United States in particular. It is too soon to properly evaluate how effective these efforts are.

Doing whatever horrible things Russia has
done to us since I finished this book

The point of these lists is not to show which side is worse or which side started it. It's to demonstrate that we're failing to look at our own actions when we conclude that we're always blameless, that the Russians are always the aggressors, and that we only act defensively. That's what each side always thinks in a conflict. In fact, we have been at the very least equal partners in the cycle of attacks between our country and the Soviet Union/Russia.

Although the mutual attacks were usually restrained during the Cold War—no one wanted to get into a full-scale war—they originated in a clear desire to destroy each other that undergirded the entire relationship. Both sides accepted and understood this was each country's goal. The seriousness of the effort to literally destroy each other waxed and waned throughout the life of the Soviet Union, but you have to be careful if you think such a plan is ever really waning. Dreams like that are too big, too uncontrollable to harness. Some people on both sides fully dedicate themselves to destroying the other nation.

Take Ronald Reagan. In his effort to destroy the Soviet system, he took covert actions that boggle the mind. Supporting the Mujahideen attacks on Soviet territory (and bombing a Trans-Siberian gas pipeline, if it happened) seem like outright acts of war, and were so irresponsible it's hard to believe a competent president ordered or allowed them. (What if the Soviets had supported a group of Sandinistas who hiked into Mexico and launched cross-border attacks on the U.S. mainland?)

If we match our most gonzo effort—since we're not sure if the Trans-Siberian pipeline was actually blown up, let's settle for our role in the Mujahideen attacks inside the USSR—with their oddest effort, let's say spreading the malicious rumor that we engineered and spread the AIDS virus on purpose—I see two adversaries that are out of control, out of touch, and very dangerous.

Some Russians today see our past efforts to destroy their former country as part of a continuum. They think we want to destroy them now too. And who can blame them? Their attack on our 2016 presidential election—or counterattack, or whatever—hit a real sore spot for us, since our elections are a source of great national pride, a cornerstone of our democracy. But we can hardly expect our elections to be sacrosanct to them.

We have responded as if this Russian attack came out of nowhere, as if our two countries hadn't been attacking each other for many decades, both throughout the Soviet period and since Russia has been an independent country. But Russia's interference in our elections was just another move in a long-lasting conflict. It was as justified, or unjustified, as anything else they've done, or anything else we've done. Our surprise and aggrievement make little sense.

WHAT WE SHOULD DO

POLICY IN A
STRANGE NEW WORLD

I s our conflict with Russia somehow unalterable? Why? The Russians are not fascists. There is an extremely anti-Western, nationalist, possibly fascist ideological movement there, and it has Putin's ear to at least some degree, but this movement isn't what animates the Russian system, and it's hard to know how popular it would be if we weren't fanning the flames of mutual hostility. Is there a moral conflict that requires us to be enemies with Russia? Russia's internal policies are problematic, but don't justify our level of enmity. Our problems with China, less serious and less persistent, are mostly about money, even though they treat their internal political opposition as badly as Russia does, or worse.

I have argued that the Cold War between the Soviet Union and the United States was to a degree the product of fundamental misperceptions, but at least it was about something—whose system would prove to be better, whose system would spread and dominate. Our conflict with Russia today lacks even this basis.

Mostly, Russia (the leadership and a majority of the people) want us to leave them alone. And we should leave them alone. Instead of fighting Russia, we should spend our time and energy on ourselves. First on seeing ourselves as clearly as possible, then focusing and working on our own internal problems. Hopefully Russia will do the same.

No part of this is easy. It isn't easy to let go of the struggle with Russia. It isn't easy to look ourselves squarely in the eye, and we don't all see the same thing when we do. And it isn't easy to take on whatever problems we see when we look at ourselves.

A self-aware politics advocates for starting with what each one of us, personally, sees. Having let go of the Russian enemy that was clouding my own vision, but having been profoundly influenced by the struggle I went through with that enemy, here is what I see when I look America in the eye.

We have enormous political and moral strengths, centered on a tremendous and somewhat rare level of broad-based freedoms. We have a powerful and cohesive economy that supports many of us and our vital state institutions exceptionally well. We have a stable series of layered governments and bureaucracies that usually function with a fairly high degree of competence. We have a judicial system where you can get a fair shake in civil trials. We have an ability to demand progress and improvement, and use our openness and creativity to fight for it.

These are all great civic strengths, and should not be taken for granted. Our lives would be indescribably worse without them.

On the problem side of the ledger, here's what I see.

We're often self-righteous, still believing in American exceptionalism and looking down on others (none of this applies to everyone—I'm saying I see it, and it's a force). A growing chasm between the wealthy and the poor is destabilizing our system, which is losing the strong and large middle class it relies on for stability. We have serious problems with how we treat our citizens and always have, but our (partly true) national myths about equality and opportunity work against reckoning with fundamental injustices in our country.

This is not the place for a deep exploration of these problems, but just to take a single example of our state mistreating its citizens—there are millions of people in prison all across the country, many of whom are victims of racial and other kinds of injustice. These injustices are different from the injustices that took place in the Soviet Union under Stalin, another time when a country incarcerated mass numbers of its people. There, most of the imprisoned literally hadn't done anything. Here, the injustice is based on throwing away people who had little or no opportunity in life. Not all of them, but many of them. We also have a far different level and kind of brutality inside our prisons from what took place in the camps of the Gulag. These two examples of incarceration are different, but so what? It's more important to see the commonalities and learn from them, not to insist on the differences. I'm emphatically not saying our prison system is as bad as the Gulag. The point isn't to compare the two, the point is to think about the Gulag in order to help us see ourselves. The point is to see the suffering that came from mass incarceration in the Gulag, and understand that we, too, have mass incarceration that results in unimaginable suffering.

Looking inward, focusing on ourselves and our internal problems, does not mean isolationism. Isolationism suggests a prioritization of one's country far above the rest, not just staying out of each other's affairs but not caring too much about other countries. This is not the looking inward I am proposing. I suggest turning inward in part to engage more fully and productively with other nations.

Directing most of our energies toward our internal problems also doesn't mean we can't respond to inhumanity in other countries. I am not advocating that we turn a blind eye to repression around the world. Nations can act as checks on one another, just not through scolding and punishment, which are usually ineffective at creating change, get people's backs up, and create fertile conditions for war.

Groups like Amnesty International and Human Rights Watch, as well as private individuals should play the primary role in standing up for the victims of state repression around the world. Independent groups and individuals are generally better suited to this role than are governments, which often create international conflict and stumble under the weight of hypocrisy when they try to support citizens of other countries. Groups can also be transnational in ways that governments obviously can't be. Speaking out against brutality and repression of all kinds is a job for citizens and groups from all countries, standing up to any and all governments (obviously including our own).

Once we let go of constantly criticizing other countries, what can our government and we as citizens do to help victims of repression, or people who just want more freedom than their government will allow?

We should work toward:

1. Attaining a higher level of decency and peace in America, using the freedoms we have.
2. Being less aggressive and more peaceful abroad.
3. Cultivating understanding with foreign leaders so they feel less afraid of us and less threatened in the world in general. (This may be the only workable long-range approach to North Korean nuclear proliferation, for example.)

———

Opening up to our own flaws and imperfections should make us more open to collaborating with other imperfect leaders and imperfect nations. To start with, I think we are missing—or have already missed—an opportunity with Putin. I think he would be willing to negotiate truly significant arms reductions, including nuclear arms reductions. I think he would cooperate on environmental treaties, and certainly make joint progress on terrorism.

Putin has said over and over again that he is willing to cooperate with us. How do we know if he means it? As long as we believe that Putin is just putting up a front when he speaks reasonably or offers cooperation, and that he is in reality a villain, we will keep acting aggressively, and in all likelihood Russia will too. The only way to find out if Putin is sincere is to respond to his overtures with our own efforts at cooperation, and see what happens. I believe we have a reasonable chance of receiving back from Putin as much as we offer him, and there is hardly any risk in trying. If we don't try, we may be letting a great opportunity slip away—with all the anti-Western currents in Russia today, the next leader may not be as open to us.

It is also possible that we've missed our chance. As detailed earlier, Putin was more open to the West early in his presidency. His hostility is now significant, and may reflect a changed worldview that won't change back. But there's only one way to find out.

If Putin is open to a rapprochement with the West, it doesn't mean we should ignore his various flaws, faults, and cruelties. But we don't need to arrive at a final, black-and-white judgment about him any more than we need to arrive at a final judgment about ourselves.

In place of judging, we need to understand that strong state/strong leader systems are a common form of government and politics and likely here to stay. We have to accept that this type of system can function, that it can manage an economy, guide relations with other countries, and provide the basic stability necessary for a country to be a coherent place. In other words, strong state/strong leader systems can manage a country. We have to stop demanding that every system be a representative democracy just like ours.

———————

This demand that Russia be like us, sometimes openly driving policy and sometimes guiding us in a more subterranean way, has undergirded the attitude toward Russia of every American president since the Soviet collapse. It has fomented almost uniformly negative and damaging policies, and engendered strong and steady hostility. NATO expansion under Clinton was particularly harmful. Bush did more of his damage through the war in Iraq and America's reemergence as a country willing to wage reckless and devastating wars. When Obama's reset failed, he was openly patronizing to Russia, labeling it "a regional power." Overall, American presidents never escaped their own Cold War attitudes enough to see Russia as a fully legitimate state that we could have a positive relationship with. They followed confrontational policies with occasional halfhearted attempts to "hit the Reset button," with Russia expected to do most of the resetting. To actually reset a relationship, you have to change the way you look and think about the other nation, and change your habitual responses to them. Under Obama, when Russia acted in ways that conflicted with U.S. desires and interests—passing anti-gay legislation, granting asylum to Edward Snowden, intervening in Ukraine—the American leadership felt that Russia hadn't changed the way we wanted, or as quickly as we'd wanted. The reset was dead.

And then came Trump. Here was an American president who genuinely lacked any hostility toward Russia, and wanted to create a new and different relationship between our countries. Before he even took office, Trump was working to undo the sanctions regime that constituted our worst ongoing attack on the Russian state.

But what a strange messenger for rapprochement. For starters, Trump didn't seem to think much in terms of policy. He was a chummy businessman, and approached the world this way. There were some potential advantages to this—if Trump had worked with Russian businessmen and liked them, and this fed his instinct that we could get along with Russia—well, good. Trump's opponents theorized there was something more here—that he was being blackmailed, or that his political attitudes were based on debts or other financial obligations to Russians. But there was no actual evidence of blackmail or debt. And there was no reason to assume

Trump was insincere even if his views on Russia were influenced by financial relationships. Trump was a financial creature. He saw the world in part through the lens of money. If he knew and liked Russian businessmen, that isn't any worse a place to get your political instincts from than the myriad other potential sources of our politics.

Even if Trump's instincts about Russia came from a more self-interested place, we still had a president who was willing to work cooperatively with Putin, and didn't think of Russia as an enemy. But Trump didn't know how to question or utilize his instincts, so he never formed a coherent policy to ease tensions with Russia. Without any concrete ideas to work with, he likewise didn't know how to use his political acumen to find support for instituting such a policy.

There were specific places he went horribly astray. First, Trump's accurate instinct that Putin was not as bad as most people in America thought, probably coupled with admiration for Putin and his style of leadership, somehow morphed into believing virtually anything the Russian leader said. This political naïveté turned the president into a dupe. It was Trump's own version of black-and-white thinking. Putin wasn't as bad as people said, so he was great, and fully trustworthy. Trump could not manage or understand Putin's complexity.

Trump's admiration for Putin also seemed to evolve into an effort to emulate him in America. I say "seemed to," because Trump's mind and deeper motivations were always mysterious, to the public and probably to the president himself. Maybe Trump wanted to be like Putin, and so he acted like him. But maybe he just was like Putin, and so he liked the Russian leader. Maybe it's a distinction without a difference.

Either way, Trump's efforts to become a strong-arm-type leader were threatening to many Americans, who would never follow Trump into a rapprochement with Russia when they feared he was actually going to make America more like Russia.

Finally, Trump's behavior in international affairs further alienated the political leaders and followers he needed to radically change U.S. relations with Russia. Trump vocally supported authoritarian leaders in countries torn between democratic and anti-democratic ideals, and he constantly trashed democratic leaders in Western countries. It was bizarre to see an American president acting this way, and it was never clear exactly what his reasons were. The assumption that Trump simply liked autocrats, and wanted to be one himself, sprung from his lack of a coherent (or really any) explanation for his string of insults against liberal democrats abroad, as well as his frequent supportive words for autocrats.

These actions out in the world reinforced the idea of Trump as an authoritarian wannabe. And that meant the political base he would have needed to make peace with Russia would never go there with him.

Even the most savvy and experienced political leaders, who understand and clearly articulate their own political reasoning, struggle in the world of foreign policy, where so many factors contribute to thwart plans, and unintended consequences lurk around every corner. But it's sad that the only president in recent memory with the instincts and political openness necessary to repair relations with Russia was unsuited to accomplish that goal.

Instead, things got considerably worse under Trump, as Russian attacks on our foundational systems of governance and our society in general reached maniacal proportions. This can't be laid at the feet of a president who, left to his own devices, might have repaired relations enough to prevent all of that happening. Mainstream American opinion, and a long and broad series of political leaders, bought into and sustained the conflict with the Soviet Union and then Russia. Trump's unique contribution to the fight was making an attempt to repair fences with Russia so unappealing. Even I, a staunch supporter of improving relations with Russia, couldn't follow Trump there.

I understand that the following suggestions for a new policy toward Russia sound soft and touchy-feely, and that no politician would take them seriously. In the middle of a conflict, looking for a moderate, emotionally sound way to behave is rarely popular, and can seem laughable in the context of the dangerous, harmful actions the adversaries are taking against each other.

But the only way to get out of a long and bitter fight is to change both your attitude and your actions. A self-aware politics begins with the attitude. But it has to lead to new policy. I believe these actions might be effective in dealing with Russia and help us get out of the second cold war.

We should:

1. Make a conscious decision to stop fighting Russia. We should remove ourselves from the conflict. We should defend ourselves not with counterpunches, but by refocusing our energies and resources on other problems. Even if Russia remains aggressive, becoming genuinely stronger—increasing our social cohesion, using our vast wealth to improve life in America—will help us withstand whatever they throw at us more than fighting back will. In the long term, Russia will also be less likely to keep fighting us if we're not participating.

    I do not suggest immediately withdrawing from our regional alliances, but rather working to limit any ways in which they are confrontational versus purely defensive (never an easy distinction) over the long term. If we successfully deescalate the conflict and a new, improved, lasting relationship with Russia emerges, these alliances will fade away on their own, or develop into something useful in the new circumstances.

2. Adopt a less superior attitude. This means talking to the Russian leadership as equals, and even potential allies. If Russia does something that troubles us, we should discuss it with them in a spirit of cooperation. For example, our

leaders should sit down with Putin and his representatives to talk about Crimea and Ukraine, but instead of demanding they do what we say, we should focus on our own military adventures in countries near us. Our leaders should say that their actions in Ukraine are similar to things we've done in Latin America, which have caused enormous suffering, and fundamentally affected who we are as a nation and how we're perceived around the world, all for the worse.

I am not predicting this would have any short-term effect on Russia's policy in Ukraine. But it might have a long-term positive influence on our relations with Russia. And if Russia feels more respected and less threatened by us, their policies might also change more broadly in the long term.

3. Join Russia in areas of mutual interest, such as fighting terrorism, protecting the environment, and reducing both nations' nuclear forces. Goals for such reductions are always preposterously low. We should aim for a reduction in total nuclear forces that eliminates the absurd capacity to destroy any adversary over and over and over again—perhaps a 90 percent reduction to start. We should attempt to re-enter/renegotiate the ABM (anti-ballistic missile) and INF (intermediate-range nuclear forces) treaties. We should negotiate reductions and improved controls on biological and chemical weapons.

4. Remove our antimissile defenses from Eastern Europe. If we truly feel we need these systems to protect against threats from the Middle East, they should be deployed in a way that isn't directly threatening to Russia. The most obvious way is to build them in cooperation with Russia, which isn't possible now, but could be possible down the line if our relationship improves.

5. End sanctions against Russia. Efforts to harm the Russian economy are not an appropriate response to Russian activities we don't like. Americans should imagine what it would

be like if a foreign power had the ability to severely undermine our economy in response to our disastrous foreign-
policy mistakes, such as the war in Iraq.

6. Eliminate human-source spying on each other, and vastly
reduce all kinds of spying.

I'll go into greater detail on point number 6, because I worked
at the CIA for several years and came away with strong feelings and
a small amount of experience on these issues (I don't say that with
false modesty, it was a small amount).

LETTING GO OF ESPIONAGE

I remember the first time I set foot in CIA headquarters. It seemed like the most special and exciting place in the world. That feeling faded, and I wasn't there a long time—just a few years— and most of that time was spent as a trainee. But it left me with strong feelings about espionage.

Espionage does incredible damage to the fragile trust between nations, ally and adversary alike. I believe its benefits are marginal, as I'll argue in the coming pages. And it puts lives at risk, nominally in the interests of national security, but more often to further bureaucratic imperatives.

I believe we should move away from spying as a tool in international affairs. Specifically, we should work toward a truce between the United States and Russia, where we both agree not to recruit any more people to spy on each other. It's unlikely anything very valuable comes from this human-source espionage for either side, but it sows deep anger and suspicion. This is true of human-source espionage against most countries, not just Russia, but it should be particularly easy to call it off with Russia because the roots of our mutual strategic threat are far from irreconcilable. We have more stubborn and substantive conflicts with a few countries, where there may be some truly valuable information attained through human-source espionage—for example, if we're able to get spies to provide information on Iran's nuclear program, that could really matter (although even with Iran, we have to ask if human-source espionage is doing more harm than good.)

But what information could we steal from Russia that would be truly vital? It's important to know about Russia's political intentions, and the state of Russia's weapons of mass destruction, but I'm dubious we get information from spies on these topics that we can't figure out just as well, and more reliably, by looking at their behavior, listening carefully to what they're saying, and judiciously using the tools of satellite imagery and communications intelligence. We can follow their efforts to spread disinformation in the same way, by paying attention, without using human spies.

After reining in human-source espionage, and assuming the overall relationship between the United States and Russia improves over time, both countries should strictly limit and perhaps ultimately eliminate cyber operations and all forms of electronic eavesdropping against each other. Satellite surveillance is the one type of spying that may actually serve the cause of peace, since it keeps everyone more aware, and therefore less scared, about what an adversary's military is up to.

I became skeptical about espionage in general, and human-source espionage in particular, soon after I joined the CIA. As I've said, I spent most of my short time at the agency in training, but training sometimes involved real work. On what was called an interim assignment, I met with a former foreign agent whose cousin had been killed in their homeland during the Reagan era. This was exciting for me—a real agent meeting. I traveled to the meeting site, and wore a disguise. At the meeting, the former agent explained to me that he was concerned he was the reason his cousin had been killed, that it was an act of retribution against him for working with the CIA.

I had read this agent's file carefully, and it was impossible to know exactly why his cousin had been killed. But it was possible their country's intelligence service had suspected what our agent was doing, and had killed his relative as an act of revenge. Later, I started to wonder if the work this agent had done for us was worth this terrible loss. Having read his file, I was familiar with all of the intelligence he'd produced. I can't go into it here, and it's important to say that different people would evaluate it differently. But I didn't think anything we'd learned from this agent was worth a human life.

I asked myself another question—would a CIA officer recruiting this agent have had reason to believe he would provide intelligence valuable enough to risk dying for? Because there was no question this agent might die—he worked in a country where there was a strong possibility, if he went to work for us, he would be caught and killed. Based on his background and his job, I didn't think there was a high likelihood this man would ever produce information worth losing a life over.

When I finished the training program, before I was scheduled to start my first tour abroad, I was sent to work for a few months on a program I won't describe in detail. I was assigned to do a review of every case in the program, picking out key facts from each file. The facts I needed to find were straightforward and easy to locate quickly, but I decided to read each file in its entirety. I was curious, I was cleared for the files, and nobody cared what I was doing. It's important to note that these cases, although part of a special program, represented, in my opinion, a broad cross-section of the cases run in the division, which again represented, in my opinion, a broad cross-section of the cases run in all five of the agency's geographic divisions at the time. That is not to say they represented all cases but rather that they represented most cases. In other words, they probably weren't examples of the very best agents run by the agency. But they almost certainly were similar to most of them (I suspect they accurately represented 90 percent or more of all cases—I base this on exposure to other cases in other divisions that I knew about firsthand or learned about from others, and some guesses and estimates about certain cases with higher classification levels).

When I began reading through these cases, it was without prejudice. I hadn't yet become critical of the CIA's recruitment policies. I was just curious, eager to see who our spies were and what they were doing. It was a rare opportunity to have so much secret information at my fingertips.

Over many weeks of reading, I kept waiting to find a case that was producing valuable information (intelligence is a word for information obtained in a covert manner, but it is ultimately all information). I kept moving on to the next case, thinking this one would be better. But they never were. This is, again, my opinion. Many others would see it differently (although I was not the only person at the agency who was skeptical of the quality and value of intelligence).

I eventually developed a formula for what would make intelligence valuable: did it have a reasonable chance of actually affecting U.S. policy, or in any other way substantially affecting our actions (for example, altering military plans)? Intelligence that merely helped shape our understanding of foreign countries and world events didn't seem important enough to recruit, run, and risk spies' lives for. This was partly because using open-source material and high-level expertise was just as good or better than espionage at increasing our understanding of world affairs. But it was also necessary to have a higher bar because almost any information could be said to increase our understanding of the world in one way or another.

Of the hundred-odd cases in my file review, none met this standard. I wasn't sure they met any standard—the intelligence in them seemed worthless. I started to think that the organization I was working for believed it was worth recruiting someone to get almost any information. The risks these agents took to pass that information along to us rarely seemed to bother anyone.

As I've said, the cases I was exposed to at the CIA were a fair representation of the average case, but not of the best. But we can get a sense of who the best CIA Cold War spies were, because in many cases their identities leaked, or were released to the public, after they were executed by the Soviets. Oleg Penkovsky and Adolf Tolkachev were two of these agents, and some think the two most significant.

Penkovsky was a colonel in Soviet military intelligence. He has been referred to as "The Spy Who Saved the World," because he provided information that both helped the CIA recognize that the Soviets had deployed nuclear missiles in Cuba and understand details of how quickly those missiles could become operational. Along with other information on Soviet readiness, this allegedly "saved the world" because it allowed Kennedy to respond before it was too late, to understand the time constraints on his response, and perhaps to make tougher ultimatums because the Soviets were not yet ready for war. This supposedly prevented a nuclear war.

In "Espionage and the Cold War: Oleg Penkovsky and the Cuban Missile Crisis," Len Scott, a professor of international politics at Aberystwyth University, disputes the most basic elements of these claims. He quotes McGeorge Bundy and former CIA analyst and espionage authority Raymond L. Garthoff as saying that Penkovsky's role in the crisis was minimal and mostly involved background information. Scott uses declassified CIA documents to suggest Penkovsky did not, in fact, alert the United States to the placement of ballistic missiles in Cuba, as some reports have suggested.

Penkovsky seems to have provided other valuable intelligence about Soviet intentions and capabilities, but not of the save-the-world variety. Even if the old story about the information Penkovsky provided is accurate, it's quite a historical leap to assume that if the missiles were found later, or if Kennedy had learned they were going to be operational sooner, it would have resulted in a nuclear war.

I suspect the idea that Penkovsky saved the world is the result of espionage boosterism. People in the intelligence community, without realizing it, often exaggerate the importance of spies in order to glorify espionage, and to justify their work to others and to themselves. With little ability to check secret information and analysis, journalists and others outside the intelligence community often repeat and amplify these exaggerated claims.

There's a more compelling case to be made for the value of intelligence provided by Adolf Tolkachev. Tolkachev was a Soviet engineer specializing in airborne radar who provided technical details about Soviet military aircraft, radar, and weapons systems to the CIA from 1978 to 1985. This information allowed the United States to engineer its own aircraft to counter these threats, and to achieve a technological superiority that purportedly would have made a significant difference if the Cold War had turned hot. In *The Billion Dollar Spy*, author David E. Hoffman quotes an air force estimate that the U.S. military saved at least $2 billion in research and development costs because of Tolkachev's intelligence (back when a billion dollars was a lot of money!). I heard this same claim when I was working at the CIA. Some estimates have been many times higher.

These seem like generally credible claims, even if the multibillion-dollar estimates do make me wonder how exactly the military figures that out. But I still have some doubts about whether the military and CIA have exaggerated Tolkachev's importance to a degree. Did the military really need his intelligence to design their own planes more effectively, when virtually every type of technology was more advanced in the United States in the first place? In other words, would we have had a significant advantage in a hot war regardless? Still, the capabilities of a hostile military are indisputably a reasonable target for espionage, and within the context of the Cold War, I do not deny the value of Tolkachev's intelligence.

Most anyone would agree that the intelligence production of Penkovsky and Tolkachev looked different during the Cold War, and that this is the only reasonable way to judge it. I don't entirely disagree. But hindsight has its uses, too, and I think it's worth at the very least asking if the intelligence Penkovsky and Tolkachev provided balanced out the damage done by espionage in general during the Cold War. This is not a question that can really be answered. But we should remember that spying greatly increases mutual hostility, and because we carried it out so liberally, it did significant harm both to our ability to get along with the Soviet Union and to our reputation around the world.

Just as important, Penkovsky and Tolkachev are touted as being among the most valuable spies of the Cold War, but the historical record suggests they were spies with some real value in a sea of those without much, just as my own experience suggested. Some of this historical record is available. I can't review every case here, but I'll briefly note that information is publicly available about many of the spies executed after having been betrayed by CIA officer Aldrich Ames and FBI agent Robert Hanssen (in the same era as Tolkachev, who seems to have been betrayed by both Ames and CIA officer Edward Lee Howard). These were spies being run against our main adversary during a dangerous time in the Cold War. Knowing the jobs they held, we can make educated guesses about what information they would have been able to provide to the U.S. government. Most of it, in my opinion, was likely to be either insignificant or inside baseball—spies revealing the work of other spies. I know many in the intelligence community see it differently.

Issues beyond the value of the CIA's assets and the quality of the intelligence they provided started to trouble me when I worked at the agency. The CIA, to its credit, completed exhaustive internal reviews of counterintelligence failures in East Germany and Cuba. Over the course of several years, most of the assets (and possibly every single asset) being run by the CIA in those countries was actually a double agent being run against us by the East German and Cuban intelligence services. Reading these internal reviews, I thought more about the counterintelligence issues we were trained to consider with all assets. It seemed to me the chances of any asset being a double were so high, and so difficult to guard against, that the odds were slim of ever knowing whether most of the intelligence we obtained was credible. That meant that even in the rare event intelligence was valuable, you usually still couldn't trust it. I remember telling a friend who worked in counterintelligence that I was starting to think a third of all agency assets might be doubles. "More," she said.

When I joined the CIA, I thought that I would find the truth there about how the world really worked. Not a conspiracy, but secrets that would reveal answers to the puzzle of world affairs. That key, of course, wasn't there. Instead, I found a lot of conspiratorial behavior that mostly served to worsen relations with the other nations of the world.

I have written about the value of focusing on oneself and one's own country in a self-aware politics, and how shifting focus away from judging an enemy makes it easier to see oneself. A fundamental corollary of this self-focus is taking a greater degree of responsibility for one's own actions. In trying to think in a more self-aware way about espionage and its consequences—in trying to take responsibility—I find it useful to think about Ames and Hanssen, who turned over the identities of multiple Soviet citizens spying for the U.S. government, many of whom were then executed. Ames and Hanssen were eventually caught, and are serving life sentences.

In the intelligence community, I often heard Ames and Hanssen referred to as murderers. This was correct. They had provided information they knew would likely lead to the executions of the people they betrayed. The KGB and the Soviet state, which carried out the actual killings, of course shared responsibility with Ames and Hanssen in most people's minds. But what about us? U.S. intelligence agencies had recruited most of the dead Soviets. They had used various tactics of manipulation, and in at least one case blackmail, to get them to spy for the United States. They had done this convinced (wrongly, in my opinion) that we would receive vital information from these people. Recruiting officers may have played up the degree to which their clandestine methods could keep their agents safe (I don't know this for a fact, and don't suspect it was the case with every one of these Soviet spies, but I believe it was a pattern in CIA recruitment). Caught in our Cold War mania, we had put many lives at risk, and those lives had been lost. This is not to diminish the responsibility of Ames, Hanssen, the KGB, and the Soviet state for what happened. It is to add us to the list. Without us, those murders never would have taken place. This is a similar dynamic to what happened when KAL 007 was shot down, and we decried the Soviet murderers without taking notice of the role we had played by fueling suspicion and paranoia by carrying out numerous spy flights over and around the Soviet Union. As we work toward a more human and complex view of ourselves, we should watch out for apportioning blame entirely to others in the international arena.

I believe we should consider freeing Ames or Hanssen, and letting them go to Russia. This would be a straightforward goodwill gesture, intended to send the message that we want to improve our relationship with Russia. Ames and Hanssen have both served over two decades in prison at this point, and since we are not guilt-free ourselves for the damage they did, this would be a potentially useful and positive end to a terrible series of tragedies.

We could also begin trying to forge a new relationship with Russia by suggesting that both countries agree not to spy on each other going forward. This could be a first step and a test case for a more direct and open foreign policy that leaves espionage behind everywhere.

WHAT THEY SHOULD DO

I've said what I think America should do. That's my focus, since I am an American, but I will also briefly say what I think Russia should do.

My intention here is to directly address Russians and the Russian leadership, and I want to give four caveats before offering them advice and ideas on their internal affairs.

1. Russia's choices are primarily its own business, and I'm discussing them here, to the best of my ability, as a friend of Russia.
2. I am limited in my knowledge and understanding of the Russian perspective by not living there, not speaking Russian, and the frequent difficulty of seeing fully and clearly through the eyes of someone from a different country.
3. As Americans, we tend to be judgmental. I am aware of this.
4. All of the principal issues between the United States and Russia should be seen in their historical context, focusing on understanding instead of blame, and with each country taking responsibility for its mistakes and shortcomings.

With these considerations in mind, I suggest that Russia:

1. Think more about themselves, and worry less about us, even if we're being aggressive. This is a hard case to make—an international version of turning the other cheek—but I think Russia will be better off if it focuses less on us and our behavior. We should do the same, but we will or we won't. Russians need to get us out of their heads either way. If some Russians feel destructive and aggressive behavior toward the United States is warranted because we tried to wreck the Soviet Union, they should let go of seeking revenge, or of trying to attack us. If they can become more generous instead, if they can hope for the best for us, that we succeed and thrive and reach our potential, that will ultimately be better for them, regardless of what we do. Russia has a choice between looking at itself more carefully or spending its time and energy being mad at us. Being mad at us is okay, and to some degree justified, but shouldn't distract Russia from facing its own problematic sides and the ways in which it hurts itself and others.

2. Look into what they've done right and wrong in the world, specifically what nations they've harmed, and what they've done to the United States that hurt us and damaged our relationship. It does not help Russia to assume it's always right or blameless in all conflicts. America's job is examining itself, and Russia's job is examining itself.

3. Try to grapple with and overcome feelings of paranoia and the sense that the country is encircled. These feelings are based on some concrete and understandable realities, but are probably playing too great a role in shaping the worldview of many Russians and the actions of the Russian government. Fear and anxiety of Western influence and aggression, and feeling pushed into a corner, may be causing Russians to lose sight of their country's potential to grow

and thrive in ways that are hard to do when a nation is overly focused on defending itself.

4. Look at its support for far-right political parties throughout Europe—in Hungary, Greece, France, Bulgaria, England, Italy, Austria, Germany, Belgium, and Slovakia. According to Antonis Klapsis, an assistant professor at the Department of Political Science and International Relations of the University of the Peloponnese and author of *An Unholy Alliance: The European Far Right and Putin's Russia*, the alliance between these parties and Russia seems built on mutual antipathy toward the EU and NATO; a Russian desire to champion and spread social and political conservatism around the world (after communism for them and democracy for us, this is the latest thing to try and "spread"); the fact that the far right European parties would like to see strong leader/strong state governments like Russia's in their own countries; the publicity and legitimization the leaders of these parties get when they appear in Russian media, interacting with representatives of a major power; the political parties' desire to receive funding from Russia; Russia's desire for greater influence in Europe by whatever avenues it can find; and increased legitimacy for elections in disputed regions of Russia as leaders of these foreign parties often agree to act as election monitors. But support for these parties is likely a bad idea and potentially dangerous for Russia. Russia should consider its own history and what fascism did to it. Russian leaders don't believe these parties are fascist and frequently call their own opponents fascists to delegitimize them. But there is a strong possibility of conjuring real fascists by striking bad alliances and muddying one's own sense of what fascism means. Trying to destroy the EU, which at the end of the day will never physically attack Russia, is a terrible mistake, and may unleash far worse demons than Russia imagines the EU to be.

5. Find a way for the leadership to communicate with and
   open up to the opposition. The goal here does not have to
   be liberalizing the nation, but rather making the minority
   feel heard, making them feel like they're a part of the country. This will create a stronger and healthier political cli-
   mate, and may have a trickle-down effect to Russians who
   aren't aligned with opposition groups but would still feel
   less apathetic about politics if the system were more inclu-
   sive. I wouldn't expect reaching out in this way to be easy
   or simple. If opponents of the regime are going to remain
   cut off from any actual political power or influence, it's
   hard to say if they will embrace just talking. But talking
   and listening do offer a measure of inclusiveness, and Putin or any future president may find, if they listen openly,
   that the opposition has a valuable contribution to make to
   governance.

I don't think Russia is any more likely to take steps like these—
to bring greater self-awareness and less judgment into our international politics—than we are. If Russia did pursue a more measured,
conciliatory path, I don't know if America would follow suit. But I
hope one of our countries will eventually find its way to rethinking
and then pulling out of the perennial conflict we're in. Whoever
makes the first move in this endeavor will be doing both countries
a great service.

CONCLUSION

Politics and Personality *or, Am I Upside Down?*

In this book, I have looked at a set of political beliefs I held for most of my life about the Soviet Union, and asked where they came from. I found that the sources of my politics in this area were problematic, both those that stemmed from my own inner psychology and upbringing, and those that came at me from the outside, from our culture and society. I've looked at our country's current attitude toward Russia in light of my (and sometimes our) misunderstandings about the Soviet Union. And I have suggested that a higher level of self-awareness about the wellsprings of political beliefs—both where they come from and how they operate— can produce a more thoughtful and honest politics, better suited to our internal and international affairs.

But political self-awareness is a rough business. You can't just pick the insights that feel good, or that fit neatly into your worldview at any given time. You have to face down contradictory feelings and impulses, the possibility that you are still missing something that could be key to self-understanding (surely you are missing things—self-awareness is a lifelong effort, not a fixed state any of us will achieve). You also have to guard against constructing new edifices, which are likely to be as shaky as the old ones.

With these opportunities and pitfalls in mind, I have one more layer of myself to excavate here, one additional act of looking inward and reckoning.

I wrote this book knowing that certain aspects of my personality might be pushing me toward the conclusions I've reached. These are less the deep-rooted psychological factors I've already discussed and more sides (almost quirks) of my personality that have developed alongside them.

Exploring these personality traits is a final test of what I've written so far, and revealing them is intended as an act of faith with the reader. I am agreeing, to the best of my ability, not to hide anything about who I am, so that you have as much information as possible to use in considering my ideas.

Political views stem from a complex variety of factors, as I have discussed throughout this book. This is true for me, and it's true for you. So by investigating some of these potential sources of my thinking, I am trying to evaluate my views even more closely, looking for any final pieces of the puzzle, even if they don't fit.

As I've said before, I am less interested in proving my points or convincing you of their truth than in communicating in a more psychological and emotional way about politics.

MY IMPULSE TO BE A COUNTERINTUITIVE THINKER COULD BE WARPING MY JUDGMENT

For much of my life, when I talked to people about politics, or really anything, I often found myself arguing a point simply because it was the opposite of what everyone else thought. I don't do this much anymore (although my friends might disagree). But I used to do it a lot. It didn't matter so much what I actually thought or believed in a discussion. Most arguments were instead, for me, a crusade against groupthink.

Looking back on what I was after when I argued this way, I don't think I was interested in exploring topics with people. I was interested in proving people wrong. Or in being right myself. Even when I asked questions, I was often testing, to find out what other people knew so I could attack their weak points.

Although that approach seems obnoxious to me now, and it bothers me when I hear other people using it, there was something useful about this counter-groupthink. It demanded at least a mildly more original way of looking at things, and so had the potential to develop into a more valuable type of counterintuitive thought. Still, the line between useful and destructive counterintuitive thought is thin and can be hard to see. Counterintuitive thinking often becomes a mechanistic device for trying to think for yourself—in other words, it's easy to become trapped in the device itself, and then you're still not thinking for yourself.

I'm still bothered by groupthink, but I've found better ways to deal with it than arguing the opposite of what everyone else is saying simply for the sake of trying to prove that the mainstream view has holes in it. I hope I've crossed the bridge into truly independent thought. But it's not the easiest thing to judge.

And so I have to ask myself if I'm still falling prey to reflexive counterintuitive thinking in this book.

I don't think so. My ideas and feelings about the Soviet Union and Russia are deeply, or more fully, felt in a way that distinguishes them from positions I've taken or attitudes I've had on other political issues, especially in the past. I'm not even sure my feelings here are exactly political—they feel, in some ways, beyond politics.

Still, I can't deny a certain pleasure at having ideas that are my own, and that fall somewhat outside the mainstream. So that remains. If I do still have some tendency in the counterintuitive direction, I hope it's serving me now rather than guiding me.

MY DESIRE TO IDENTIFY WITH PEOPLE I SEE AS MISUNDERSTOOD COULD BE WARPING MY JUDGMENT

I worked on this book with a specific anxiety that people would say I was defending Putin. That is not my intention. I want to understand him, and to challenge the general understanding of him in the West.

But to be sure those are my actual motives, I have to grapple with the fact that I have always identified strongly with people I felt were misunderstood. I felt deeply misunderstood as a child, which is surely one of many reasons for this affinity, and one of many reasons I write in the first place—to be understood.

Whereas I don't think my old habits of counterintuitive thinking provided much of a motivation for the ideas in this book, I do think my tendency to identify with those I see as misunderstood is active in the thinking, arguments, and underlying psychology of what I've written here. It is in part a book about explaining "misunderstood others" to the reader.

These inclinations travel extreme curves and byways in my mind. It's not uncommon for me to walk the streets daydreaming about lengthy encounters or conversations with Putin, where I explain what's really going on in America, or more to the point, demonstrate my deep understanding of what's going on in Russia. In these talks, we share certain mutual frustrations. Through my empathy and understanding, I am able to moderate his more extreme sides, and open him up to dialogue or even cooperation with the Russian opposition. (Or sometimes, in these fantasies, he puts me in prison.)

In any case, watch out. These feelings run deep, and I've had them a long time. Am I missing certain things because of them? Deemphasizing things I shouldn't? Giving people the benefit of the doubt when they don't deserve it?

I MAY BE HAVING A KIND OF MID-LIFE REASSESSMENT, WHICH COULD JUST AS EASILY GO THE OTHER WAY

Jung writes about middle age as a turning point, when one's life and views are reevaluated and often turned on their head.

I have been prone to extreme swings in my political viewpoints, at least in the realm of foreign policy. I grew up with fairly standard liberal views, then sometime around college I shifted to fairly standard Reaganite conservative views, and after that, I don't even know. Back again? I eventually lost interest in labels.

What I am aware of now is that, as I look at my views on the Soviet Union, I am tracking a position from very harsh critic to someone with a more complex view, someone who sees a full society where before I didn't. I also have a lot of empathy that was previously absent. These changes suggest that I need to reckon with the possibility that, if I'd had a softer, more forgiving view of the Soviet Union earlier, I might be changing course now and reevaluating the country in the other direction. I might be seeing its darker side for the first time, and coalescing a set of ideas around that.

Is my primary impulse, then, simply to reevaluate? As opposed to what I think is happening, which is that the depth and complexity of my views is progressing?

I can't answer this, but I think it's possible.

There may also be a less extreme version of what Jung points to, which is that I'm simply opening up as I get older. In this case, I may still be at an acute early stage of discovery, where I'm so excited about what I'm seeing and feeling and learning that my views aren't balanced out yet. In other words, I've newly discovered the complexity and the positive side of the Soviet Union (and Russia), so I'm paying less attention to the problematic sides, which will reassert themselves later.

This notion of reassessing is also fundamentally connected to the idea of a more self-aware politics that I advocate throughout this book. In a sense, I would expect and even hope that in ten years I will look back on what I've written here and see things I've missed, or maybe even have a radically new perspective. That would indicate I've continued to grow and learn.

Either way, what I write now can only be a snapshot of my thoughts and feelings at this moment.

MAYBE I HAVE AN UNCONSCIOUS
SOFT SPOT FOR DICTATORS

I have tried to present a portrait of Putin as complex—a leader with good sides and bad sides, who is somewhat middle-of-the-road as far as world leaders go. This is such a minority view in America—and what can fairly be called Putin's bad side is so substantial and troubling—that I find myself wondering if it's possible that I have a soft spot for, or even some kind of attraction to, dictators or strongmen.

Although this idea seems absurd to me, I know where my concern comes from. When I was eleven or twelve years old, before I thought much about politics, I read or heard somewhere that the writer Graham Greene had gotten too close to the Panamanian dictator Omar Torrijos. I didn't know who Greene was at the time—although the accusation made clear he was a writer—and I didn't know who Torrijos was either. But the implication of Greene "getting too close" to a dictator was clear to me—writers and artists were prone to being naïve, and these "dictators" could take them in. I also concluded that there was something about the world itself that was incomprehensible to the artist, who would always be out of their depth in it. (I don't know whether I thought of myself as an artist yet at this point, but I was writing already, and I may have.)

The exact source of this odd, out-of-context line—Graham Greene had gotten too close to Torrijos—remains a mystery. Did I hear it from my father? He read Graham Greene, and often spoke to me like I was an adult. It doesn't quite sound like something he would have said to me, but maybe I overheard him saying it to someone else. As I was googling around recently trying to sort through all of this, I found a 1977 article by Greene about Torrijos in the *New York Review of Books*, so maybe the accusation was in a letter to the editor there, and I read it in the bathroom.

Wherever it came from, this memory of Graham Greene as dupe is like a time capsule for me, because I barely learned a thing about him or Torrijos between then and when I started writing this book. My thinking about them, and my broader conclusions about writers and artists, were encased in mental amber for more than forty years.

Looking into it now, I find Torrijos was complicated. He was a kind of socialist, a moderate and progressive. In the first few years he was in power, there were significant human-rights violations in Panama as he fought his enemies. But that subsided. Despite the obvious horror of what happened early on, no lasting pattern of human-rights abuses developed. Torrijos seemed to inhabit the gray zone where many leaders live, and maybe he was even on the good side of gray. (After Torrijos died in a plane crash in 1981, Greene wrote a book about their relationship, called *Getting to Know the General*.)

In college, when I was starting to harden into a staunch believer that America was always right about everything, I started to hear about another famous writer and dictator with a close relationship—Gabriel García Márquez and Fidel Castro. Again, I only heard rumblings about this, I never really looked into it. I just assumed that another naïve artist had been duped.

While writing this book, I read what Márquez actually thought and said about Castro, as opposed to what other people said he said. I found him to be reasonable. Márquez had a thoughtful and complex view of the world, and was a firm supporter of basic rights and dignity for all. He may have made a moral error in defending Castro too much, I'm not sure. Castro was consistently repressive, but somehow he was popular with much of the population all over Latin America, a champion of the poor and an anti-colonialist leader. He was, of course, reviled by many as well.

Back when I was offended by Márquez's friendship with Castro, I would have done better to ponder Castro's popularity instead of denying it. Castro was another good example of a complex leader. He was personally responsible for a range of immoral, devastating human-rights abuses, in particular the incarceration of political opponents. And yet I shouldn't have dismissed him as a one-dimensional villain simply because he was repressive and undemocratic.

Some leaders routinely brutalize their own people, torture their opponents, steal and suck up all of their nation's wealth. Some advance the welfare of their countries. Some do various degrees of both of these things. Over the years, I've watched every American president of my lifetime have friendly relationships with leaders who were truly awful. I used to tell myself a story that these leaders weren't as bad as Castro, but I think I knew that wasn't true. I also told myself that we supported, and that I sort of kind of supported, repressive leaders and governments to stave off even more repressive leaders and governments. This frail house of cards probably stood so long for me because I didn't have anything to replace it with.

Looking back on Greene and Torrijos, and my own early confusion about them, I don't see any evidence I was or am attracted to dictators. (Having now read more of and about Greene, I don't think he was, either—he seems interested in politics, people, and the world, anti-American, and as his friend and writer Bernard Diederich put it, sympathetic to the underdog.) I am, instead, wary that we use the word "dictator" indiscriminately to put down any leader who isn't democratically elected. What exactly is a dictator? The word implies malevolence along with unchecked power. There are, of course, leaders who fit this bill—Stalin was one of the few to really have unchecked power, and he was certainly malevolent. Torrijos had less control than Stalin, and was much less brutal. It's confusing to call them both dictators.

Leaders with great power in nondemocratic countries have enormous influence in the world. We call them autocrats, dictators, sometimes presidents or leaders. But if they weren't democratically elected, we tend to assume, in one way or another, that they're entirely bad. This is another example of our overall vision of ourselves as virtuous, a virtue shared only by those who are the most like us.

I MAY BE PRONE TO GRANDIOSE THINKING— BELIEVING THAT I AM THE ONE WHO KNOWS THE TRUTH, AND WHO CAN FIX ANY PROBLEM

Why am I writing this book in the first place? Isn't the very premise of the project that I know better than everyone else? That I'm smarter than everyone else?

I don't think I act like I have this attitude out in the world. I'm not known as an arrogant jerk (I don't think). But maybe, at least, on this subject, I do think I'm right and everyone else is wrong. Or maybe I still have a complex need to see myself as superior, and it's cast everything in a distorted light. Maybe the conclusions I present here about the Soviet Union and Russia are the consequence of this distortion. (Although it's worth noting I am not literally alone in my general beliefs about the Soviet Union and Russia.)

I think grandiosity is loosely (or maybe closely) connected to a proselytizing instinct—*I, who as a child struggled to fit in, will now guide you. I, who felt in many ways muted, will now speak loudly, showing you the right way to do things.* I proselytize as I try, like the conspiracy theorist or the demagogue, to construct a system for understanding a complex world. I, too, am trying to create order from chaos. This is arguably also the goal of therapy—to create a map to follow through the confusing world. But in therapy, you construct your own map. Books, like religions and conspiracy theories, hand you one. And it is a risky business to suggest others follow a map you've made, really, for yourself.

————————

A self-aware politics requires openness and honesty about mixed feelings, about doubt and uncertainty. I have tried to be vigilant about seeking out the sources of my views, old and new, and hopefully that has allowed me to see somewhat more clearly. My claim is not that I am right but that the ideas in this book have value, and are worth incorporating into our overall vision of the conflict we have been in for such a long time, first with the Soviet Union and then with Russia.

What about right and wrong, true and false? I believe in facts, and in truth, but locating them isn't always simple. A rigid insistence that our beliefs are "true" is problematic. Beliefs do not rest solely on facts and truth but also on our personalities, our experiences, our emotions, our biases and prejudices, all interacting with the information we're exposed to, accurate and inaccurate. This all starts gelling into certainty, at which point we feel it's important to be right, not wrong, which strips the nuance out of our thinking. The end result is not the truth. It's an endless intersection of our disposition with our experience, which we call our beliefs.

In a self-aware politics, beliefs gain value when tested against our biases and predilections, against life experience and cultural forces, and against our own sideways and byways of personality. In other words, awareness and exploration of the multiple sources that our views develop out of is the necessary test that our beliefs should be put to.

What results is still belief and conviction, but of a softer variety than we usually see in politics. We can have our views, but accept that the political world is not black and white, is not entirely made up of truth and falsehood. In a self-aware politics, our beliefs remain somewhat malleable, open to the ideas of others. We fully accept that other people see the world differently.

If I am more open and flexible in my politics, and less devoted to being right, does that mean I have doubts about the basic ideas in this book? Do I wander the streets wondering if they're wrong, off-base, even damaging?

Of course I do.

I am particularly afraid that I could be providing fuel to anti-Semites, who might take my argument that the Soviet Union was less anti-Semitic than generally believed and use it against the Jews. Many anti-Semites love to deny their anti-Semitism, and I hate to make it easier for them.

I am also afraid that I am breaking faith with those I'm closest to in spirit and outlook. Socially, psychologically, culturally, I have a lot in common with Soviet dissidents and Russian liberals. Yet somehow, in this book, I take many positions that would probably be abhorrent to most of them. Is this entire project a betrayal of those who are most like me, of people who have fought in the past and fight now for freedom and basic decency? Many of whom have paid a high price for their courage, while I have never had to sacrifice anything.

Another fear—I am well aware that people who have strained to understand brutality and oppression can look not just naïve later on but even complicit. There is a particularly distressing tradition of this related to Stalin. Many Americans and other Westerners talked themselves into not seeing what was happening in the Soviet Union as Stalin decimated the population. These people wrote books and articles painting him in a positive or benign light. This is especially troubling because these writers had access to enough information to know the truth.

As an American in a free media environment, I have access to a virtually limitless amount of information. Have I gone too far in trying to understand Stalin's supporters, and in trying to understand Putin?

There's no way I can answer this question. I can only repeat what I've said before and what I made sure to remember as I wrote this book—I abhor all brutality and would never excuse even a single instance of it. Part of my project here has been to examine the way many of us excuse our own brutality and judge it only in others.

Judging versus not judging in politics is its own kind of binary. The trick, for me at least, is to try and hold both at the same time—to judge cruelty, atrocity, and infliction of suffering, while at the same time trying to observe and understand perpetrators and resist the impulse to judge. When there is too much focus on judging alone, it kills complexity, makes cooperation hard, leads to dangerous conflicts, and can make you lose sight of your own flaws and faults.

———————

When I began writing this book in 2015, America seemed strong and stable, despite its many problems. No one I knew was seriously concerned about any kind of national collapse. Then Trump was elected, and I started hearing people on both sides of the political spectrum exploring a voluntary dissolution of the United States, or more precisely, a reconstruction as two separate countries, one red and one blue. This was a fringe idea, though, usually discussed more out of frustration than with any actual intent to seek change. Even as a fantasy, it revolved around making a decision to dissolve the Union, not a national collapse.

As I edit the final draft of the book, a wide-ranging assault on the 2020 presidential election, coupled with a physical assault on our nation's capital, at least in part instigated by our own president, recently came close to undoing American democracy. Not long before that, protests, rebellions, and riots broke out across the country. Many have lost faith in the fairness of our elections. Most people I know are now asking basic questions about whether our system works, and whether our country will survive. America seems to be wobbling, more fragile than at any previous time in my life.

And yet, for all this, as 2021 begins, most of our institutions continue to function. Our bureaucracy has been challenged, but remains largely intact. Our economy tumbled due to coronavirus, but it's tumbled many times before, and then recovered. There has always been something huge and solid about America that proved to be greater than all the forces that shook it. Is there still?

It's useful to think one last time about what happened to the Soviet Union. A powerful nation, that seemed stable, fell apart quickly and unexpectedly. Their internal problems—everything from economic stagnation to plummeting ideological commitment—were left unaddressed for years, and the few voices who recognized these problems as existential were ignored almost until the end. The Soviets focused much of their attention, and their money, on fighting us.

This sounds a little too familiar. In the United States, we, too, are failing to address our most pressing internal problems. There is a widening wealth gap in our country, and a long-standing failure to use our vast resources to fight poverty. Mass shootings have become commonplace, many of them in schools and places of worship (once you feel a need to highlight where a mass shooting took place in order to get across how horrible mass shootings are, your country has a problem). Children are killed regularly in struggling neighborhoods. Racial tensions alternate between simmering and boiling.

Yes, we also face an external threat from Russia. This threat is important, and has to be faced. Part of it is indirect. Like some other strong state/strong leader countries, Russia is in some ways becoming less brutal. That doesn't mean they're becoming less effective at solidifying and using power, it means they're getting better at it. Russia is raising its game. This alternate style of government could become more appealing—seems to be getting more appealing to many—even in the United States. It appeared for a long time like democracies could pull strong leader/strong state systems toward their way of doing things, but not the other way around. In fact, it is a two-way street, as we now see. The implications of this for our democracy are frightening.

A more obvious and direct threat comes from Russian efforts to pull our society apart. Russia is directing a substantial amount of its fighting resources—the most creative part—at publicizing and exacerbating our internal social troubles. It spreads propaganda and misinformation, which are playing at least some role in dividing us. The Soviet Union tried to do this, too, but their efforts were clumsy and for the most part unsuccessful. Now this effort is working better, in part because of transformed technology and the new ways we acquire information.

Russia's attempt to undermine our society creates a powerful cycle of subversion, because our focus on the Russian assault distracts us from the very internal problems the Russian propaganda and misinformation prey on. This distraction itself is probably the greatest threat. In fact, I suspect that we embrace the conflict with Russia in part so that we can look away from our social failures. Then we focus on, spend on, and fulminate about Russia, instead of working on our real problems here at home.

I certainly used the Soviet Union as this type of distraction. My deep passion for the history and affairs of another country was always in part a way for me to avoid our own country's problems. If I wasn't focused on what was happening here, I didn't have to act, I didn't have to do anything about what plagues us. I became almost helpless, because the Soviet Union's problems were far away and acting on them more or less impossible. The way I set it up, there was little I could do except talk, talk, talk about problems far, far away.

I want to clarify that this type of distraction was not total for me and, to the extent it was a broader American issue, did not prevent us from paying any attention at all to our internal issues. But it does seem to me that we faced the Soviet enemy with a commitment and passion that were lacking in our approach to our own internal problems. The Cold War ate up resources and energy that could have vastly improved and strengthened America.

This same mistake—getting overly distracted by us—cost the Soviet Union its existence. We should be careful not to repeat this mistake in our conflict with modern-day Russia. As a first step, we can try to increase the personal and societal level of self-awareness in our politics. Then we should address our internal problems with the same unity and vigor we summoned to fight the original Cold War, while leaving the distraction of the second cold war behind us.

I'm not sure I ever would have gotten past my binary view of the world if I hadn't gone into therapy and started to discover more complex layers inside myself. Breaking open personally was, not surprisingly, indistinguishable from breaking open politically. If I was more complex than I'd realized, so was everyone else, and so was the world. As I opened up emotionally—to myself, my family, my friends—my interest in the Soviet Union remained, but my extreme level of judgment waned. This allowed me to see more of the Soviet Union and Russia than I'd seen before.

Everyone grows up in one political system or another. We can divide people into those who start questioning their own system at a young age, those who start questioning it when they're older, and those who never question it. I fell into the middle category.

I didn't question our system earlier in part because I was fully enfranchised in it—it was working for me. But I also failed to think critically about our system because I was prone to seeing political conflict as good versus evil, which in turn allowed me to think of myself as good, as part of the good side. That was not something I could give up easily.

I've already written about this binary thinking and how it developed in me. But I can explain it in another way that I think is useful. I recently reread a book of essays edited by Connie Zweig and Jeremiah Abrams titled *Meeting the Shadow: The Hidden Power of the Dark Side of Human Nature*. This book was my first detailed exposure to Jung's idea of the shadow self. According to Jung, many human beings suppress their dark side, driving it out of conscious awareness—this includes dark desires, feelings, and impulses—while remaining consciously aware only of our positive, bright sides. This suppressed side is called the shadow.

We all have this shadow self. When you're attacking a friend or political leader, or really anyone, for specific actions and character traits you abhor, much of the fuel of that indignation comes from the fact that you are fighting hard to deny the sides of yourself this other individual is acting out. We are all dark, violent, angry, jealous, gluttonous, you name it. If it's generally perceived as negative, it's in us somewhere. It's part of our human inheritance. But most of us get along in society by hiding these dark aspects of our personalities from ourselves, and as best we can, from everyone else.

One particular essay from the book, "The U.S.-Soviet Mirror," which I'd long since forgotten, clearly had a significant impact on me. It was an excerpt from another book called *Power and Politics: The Psychology of Soviet-American Partnership* by Jerome S. Bernstein. Bernstein, writing in the 1980s, argued that the Soviet-American relationship was a political manifestation of the shadow. Although usually seen as an individual dynamic, the shadow also functions collectively, and was driving the conflict between the two countries. While we saw ourselves as free, open, democratic, honest, and good, we saw the Soviet Union as the opposite—they were intolerant, closed, autocratic/totalitarian, aggressive, violent, and just plain evil. In other words, they were the embodiment of everything negative we were unaware of in ourselves. They saw us in the same way, as the inversion of their self-image as a nation. In their eyes, they were communal, progressive, democratic, socially conscious, and good. We were selfish, reactionary, racist, uncaring, stratified, aggressive, violent, and evil.

Neither of these visions was true. Each rested on one country focusing solely on its own positive side while seeing only the other country's negative side, and simultaneously failing to see or focus on its own negative sides. We were each other's shadows, or more precisely, each country used the other as the mirror for its own shadow.

The rhetoric, attitudes, and actions of the United States and the Soviet Union, it seems to me, completely supported this analytical framework. It explains our nation's collective adoption of the Soviet Union as an intractable enemy and font of evil in the world. And since the Soviet Union was our nation's choice for an enemy, it was the most obvious choice for the personal enemy that could help me avoid facing my own dark side too.

A number of years after I was first exposed to Jung, I started reading the work of teachers from the Insight Meditation Movement. These were mostly Americans who had spent time in India and other Asian countries studying with Buddhist priests. They came back to America and adapted much of what they learned for our culture, to a degree removing much of the religious doctrine and practice, and focusing on the incredibly powerful elements of psychology in Buddhist teaching. They seek self-awareness and self-understanding, in certain ways like a therapist would, but with less focus on an individual's past and more on how we all work generally as human beings.

These teachers also explore how to disassociate oneself from black-and-white thinking, and what they call our addiction to our strong views and opinions. This is similar to the attitude of "I am so good; they are so wrong" that easily turns into enemy-making and aggression. The Insight Meditation teachers look for ways to be a little more relaxed, to stop insisting on being right while other people are wrong. They teach techniques for assiduously checking in with and understanding ourselves. Notably, they tend to stand against idealism or utopianism, which they think block us from accepting and being fully present in reality as it is. They're not opposed to seeking and working toward justice, but think the best way to do it is for individuals to become more enlightened and less aggressive themselves.

What would it look like if we used these ideas to face our current national conundrum? Left and right, liberal and conservative, Trump and anti-Trump, all have turned on their political opponents with a vengeance, casting each other in the role of the dark and evil object that the Soviet Union used to play. Binary thinking has seized us all. To move away from this, we ought to take our gaze off of the "other side." We need to look at ourselves instead. How have we been fooled, lost our minds, become conspiracy theorists, become addicted to rage, all while accusing the other side of these exact same things? Instead of accusing "the other" of delusion, insincerity, and trying to destroy our country, let's explore if we may have acted in any of those ways.

To start, let's look at what happened during the Trump presidency. Most liberals were entirely tuned into Trump's anger, victimhood, and self-centeredness—while most conservatives paid it little heed, focusing almost entirely on his clarity, determination, and successful use of power to make America better, in their eyes. Almost everyone, then, was caught in a one-sided illusion in which all of our dark shadow selves were projected onto the other, in which we were virtuous and the other side was abominable. Pro- and anti-Trump individuals alike became aggrieved, angry, aggressive, addicted to calling each other liars, and convinced the other side was destroying America. In a sense, we all became Trump's dark side.

How can we break free from this almost magnetic force? Liberals should focus far less on Trump supporters' relationship with the truth, and instead ask how so many liberals fell for a conspiracy theory that he was a Russian agent, a lie that was never supported by evidence (a baseless accusation confidently repeated without evidence is a lie). In fact, consciously or unconsciously, were Trump's efforts to delegitimize the 2020 election not linked somehow to liberals' long and powerful effort to delegitimize the 2016 election that he won? Conservatives, on the other hand, are aggrieved by liberals' promulgation of this false narrative—that Trump was a Russian agent, that Russia stole the 2016 election for him—but instead of focusing on that, they should explore why they elected a president who promulgated an equally false conspiracy theory that his predecessor in the White House was not an American citizen, and then they should look at their own complicity in undermining confidence in the 2020 election (not all of them did this, of course).

Beyond the issue of truth and lies, almost everyone in America has hurt feelings now, and blames the other side for it. Many conservatives feel tremendously denigrated by liberals, and respond to this feeling by denigrating liberals. Liberals rarely examine their own snobbery and self-righteousness, which feeds this conservative pattern. Many liberals are convinced they are the victims of conservative racism, sexism, and homophobia, and lash out in response with name-calling and demands that everyone accept their way of understanding race, gender, and issues of sexuality. Conservatives feed this liberal pattern with an insistence that anyone who focuses too much on America's flaws is somehow unpatriotic.

And on and on. Both sides are caught in very much the same mental circles and traps. The blaming, the self-righteousness, the name-calling, the victimhood—none of this is solely Trump's fault at the end of the day. We are all responsible for ourselves.

In *Don't Bite the Hook*, Pema Chödrön, one of the best known Insight Meditation teachers, says that when eighth-century Indian philosopher and yogi Shantideva looked at all the violent, cruel, shady things that certain people did, rather than blaming them or getting indignant, he was interested in the question "How did the people get like that, and do you want to get like that too?" In other words, how does your reaction to violence, cruelty, and other people acting in their own extreme self-interest strangely enough send you down the same path?

Most of us have traveled far down this path lately. The work to get off of it is what the meditation teachers might call a practice. It is endless. The voice saying you are right, they are wrong, you are good, they are bad, is like some mythological temptress. Lately, I have to push back against this voice ten times a day. Sometimes more. When my brain produces the idea of my own superiority and victimhood, I don't get into a logical argument with it. I just block the door (to my heart, and my mouth) with deeper feelings and understanding, with what I really feel and believe.

Self-examination, followed by strenuous efforts to resist our impulse to vilify, may be able to pull us out of these endless circles, and allow us as individuals to get a hold of ourselves. If enough of us can accomplish this, our nation will get a hold of itself too.

EPILOGUE

What happened to the Soviet Union?

Many explanations have been given for the country's collapse: its weak economy couldn't support the nation any longer; its failure to keep up with the West economically led to widespread disaffection; the country was brought down by corruption; it fell apart because it was a moral failure; the war in Afghanistan further eroded an already troubled society; the republics took their opportunity to split off and that was the end of a coherent communist country. I have already repeated Stephen Kotkin's quote from a former high-ranking KGB officer and analyst who believed the most significant factor in the Soviet collapse was lying—"Lies struck at all aspects of our existence, becoming a fatal disease in our blood, destroying our soul."

There are elements of truth to every one of these explanations, and in aggregate, they certainly weakened the state considerably. But the Soviet Union probably did not fall because an embittered Soviet population, worn down from years of financial and moral depredation, brought it down. The majority of ordinary citizens likely didn't even want the state to dissolve.

The Soviet collapse was, instead, a revolution from above (at least, this is one of the more convincing theories). First Gorbachev, then Yeltsin and the country's elites, changed and ultimately dis-

mantled the country. Yes, Gorbachev was to some degree responding to the needs and desires of the population, and widespread
political apathy meant he could experiment with reform without
encountering too much popular opposition. But only the Soviet
leadership, not the people, really had the power to bring down the
country.

Stephen Cohen writes that most Russians think three "subjec-
tive" factors led to the collapse of the Soviet Union:

"The unduly rapid and radical way—not too slowly and cau-
tiously, as is said in the West—Gorbachev carried out his political
and economic reforms; a power struggle in which Yeltsin overthrew
the Soviet state in order to get rid of its president, Gorbachev, and
to occupy the Kremlin; and property-seizing Soviet bureaucratic
elites, the *nomenklatura*, who were more interested in 'privatizing'
the state's enormous wealth in 1991 than in defending it."

Cohen sees what happened as "authentic democratic, market
and nationalist aspirations" losing a battle with "cravings for power,
elite avarice, extremist ideas and widespread popular perceptions of
illegitimacy and betrayal."

It's not as surprising as it sounds that the Soviet elite destroyed
their own country. Revolutionary change is often instigated by determined minorities, and by elites. In this case, many of those who
supported the Soviet system were also resentful or apathetic, and
they didn't muster the will to save their country. And that was that.

Afterward, many regretted the unraveling, but many didn't.
People's feelings changed over time too—some who regretted the
collapse felt differently later, and vice versa. There was and is no
consensus.

Could the collapse of the Soviet Union have been prevented if
Gorbachev had implemented his changes more slowly? Or more
quickly? Or if he had tried an approach more like China's, allowing
a slow capitalist transformation without giving up the party's grip
on power? We'll never know what might have been. But the general stability of the Soviet state throughout the decades before the

collapse, and the general attitudes of the population, suggest that the country could have lasted a lot longer, maybe even truly lasted.

––––––––––

It's important to get over the self-centered idea that we—and especially Ronald Reagan—were responsible for the demise of the Soviet Union. This is a grandiose notion, possibly stemming from a desire to believe we acted appropriately and successfully in our relations with the Soviet Union, and won the Cold War as a result. That's not to say a kind of moral attack that we waged didn't put some pressure on the Soviets. And our relative prosperity created even more pressure. But the idea that Reagan spent them into oblivion, or that his hardline anti-communist stance brought them to their knees, doesn't fit the evidence.

Let's focus on the most common claim: that the Soviets couldn't match Reagan's huge military buildup and that they destroyed an already tenuous economy by trying to. Soviet military spending can be analyzed as an absolute amount spent, as a percentage of GNP or as a percentage of the state budget. I think the easiest statistic to understand, and the one that gets most clearly at the Soviet Union's problem with military spending, is how much was spent on the military relative to the entire state budget. Like all questions about the Soviet budget, experts have not reached a consensus here, but some estimates suggest the Soviet Union spent around 40 percent of its total budget on the military (Volkogonov claims it was 70 percent under Andropov!). For comparison's sake, the United States spent around 25 to 30 percent of our national budget on the military in the late 1970s and early 1980s. Whether we could afford this is an almost abstract question. It's hard to calculate how much damage we did to ourselves by not spending some of this money on pressing social problems. But one thing is clear—the Soviets spent a considerably higher percentage of their budget on the military than we did, and they couldn't afford it.

Doesn't this suggest, then, that Reagan's military spending essentially bled them to death? Not really. For one, experts disagree on whether or not already high levels of Soviet military spending increased significantly in the early 1980s after Reagan took office. They likely did not. But even if they did, I have never seen economic statistics that show a precipitous decline in the Soviet economy based on this increased spending. Soviet military spending in fact declined under Gorbachev starting in 1986, when a change in military doctrine allowed the Soviet Union to stop preparing for a war fought in the West. This shift under Gorbachev doesn't seem to have made a huge difference to the Soviet economy either (although it's hard to disentangle from all the other facets of his economic reforms).

The entire Soviet economy creaked and groaned for decades. To the degree that economic weakness contributed to the Soviet collapse, it wasn't caused by or necessarily even exacerbated by the effort to match Reagan's military buildup.

Thank God their dissolution was, at the end of the day, their own doing.

Most people in the West think that Gorbachev was a great man and a great leader. They believe that he tried to bring Western-style freedoms to his country, which was a noble enterprise, and that it doesn't matter that he failed and the country collapsed, because really it was a lousy country anyway.

But we have been wildly out of step with the Russian population and a significant portion of the previously Soviet population in our estimation of Gorbachev. Although the extreme animosity toward him seems to be fading lately as the generations turn over, his time in power has been perceived by most Russians and former Soviets as an unmitigated disaster that led to the collapse of their country. There's no denying the validity of this interpretation.

Gorbachev was an extraordinary human being, a fully decent person who vastly reduced repression in the Soviet Union and finally took on problems that had been festering for decades. But he not only presided over the country's collapse, he was at least in some ways responsible for it. He may have moved too fast in carrying out his reforms, and people around him report that he often barreled forward without listening to those who disagreed with him. He seems not to have had a fully thought-out plan for the massive changes he was engineering, trusting instead that things would simply work out. It's true that he was in an almost impossible situation, but he failed at what he set out to do, and leaders who fail are usually held responsible.

Historian and Gorbachev biographer William Taubman argues that calling Gorbachev a failure is too simplistic. He believes that, although Gorbachev didn't accomplish everything he wanted to, he brought a new measure of freedom and democracy to the Russian people, and changed the world by ending the Cold War.

Fair enough. But imagine if Lincoln had let the South leave the Union instead of prosecuting the Civil War. If slavery in the South had diminished on its own within several decades anyway, he might have been seen there, as well as abroad in America's former great power rivals, as a thoughtful and moderate man who let the Confederacy go rather than risk bloodshed and war. But in the North, he would probably be seen as the man who let the country dissolve.

We'll have to see how history judges Gorbachev, there and here. But one part of his potential legacy is particularly troubling. Gorbachev was a special kind of politician. He was idealistic while knowing and avoiding the dangers of utopianism. He rejected violence as a political tool, and refused to use it in instances when many other leaders likely would have, for example as Eastern Europe broke away from the Soviet Bloc. He did violate his principles here in a few instances as the Soviet Union was nearing collapse, but ultimately he chose not to use widespread state violence even to preserve his own country. The fact that this broadly enlightened and humane approach was politically unsuccessful is a great tragedy, and hopefully will not be the primary lesson future generations take away from the Gorbachev era.

No matter how much we want them to, political systems do not last. It's a rule of history. Eventually, every single one declines, explodes, transforms, or in one way or another changes enough that it is no longer what it was. As much as we might not want it to, this is going to happen to our political system as well. Maybe it will be sunk by an idealistic revolution, maybe it will break out into a civil war, maybe it will crumble after economic decline, or even find some brand-new way to fall apart. But fall it will.

One last perspective on Gorbachev's potential legacy: He has set an example for how a superpower might best disintegrate. The notion that the collapse of the Soviet Union was nonviolent is incorrect. Although Gorbachev rarely used it as a tool of the state, there was violence before, during, and after the breakup, including terrible ethnic violence and a number of small all-out wars. Brutal as it was, though, the Soviet collapse was mild compared to what might have been expected. The cataclysmic violence that might easily accompany the collapse of a large and powerful state never took place. And this was largely because Gorbachev would not commit it, or allow it. This is an example for all countries to follow, including our own, if the day comes when similar decisions have to be made.

I do not mean to imply by this assessment that the use of violence by a state is never acceptable in a political context, as much as I personally believe it is almost always unnecessary. But a self-aware politics is not an enlightened liberalism that precludes all the tragic and unsavory measures that have always been a part of politics. Rather, it's important to understand one's personal motivation to use violence instead of just assessing its use in strategic terms. One would hope this approach would reduce political violence, but human nature ensures it will not eliminate it.

I'm sorry that the Soviet Union collapsed. I agree with Putin's sentiment that it was a major geopolitical catastrophe of the twentieth century (though not the greatest). I'm happy for the Soviet peoples that wanted their freedom and now have it—Latvians, Lithuanians, Estonians, Georgians, Armenians, Ukrainians. It's wonderful that these people achieved a widely held aspiration for independence. But I wish the Soviet Union had managed to go on without them, that it had carried on for the rest of the republics and peoples, for Russia and the Central Asian republics and the rest.

I don't mean I'm sorry that the country of Stalin is gone. If the Soviet Union had collapsed during his era, I wouldn't feel this way. I'm talking about the country of Gorbachev. And yet it's silly to separate the two, because Gorbachev's country was the country of Stalin, at a later stage in its historical evolution. Gorbachev's Soviet Union was Stalin's Soviet Union going through radical change, and reforming in profound ways. It was shedding the worst things about itself and embracing the many good things. I wish that country could have survived and progressed.

If the United States had collapsed right after slavery ended, or during the civil-rights movement, really at any time when it was trying to change and get better, it would have been a terrible tragedy. Instead, we survived and got to progress, got the chance to overcome some of our worst impulses, and to continue struggling with our remaining problems. The Soviets didn't get that chance. They lost everything that was good in their country along with everything that was bad. They lost a future that might have been better.

ACKNOWLEDGMENTS

I would like to thank my parents (no longer with us). My father was a sharp, focused, and rigorous thinker. He was also open-minded and curious, a voracious reader of virtually anything (and often, it seemed to me, everything). My mother was sharp and focused in her own way, but was first and foremost an out-of-the-box thinker. They rarely argued, but one night, they were getting into it over my mother's failure to record checks she'd written in her ledger. My father, in a lawyerly fashion (he was a lawyer), rattled off three or four proofs about why my mother's position was wrong. Exasperated, she looked him in the eye and said, "Well, I like to be wrong!" This book owes a great debt to that moment.

Jacob Weisberg: Always my first reader, who makes sure I don't seem crazy to my second reader. Brother, friend, tireless supporter—the best possible companion from birth on.

Artemy Kalinovsky: Despite my decades-long immersion in Soviet history and culture, I am not a historian. Artemy Kalinovsky, a professor at Temple University, is. His thoughts and comments on the manuscript allowed me to avoid serious mistakes, as well as to clarify many muddy points. More generally, his thoughts (and his parents' experiences) on being Jewish in the Soviet Union, as well as his comments on how younger readers would respond to the book, were especially helpful.

Sergei Kostin: When I first read *Farewell*, the book that Sergei co-wrote on Vladimir Vetrov, I felt a very special person and thinker was behind it. Later, when we asked Sergei to consult on *The Americans*, he said no. Happily, we were able to talk him into it. Sergei's thoughts, edits, and corrections on this book were not just those of an insightful reader but also of a good friend. I feel extremely fortunate that our paths crossed, and then converged.

Alex Hazanov: For reading and commenting with great acuity, and knowing the answers to questions that nobody else knew. Alex's wonderful and esoteric interests coincided exactly with some of my own.

Robert van Voren: Robert was extremely helpful and gracious in clarifying my understanding about the punitive use of psychiatry in the Soviet Union and modern-day Russia.

Larry Bogoslaw: Larry went to great lengths to help me understand and write about the current state of the Russian media. He was among a number of complete strangers who acted more like old friends in lending a hand on this project.

James Graham Wilson: A historian at the Department of State, Wilson has compiled multiple volumes of official documents concerning the Foreign Relations of the United States (FRUS). I was extremely fortunate to have him apply his wide-ranging knowledge and acute perception to my manuscript. As to his friendship, all I can say is, he carefully reviewed my book in the days right before his baby was born.

Andrei Soldatov and Irina Borogan: Please do not think their inclusion here implies any endorsement of or agreement with the ideas in this book. Rather, like true friends, Andrei and Irina helped me say what I was trying to say better and more accurately, despite profound disagreement.

Joel Fields: Joel added a profound level of calm, organization, collaboration, and joy to my regular workday without which I never would have had the mental energy to work on this project in my off hours. He was also an open and generous reader of this book.

John Landgraf: For many years, John lovingly pushed and prodded Joel Fields and me to make *The Americans* better—he showed us how to dig deeper, tell better stories, and find ever more feeling. He used his insight and kindness again here to help me tell this story. (He also introduced me to the concept of the "narrative sandwich.")

Joe Cohen: My career in television—which made this work possible—depends on the help, guidance, and unique genius of Joe Cohen.

Bruce Feiler: A friend and advocate over many years of writing, who always helps me figure out what exactly to do with these books.

Keith Melton: One of the world's foremost experts on espionage, who has done his best to keep me from going astray in this area (and is not responsible if I do anyway).

Darrell Blocker: Darrell helped me realize I wanted to write this book.

Ben Kalin: By the time Ben came on to fact-check this book, I was mentally exhausted, and unsure I could do any more thinking or writing. But the rigor and clarity of his work woke me up, and got me through the final passes.

The team at PublicAffairs: Michelle Welsh-Horst, Brooke Parsons, Lindsay Fradkoff, and publisher Clive Priddle.

Rachelle Mandik: For invaluable copyediting, and getting me to rethink the comma at this late stage of life.

Christy Fletcher: It is fair to say that the virtues of this book were not immediately apparent to all of its early readers. I am enormously grateful that Christy saw what was there, and what could be there.

Ben Adams: Ben, too, saw the potential of this book, and played an enormous role in making sure that it was (at least to some degree) realized. I could spend pages on his contributions, but I will settle for this particular one: I had, in early drafts, dug a series of rhetorical pits, then jumped into them. Ben patiently showed me where each one was, then handed down a ladder.

Remodeling: A.S., F.L., C.Z., J.C.

Julia: Out of adversity . . .

Rosa: when the moon rises, or even before

ANNOTATED BIBLIOGRAPHY

I suppose all writers rely heavily on the sources they cite. But I can't help thinking that my debt is especially great. I am not a historian, and with very few exceptions, did not work with primary source material. The books, papers, articles, and podcasts below were the source for most of my facts and information, as well as much of my analysis. I understand there is a certain blurriness in the book about where the analysis from my sources leaves off and mine takes over. This gives me pause. I want to give full credit to the writers and thinkers below, try not to take credit for their work, and make sure they will not be blamed for any of my own ideas. To that end, I want to make clear that almost everything I have ever learned about the Soviet Union and Russia comes from the work of academics, journalists, émigrés, and other thinkers and writers. This bibliography is dedicated to them, with deep appreciation.

THROUGH THE FOG, I SEE A COUNTRY

Books

Hoffman, David E. *The Dead Hand: The Untold Story of the Cold War Arms Race and Its Dangerous Legacy.* Doubleday, 2009.

Sell, Louis. *From Washington to Moscow: US-Soviet Relations and the Collapse of the USSR.* Duke University Press, 2016.

Garthoff, Raymond L. *Soviet Leaders and Intelligence: Assessing the American Adversary During the Cold War.* Georgetown University Press, 2015.

Raleigh, Donald J. *Soviet Baby Boomers: An Oral History of Russia's Cold War Generation.* Oxford University Press, 2011.

    A wonderful, oral-history-based book about the lives of Soviet citizens in two different cities.

Volkogonov, Dmitri. *Autopsy for an Empire: The Seven Leaders Who Built the Soviet Regime*. Free Press, 1998.

I relied heavily on this book for my section on the Soviet Union's post-Stalin leaders.

Alexievich, Svetlana. *Secondhand Time: The Last of the Soviets*. Random House, 2016.

An astonishing book. Alexievich uses her own unique style of oral history to present a group of disparate Russian citizens struggling with life after the collapse of their former country. There's nothing like this.

Weisberg, Jacob. *Ronald Reagan: The American Presidents Series: The 40th President, 1981–1989*. Times Books, 2016.

A great account of Reagan's presidency, with brilliant insight on how he did and didn't change in his approach to the Soviet Union. By my brother!

Miller, Chris. *The Struggle to Save the Soviet Economy: Mikhail Gorbachev and the Collapse of the USSR*. University of North Carolina Press, 2016.

Wilson, James Graham. *The Triumph of Improvisation: Gorbachev's Adaptability, Reagan's Engagement, and the End of the Cold War*. Cornell University Press, 2014.

Wilson makes a compelling case for how improvisational leadership, rather than fully fleshed-out and fully implemented policies, ended the Cold War. An honest and convincing look at the strengths and weaknesses of leaders on both sides.

Applebaum, Anne. *Gulag: A History*. Doubleday, 2003.

A historical masterpiece. Applebaum digs into the history and answers almost every question you could come up with about what exactly happened in the Gulag. Among other things, I relied on her as a prime source in counting Stalin's victims.

Cohen, Stephen F. *The Victims Return: Survivors of the Gulag After Stalin*. PublishingWorks, 2010.

A profoundly moving and insightful account of how Soviets returning from the Gulag struggled to fit back into society, and how society struggled to fit them back in. I first encountered the idea that a great number of Soviets were unhappy about the collapse of their country here. This is one of the most beautiful and moving books I've ever read. There are so many reasons to study history and politics. Work like this, that brings you into the heart of the human experience, is one of the best.

Braithwaite, Rodric. *Afgantsy: The Russians in Afghanistan, 1979–89*. Oxford University Press, 2011.

A great, humanizing book. Makes it hard not to relate to and sympathize with not just the Soviet soldiers who fought the war but also the Soviet leaders who made the mistake of getting into the war.

This was also the book where I first encountered the idea that the Soviet press was something more than just a propaganda outlet, that it also functioned as a recourse for Soviet citizens who were in many circumstances able to send letters of complaint to the newspapers, and sometimes even get action taken for various injustices through the press.

Also, in many years of reading, this may contain the only story I've seen suggesting Chernenko was a smart and decent man (or at least had a smart and decent side) rather than being the fully sclerotic leader he's generally portrayed as.

Slezkine, Yuri. *The Jewish Century*. Princeton University Press, 2004.

A staggering, revolutionary way of thinking about history in general, and specifically the Jewish people.

Martin, Terry. *The Affirmative Action Empire: Nations and Nationalism in the Soviet Union, 1923–1939*. Cornell University Press, 2001.

Bubbling over with insight and originality.

Cherkashin, Victor, and Gregory Feifer. *Spy Handler: Memoir of a KGB Officer—The True Story of the Man Who Recruited Robert Hanssen and Aldrich Ames*. Basic Books, 2005.

I've written in the text about how this memoir influenced me enormously.

Andrew, Christopher, and Vasili Mitrokhin. *The Sword and the Shield: The Mitrokhin Archive and the Secret History of the KGB*. Basic Books, 1999.

Vasili Mitrokhin stole much of the KGB's archive, copying it by hand over many years and then smuggling it to the West. This book tells the story of KGB operations through this archive. It's incredible that we have this resource; there's obviously nothing else like it.

Andrew, Christopher, and Vasili Mitrokhin. *The World Was Going Our Way: The KGB and the Battle for the Third World—Newly Revealed Secrets from the Mitrokhin Archive*. Basic Books, 2005.

Van Voren, Robert. *Koryagin: A Man Struggling for Human Dignity*. Second World Press, 1987.

An original and deeply moving book about a Soviet doctor fighting for his patients, his country, and as the title states, his human dignity. Key to my understanding of Soviet dissidents and the punitive use of psychiatry in the Soviet Union. (I also had a private email exchange with van Voren—my description of the abuse of psychiatry in Russia today is mostly based on these emails.)

Snyder, Timothy. *Black Earth: The Holocaust as History and Warning*. Tim Duggan Books, 2015.

A stunning revisionist history of the Holocaust. Snyder explains the human catastrophe in a new and deeply compelling way.

Snyder, Timothy. *Bloodlands: Europe Between Hitler and Stalin*. Basic Books, 2010.

Looks at the relationship between the mass murders committed by Hitler and Stalin in the areas of Europe where both held power, including places where Germany and the Soviet Union took turns in control. The circuitous way the final solution took shape, and details about the Red Army, not the Allies, liberating the death camps are from this book.

Mochulsky, Fyodor Vasilevich. *Gulag Boss: A Soviet Memoir*. Oxford University Press, 2010.

Kostin, Sergei, and Eric Raynaud. *Farewell: The Greatest Spy Story of the Twentieth Century*. Amazon Crossing, 2011.

Details on the Vladimir Vetrov case and stunning specifics on how executions were carried out. A great book that looks at the Soviet Union from an unusual angle, showing how they really dealt with spies, which was different from what you would probably expect.

Solzhenitsyn, Aleksandr. *The Gulag Archipelago*. Harper & Row, 1974.

To me, this is one of the greatest books ever written. A study of inhumanity, it reveals—is a revelation about—humanity. I read the abridged version in college, and the full version more recently. It's a lot to ask you to read the full version. It's long. In total, the length of three enormously long books. If your main goal is to finish, read the abridged version. But I don't see a real difference between reading the abridged version and reading the same number of pages in the full version—in other words, this isn't a story where you have to get to the end. It is an almost endless collection of incredible stories, along with brilliant insight. So I would say read the full version, see how far you get, and if you want to, keep going.

Duhamel, Luc. *The KGB Campaign Against Corruption in Moscow, 1982–1987*. University of Pittsburgh Press, 2010.

Kotkin, Stephen. *Stalin: Paradoxes of Power, 1878–1928*. Penguin Press, 2014. And *Stalin: Waiting for Hitler, 1929–1941*. Penguin Press, 2017.

I rely heavily on these first two volumes of Kotkin's biography of Stalin. Waiting eagerly for Volume 3.

Albats, Yevgenia. *The State Within a State: The KGB and Its Hold on Russia, Past, Present and Future*. Farrar, Straus and Giroux, 1994.

A groundbreaking book on the KGB. Even if some of its interpretations are different from my own, it's full of facts and explanations about the KGB's work inside the Soviet Union that I've never seen anywhere else. I relied on it heavily, and it's the source for my explanation of the difference between recruited informants and reliable persons. Also provided or confirmed details such as the number of active KGB officers.

Knight, Amy W. *The KGB: Police and Politics in the Soviet Union.* Unwin Hyman, 1988.

Rubenstein, Joshua, and Alexander Gribanov, eds. *The KGB File of Andrei Sakharov.* Yale University Press, 2005.

Fitzpatrick, Sheila. *Everyday Stalinism: Ordinary Life in Extraordinary Times: Soviet Russia in the 1930s.* Oxford University Press, 1999.

One of the primary books that helped me see how complex life was under Stalin.

Fitzpatrick, Sheila. *Tear Off the Masks! Identity and Imposture in Twentieth-Century Russia.* Princeton University Press, 2005.

I found the Rom Harré quote I use in the section on Soviet law in this book.

Solomon Jr., Peter H. *Soviet Criminal Justice Under Stalin.* Cambridge University Press, 1996.

The primary source for my section on the Soviet criminal justice system.

Gessen, Masha. *Where the Jews Aren't: The Sad and Absurd Story of Birobidzhan, Russia's Jewish Autonomous Region.* Schocken, 2016.

A fantastic history of the Jewish Autonomous Republic that never had that many Jews in it.

Gessen, Masha. *The Future Is History: How Totalitarianism Reclaimed Russia.* Riverhead Books, 2017.

Gessen chronicles the Soviet collapse through the stories of people who lived through it. Extremely compelling and enjoyable. To single out a few of the book's many highlights, Gessen offers a brilliant intellectual history of the idea of totalitarianism, and an original and moving study of how psychologists have looked at the Soviet and Russian states. While examining this second topic, Gessen argues that there is a second kind of stability that's important in Russia beyond the obvious kind that involves avoiding wars and physical suffering. This is psychological stability, which in the Russian context means a predictable way of life, free from the anxiety produced by opportunity and possibility. Gessen suggests a need for this second kind of stability accounts for much of Putin's support.

Grossman, Vasily. *Life and Fate.* Harper & Row, 1986.

Michael, Robert. *A Concise History of American Antisemitism.* Rowman & Littlefield, 2005.

Just what it says it is. Very clear and easily readable. The primary source for my brief discussion of the history of American anti-Semitism.

Stember, Charles Herbert, and others. *Jews in the Mind of America.* Basic Books, 1967.

Source for some of the statistics in Robert Michael's book.

Zubok, Vladislav M. *A Failed Empire: The Soviet Union in the Cold War from Stalin to Gorbachev.* University of North Carolina Press, 2007.

A comprehensive and insightful overview. Clarified many things for me.

Harris, James. *The Great Fear: Stalin's Terror of the 1930s.* Oxford University Press, 2016.

A brilliant reconsideration of Stalin and the Great Terror.

Suny, Ronald Grigor. *Red Flag Unfurled: History, Historians, and the Russian Revolution.* Verso, 2017.

Includes a wonderful chapter on the development of academic approaches to the Soviet Union in the United States.

Beckerman, Gal. *When They Come for Us, We'll Be Gone: The Epic Struggle to Save Soviet Jewry.* Houghton Mifflin Harcourt, 2010.

A moving account of the strength and heroism of Soviet Jews and refuseniks. I have emphasized the nuance of this struggle, while this version highlights the extraordinary lived experience of many.

Figes, Orlando. *A People's Tragedy: The Russian Revolution: 1891–1924.* Viking Adult, 1997.

A true feat of political understanding, this is the most thorough and engrossing book I've encountered on the Russian Revolution.

Taubman, William. *Gorbachev: His Life and Times.* W. W. Norton & Company, 2017.

Remnick, David. *Lenin's Tomb: The Last Days of the Soviet Union.* Random House, 1993.

Hazanov, Alexander. *Porous Empire: Foreign Visitors and the Post-Stalin Soviet State.* PhD dissertation, University of Pennsylvania, 2016.

A great history full of details about how things really worked in the Soviet Union. I also follow Alex in many of my explanations of certain crucial facts and nuances about the refusenik movement. My description of official treatment of visitors to the Soviet Union largely comes from this paper.

Podcast

Sean's Russia Blog (SRB) Podcast

While writing the third draft of this book, Artemy Kalinovsky sent me an article by Sean Guillory about Richard Pipes, a prominent historian of the Soviet Union who had a great deal of political influence during the Cold War. I had agreed with Pipes's hardline views in my younger days. The article led me to Guillory's podcast, which in turn exposed me to the work of a lot of historians and writers I didn't know, and also cleared up what had been fairly theoretical for me, which was where Soviet historiography had gone during the years I hadn't been following it. It also led me to the work of Ronald Suny, which further cleared up this same question.

The podcast also provided insight into a wonderful range of topics, from what it was like to be deaf in the Soviet Union to Soviet television programming to the workings of a school outside Moscow where foreign communist leaders sent their children. And on and on. The episodes on Soviet history help humanize and demonstrate the complexity in Soviet life and society, and the episodes on Russian politics today are deeply thoughtful and illuminating.

In the episodes on Soviet history and culture, I found that at least a few of these writers and historians told similar stories to mine—they, too, had discovered a vibrant, full society in the Soviet Union that they hadn't initially known was there. And more than a few also told of having thought the Soviet Union was a totalitarian empire until they spent time there and saw something else. They didn't join the CIA while wanting to destroy the Soviet Union, like I had—they had a different journey to get to a similar place. But it was interesting to see that I wasn't the only one who, having grown up in this society and absorbed the information it put front and center, had reached similar conclusions about a distant place we didn't really know or understand.

Here are some of the historians, writers, and thinkers whose work I was moved by on the podcast. I don't know if I got them all. I'm also continuing to work my way through the episodes. They're all fantastic.

Episodes

"American Girls in Red Russia," January 25, 2019.
     —Julia Mickenberg, author of *American Girls in Red Russia: Chasing the Soviet Dream.*
"Communist Neverland at the Russian International Children's Home," October 22, 2018.
     —Elizabeth McGuire on "Communist Neverland: New Research on a Russian International Children's Home, 1933–1991."
"Decolonization and Development in Soviet Tajikistan," October 13, 2018.

—Artemy Kalinovsky, author of *The Laboratory of Socialist Development: Cold War Politics and Decolonization in Soviet Tajikistan*.

A fascinating study on Soviet policy in a vast but sometimes overlooked (in the West) part of the Soviet Union. Artemy also explained to me how university admissions policies that were seen as anti-Semitic were sometimes about affirmative action. He also suggested that my friend Sergei's point about Jews in the KGB usually taking the name of their non-Jewish parent was explained in part by a need to establish their trustworthiness.

"Russia Beyond Caricature," August 22, 2018.

—Sean Guillory, host of *SRB Podcast*, on *The Dig* podcast.

"Nation, Nationality, and Empire," August 24, 2018.

—Ronald Grigor Suny, author of *Red Flag Unfurled: History, Historians, and the Russian Revolution*, on nationality, nation, and empire in the Soviet Union.

"The Beautiful Story of the Russian Revolution," August 31, 2018.

—Lesley Chamberlain, author of *The Arc of Utopia: The Beautiful Story of the Russian Revolution*.

"Soviet Atheism," August 10, 2018.

—Victoria Smolkin, author of *A Sacred Space Is Never Empty: A History of Soviet Atheism*.

"Communism, Youth, and Generation," October 6, 2018.

—Matthias Neumann, author of *The Communist Youth League and the Transformation of the Soviet Union, 1917–1932*.

"American-Russian Relations in the 19th Century," August 19, 2018.

—Norman Saul, editor of the *Journal of Russian American Studies*, on US–Russian relations in the nineteenth century.

"Chinese Romance with the Russian Revolution," July 20, 2018.

—Elizabeth McGuire, author of *Red at Heart: How Chinese Communists Fell in Love with the Russian Revolution*.

"Collectivization and Stalinist Perpetrators," July 13, 2018.

—Lynne Viola, author of *Stalinist Perpetrators on Trial: Scenes from the Great Terror in Soviet Ukraine*, on the Soviet collectivization of agriculture, resistance, and Stalinist perpetrators.

"Early Soviet Urban Communes," April 30, 2018.

—Andy Willimott, author of *Living the Revolution: Urban Communes and Soviet Socialism, 1917–1931*.

"The Stalin Constitution," April 16, 2018.

—Samantha Lomb, author of *Stalin's Constitution: Soviet Participatory Politics and the Discussion of the 1936 Draft Constitution*.

"Soviet Jokes Under Stalin," February 2, 2018.

—Jon Waterlow, author of *Only a Joke, Comrade! Humor, Trust, and Everyday Life Under Stalin, 1929–1941*, on Soviet jokes under Stalin.

"The Ethics of Soviet Journalism," January 19, 2018.

—Natalia Roudakova, author of *Losing Pravda: Ethics and the Press in Post-Truth Russia*.

"Deaf in the Soviet Union," January 11, 2018.

—Claire Shaw, author of *Deaf in the USSR: Marginality, Community, and Soviet Identity, 1917–1991*.

"Young Communists Under Stalin," October 21, 2017.

—Seth Bernstein, author of *Raised Under Stalin: Young Communists and the Defense of Socialism*.

"Russian and American Internal Colonization," October 7, 2017.

—Steven Sabol, author of *The Touch of Civilization: Comparing American and Russian Internal Colonization*.

"The Art of the Bribe Under Stalin," January 9, 2017.

—James Heinzen, author of *The Art of the Bribe: Corruption Under Stalin, 1943–1953*.

"The Soviet Era of Television," November 2, 2016.

—Christine Evans, author of *Between Truth and Time: A History of Soviet Central Television*.

"The 1937 Pushkin Jubilee and Stalinist Culture," September 26, 2016.

—Jonathan Brooks Platt, author of *Greetings, Pushkin! Stalinist Cultural Politics and the Russian National Bard*.

"The Paradoxes of Lviv," June 1, 2016.

—Tarik Cyril Amar, author of *The Paradox of Ukrainian Lviv: A Borderland City Between Nazis, Stalinists, and Nationalists*.

"Stalin, Clans, and Terror," November 14, 2016.

—J. Arch Getty, author of *Practicing Stalinism: Bolsheviks, Boyars, and the Persistence of Tradition*.

"The Soviet Origins of Lamaze," March 20, 2019.

—Paula Michaels, author of *Lamaze: An International History*.

"Retrospective on Stalinism." August 7, 2017.

—Sheila Fitzpatrick, author of many books including *On Stalin's Team: The Years of Living Dangerously in Soviet Politics*, on Stalinism.

"American History Through Russian Eyes," October 30, 2017.

—Ivan Kurilla, professor of history and international relations at the European University at Saint Petersburg, specializing in the history of US–Russian relations, especially during the American antebellum and Civil War period, on American studies in Russia.

"The Mitki Art Collective," April 8, 2018.

—Alexandar Mihailovic, author of *The Mitki: The Art of Postmodern Protest in Russia.*

"Stalin's Last Days," July 31, 2017.

—Joshua Rubenstein, author of *The Last Days of Stalin.*

Academic Papers and Articles

Head, Simon. "Ronald Reagan, Nuclear Weapons, and the End of the Cold War." In *Ronald Reagan and the 1980s, Studies of the Americas,* edited by Cheryl Hudson and Gareth Davies. Palgrave Macmillan, 2008.

Wilson, James Graham. "U.S. Presidents and Russia, 1917–1991."

Wilson makes the case that there was a clear continuity in approach to the Soviet Union from 1917 to 1991, with American presidents consistently subscribing to the same goal, that the United States should destroy the Soviet system. Important and enlightening.

Remnick, David. Multiple *New Yorker* pieces on modern-day Russia, including "Watching the Eclipse," August 11 and 18, 2014, and "Trump and Putin: A Love Story," August 3, 2016.

soviet78 (username). "Alexander Yakovlev, Glasnost, and the Destruction of Soviet Societal Consciousness." Posted on Soviet-Empire.com (blog) under "The Truth About Glasnost in the Soviet Union," February 12, 2012.

Worth reading not just as a curiosity to see the communist point of view, but because there is something to it. The author's main point is that the Soviet Union was a stable country with a consistent ideology and a set of moral and societal beliefs that most people bought into. He gives short shrift to the economic problems of the Soviet Union that contributed to its collapse and no shrift to the nationalities problem that likewise helped tear the country apart. The article highlights what may be the basis of Russian and Chinese insecurity, which we often think revolves around their fear of a fairly straightforward process—the people could rise up, and their countries could fall. But perhaps there is a more complex two-step process for them to fear—if leaders let people speak out and challenge basic values and ideas that the population subscribes to, those ideas and values will get undermined, and the stability of the country will quickly erode. This may explain why Russia controls the press, and how sensitive they are to opposition in general. The article also argues that the nature by which societal norms are eroded can actually be seen and understood, and it specifically charts the course of how leaders see challenges to stability potentially unfolding, starting with too much permissiveness from the top. Previously, my assumption might have been that societal norms are already less stable in a troubled country, and that this is only revealed when freedom allows people to speak. This is a worthwhile article for making an interesting case we don't hear much in the West, and that may reflect the lesson Russia and China have learned from the collapse of the Soviet Union.

Solomon, Peter H. "Soviet Penal Policy, 1917–1934: A Reinterpretation." *Slavic Review,* June 1980.

As with his book, provided almost the entire basis for my under-standing of the Soviet criminal justice system.

Roberts, Geoffrey. "Stalin's Victory? The Soviet Union and World War II." *History Ireland,* January/February 2008.

Primary source for my information on Stalin's wartime performance.

Axell, Albert. "Was 'Uncle Joe' Stalin a Great Military Leader?" *Russia Beyond,* May 5, 2015 (site owned by the Russian state).

Redlich, Shimon. "Khrushchev and the Jews." *Jewish Social Studies,* October 1972.

Wiseman, A. "Soviet Jews Under Khrushchev: Still the Total State." *Commentary,* February 1959.

Decter, Moshe. "The Status of the Jews in the Soviet Union." *Foreign Affairs,* January 1963.

Zelizer, Julian E. "Trump Needs to Demilitarize His Rhetoric." *The Atlantic,* October 29, 2018.

Immigration and Refugee Board of Canada. "Jews in Russia and the Soviet Union: Chronology of Events: 1727–1992." November 1994.

Global Security (globalsecurity.org)

Includes some KGB statistics.

The Globalist. "How the KGB Reformed Russia." May 9, 2008.

Covers Andropov, absenteeism.

Lebow, Richard Ned, and Janice Gross Stein. "Reagan and the Russians." *The Atlantic,* February 1994.

Harrison, Mark. "The Soviet Union's Military Budget: Secrets, Lies, and Half-Truths." *Hoover Digest,* 2009.

Charles, Michael A. "So Did the Red Army Really Singlehandedly Defeat the Third Reich?" Stuff I Done Wrote (blog), June 24, 2010.

Great piece (and comment section) on the Soviet role in winning World War II.

Conquest, Robert. "Stalin and the Jews." *The New York Review,* July 11, 1996.

Kalinovsky, Artemy M. "Encouraging Resistance: Paul Henze, the Bennigsen School, and the Crisis of Détente." In *Reassessing Orientalism,* edited by Michael Kemper and Artemy M. Kalinovsky. Routledge, 2015.

Cohen, Stephen F. "The Unheralded Putin—Russia's Official Anti-Stalinist No. 1." *The Nation*, November 8, 2017.

ENEMIES, AND REPEAT

Books

Aron, Leon, ed. *Putin's Russia: How It Rose, How It Is Maintained, and How It Might End*. American Enterprise Institute, 2015.
Zygar, Mikhail. *All the Kremlin's Men: Inside the Court of Vladimir Putin*. PublicAffairs, 2016.
    The kind of illuminating insider account we often see about American politics, but less often about Russian politics. The source of the Putin and Luzhkov quotes about Stalin.
Soldatov, Andrei, and Irina Borogan. *The New Nobility: The Restoration of Russia's Security State and the Enduring Legacy of the KGB*. PublicAffairs, 2010.
    Many have written about how Soviet security services reestablished their power and personnel in post-Soviet Russia. This is a particularly illuminating take on the subject, enlivened by powerful and surprising stories.
Soldatov, Andrei, and Irina Borogan. *The Compatriots: The Brutal and Chaotic History of Russia's Exiles, Émigrés, and Agents Abroad*, PublicAffairs, 2019.
    A fascinating look at Soviet and Russian émigrés and how they have been perceived (and used) as both potential assets abroad and as bitter enemies.
Dunlop, John B. *The Moscow Bombings of September 1999: Examinations of Russian Terrorist Attacks at the Onset of Vladimir Putin's Rule*. Ibidem, 2014.
Medvedev, Kirill. *It's No Good*. Ugly Duckling Presse, 2016.
Snyder, Timothy. *The Road to Unfreedom: Russia, Europe, America*. Tim Duggan Books, 2018.
    Anyone interested in Russia should read this book. If you want to make peace with people you're fighting against, you have to listen to what they're saying and be clear-eyed about what they're doing. After reading this book, I also couldn't help wondering if any Russian disinformation had crept its way into my own book. I use a few sources that might be vulnerable to this (Snyder details the way that disinformation migrates from less reputable to more reputable sources).
Adams Jr., Christopher S. *Inside the Cold War: A Cold Warrior's Reflections*. Air University Press, 2012.

Reed, Thomas C. *At the Abyss: An Insider's History of the Cold War*. Presidio Press, 2004.

An account of surveillance flights over Soviet territory. My analysis of surveillance and harassing flights come from Reed, Schweizer, Tart and Keefe, Adams, and Volkogonov.

Tart, Larry, and Robert Keefe. *Attacks on American Surveillance Flights: The Price of Vigilance*. Ballantine Books, 2001.

One of the few sources entirely dedicated to examining U.S. surveillance flights shot down by the Soviets (and Chinese).

Schweizer, Peter. *Victory: The Reagan Administration's Secret Strategy That Hastened the Collapse of the Soviet Union*. Atlantic Monthly Press, 1994.

A detailed recounting of Reagan's actions to bring down the Soviet Union. I first read about the Mujahideen attacks on Soviet soil here. I was nervous Schweizer might not be reliable because he has a strong political viewpoint (then and now), and was trying to make the case that Reagan was responsible for a U.S. victory in the Cold War. But the information in his book is logical, consistent, and well-sourced.

Podcast

Sean's Russia Blog (SRB) Podcast

Episodes

"Rich Russians," September 20, 2018.
—Elisabeth Schimpfossl on *Rich Russians: From Oligarchs to Bourgeoisie*.

"Social-Economic Life in the Donbas," September 7, 2018.
—Brian Milakovsky, consultant for international projects on economic recovery in the Donbas and writes about the economy of that region for outlets such as the Kennan Institute, the *National Interest* and *OpenDemocracy Russia* on the social and economic situation in the Donbas.

"The Russian Mafia," August 3, 2018.
—Mark Galeotti, author of *The Vory: Russia's Super Mafia*.

"Psychotherapy and Neoliberalism in Russia," July 28, 2018.
—Tomas Matza on *Shock Therapy: Psychology, Precarity, and Well-Being in Postsocialist Russia*.

"Putinomics," April 24, 2018.
—Chris Miller on *Putinomics: Power and Money in Resurgent Russia*.

"Russia's a Terrible Country," June 29, 2018.
—Keith Gessen on America's Russia hands and his novel *A Terrible Country*.

"A Memoir of Misadventures in Moscow," May 18, 2018.
—Michael Idov on *Dressed Up for a Riot: Misadventures in Putin's Moscow*.

"Love, Sex, and Porn in Russia," May 11, 2016.
—Natalia Antonova on "Russia's Porn Stars Aren't Just Hot, They're Also Ostracized and Exploited" in *Open Democracy*.

"Lukoil, Power, and Culture in Perm," March 21, 2016.
—Doug Rogers on *The Depths of Russia: Oil, Power, and Culture After Socialism*.

"Revisiting Nashi and Russian Youth Politics," December 17, 2015.
—Julie Hemment on *Youth Politics in Putin's Russia: Producing Patriots and Entrepreneurs*.

"The Murder of Boris Nemtsov," March 4, 2015.
—Mark Galeotti, author of *Russia's Wars in Chechnya*, on the murder of Boris Nemtsov.

"The Politics of Russia's Apartment Demolition," September 24, 2017.
—Maxim Trudolubov on Moscow's apartment demolition plans.

"Feminists in the Maidan," September 16, 2017.
—Emily Channell-Justice on feminist activism and the Maidan.

"Adventures in Post-Soviet Ukraine," December 12, 2016.
—Sophie Pinkham on *Black Square: Adventures in Post-Soviet Ukraine*.

"Protest in Putin's Russia," July 14, 2017.
—Mischa Gabowitsch, author of *Protest in Putin's Russia*.

"Working-Class Life in Anytown Russia," January 30, 2017.
—Jeremy Morris on *Everyday Postsocialism: Working-Class Communities in the Russian Margins*.

TV

Stone, Oliver, dir. *The Putin Interviews*. Showtime, 2017.
Charlie Rose. September 27, 2015, PBS.
Rose interviews Vladimir Putin.

Academic Papers and Articles

Qiu, Linda. "Does Vladimir Putin Kill Journalists?" PolitiFact, January 4, 2016.

Shermer, Michael, and Pat Linse. "Conspiracy Theories." *Skeptic.*

Van Prooijen, Jan-Willem, and Karen M. Douglas. "Belief in Conspiracy Theories: Basic Principles of an Emerging Research Domain." *European Journal of Social Psychology*, 2018.

Grenier, Paul R. "Distorting Putin's Favorite Philosophers." *Consortium News*, March 27, 2015.

Robinson, Paul. "The Putin Book Club." *Centre for International Policy Studies*, April 3, 2014.

Rennack, Dianne, and Cory Welt. "U.S. Sanctions on Russia: An Overview." Congressional Research Service, March 23, 2020.

Maximov, Vasily. "U.S. Sanctions Against Russia: What You Need to Know." Center for Strategic and International Studies, October 31, 2018.

Starr, Terrell Jermaine. "The American Sanctions Against Russia, Explained." *Jalopnik*, February 3, 2017.
    Most of the factual details and much of the analysis of sanctions are from the above three pieces.

Dowling, Tim. "24-Hour Putin People: My Week Watching Kremlin 'Propaganda Channel' RT." *Guardian*, November 29, 2017.

Shifrinson, Joshua R. Itzkowitz. "Op-Ed: Russia's Got a Point: The U.S. Broke a NATO Promise." *Los Angeles Times*, May 30, 2016.

Klußmann, Uwe, Matthias Schepp, and Klaus Wiegrefe. "Did the West Break Its Promise to Moscow?" *Spiegel International*, November 26, 2009.

DeBardeleben, Joan, and Mikhail Zherebtsov. "The Reinstated Gubernatorial Elections in Russia: A Return to Open Politics?" *Region*, 2019.
    On the appointment of governors and elections in competitive authoritarian societies.

Petkova, Mariya. "The Death of the Russian Far Right." *Al Jazeera*, December 16, 2017.

Klapsis, Antonis. "An Unholy Alliance: The European Far Right and Putin's Russia." Wilfried Martens Centre for European Studies, May 27, 2015.

Hays, Jeffrey. "Russian Privatization and Oligarchs." Facts and Details, 2008.
    Privatization under Yeltsin.

Rutland, Peter. "Putin's Economic Record: Is the Oil Boom Sustainable?" *Europe-Asia Studies,* August 2008.
    Russian economy and oil.

Zakharova, Olesya. "Vladimir Putin Loves Civil Society (as Long as He Controls It)." *Foreign Policy*, October 12, 2016.

Brechenmacher, Saskia. "Delegitimization and Division in Russia." Carnegie Endowment for International Peace, May 18, 2017.

Von Ow-Freytag, Barbara. "Russia's Social Awakening: A New Challenge for the EU." Carnegie Europe, April 18, 2019.

Kolesnikov, Andrei. "The Split in Russia's Civil Society." Carnegie Moscow Center, April 29, 2019.

   In my section on civil society, I rely particularly heavily on the reports from the Carnegie Endowment.

Amnesty International. "Russia: New Assault on Independent Media, NGOs and Activists Through Suffocating Fines." October 29, 2018.

Skokova, Yulia, and Havlicek, Pavel. "2018 Report on the State of Civil Society in the EU and Russia." EU-Russia Civil Society Forum, March 15, 2019.

Upadhyay, Archana. "Civil Society and Democratic Space in Russia," *Economic and Political Weekly*, November 11, 2006.

Ioffe, Julia. "What Is Russia Today?" *Columbia Journalism Review*, September/October 2010.

   An even-handed analysis of RT, which you don't see often. Back in 2010, it correctly predicted how the network's coverage of America would fluctuate along with our overall relations with Russia (which wasn't as obvious then as it seems now).

Maynes, Charles. "Russia's Elected Mayors—a Dying Breed." VOA News (Voice of America), May 27, 2018.

Gessen, Masha. "As a Gay Parent I Must Flee Russia or Lose My Children." *Guardian*, August 11, 2013.

French, Alex. "The Secret History of a Cold War Mastermind." *Wired*, March 11, 2020.

   Raising questions on the alleged attack on Siberian gas pipeline.

Michel, Casey. "The Kremlin's California Dream." *Slate*, May 4, 2017.

   Russian cultivation of European contacts on far left and right.

Smith, Ben. "How Investigative Journalism Flourished in Hostile Russia." *New York Times*, February 21, 2021.

Committee to Protect Journalists. "Journalists Attacked in Russia Since 1992." https://cpj.org/europe/russia/.

Tayler, Jeffrey. "What Pussy Riot's 'Punk Prayer' Really Said." *Atlantic*, November 8, 2012.

Kosareva, Nadezhda, and Struyk, Raymond. "Housing Privitization in the Russian Federation." *Housing Policy Debate*, 1993.

WHAT WE SHOULD DO

Books

Hoffman, David E. *The Billion Dollar Spy: A True Story of Cold War Espionage and Betrayal.* Doubleday, 2015.
    Entirely gripping account of the Tolkachev story.

Academic Papers and Articles

Upadhyay, Archana. "Civil Society and Democratic Space in Russia." *Economic and Political Weekly*, November 11–17, 2006.
Cormac, Rory, and Richard J. Aldrich. "Grey Is the New Black: Covert Action and Implausible Deniability." *International Affairs*, May 2018.
Scott, Len. "Espionage and the Cold War: Oleg Penkovsky and the Cuban Missile Crisis." *Intelligence and National Security*, January 2008.

CONCLUSION: POLITICS AND PERSONALITY
OR, AM *I* UPSIDE DOWN?

Books

Zweig, Connie, and Jeremiah Abrams, eds. *Meeting the Shadow: The Hidden Power of the Dark Side of Human Nature.* TarcherPerigee, 1991.
    A powerful collection of essays on the Jungian concept of the shadow, highly relevant to a psychological understanding of U.S.–Soviet relations, and to U.S.–Russian relations as well. The section on enemy-making is particularly germane.
Sigalow, Emily. *American JewBu.* Princeton University Press, 2019.
    A fascinating and well-told history of the Jewish influence on the Insight Meditation movement.
Haidt, Jonathan. *The Righteous Mind: Why Good People Are Divided by Politics and Religion.* Pantheon, 2012.
    Fundamental to understanding ourselves politically, in particular how politics is driven more by emotion than reason.
Chödrön, Pema. *Don't Bite the Hook: Finding Freedom from Anger, Resentment, and Other Destructive Emotions.* Random House Audio, 2017.
    How to break out of all kinds of habitual patterns, not exactly with an emphasis on political ones, but certainly including them. This is a series of recorded speeches, and seems only to exist as an audiobook.
Kornfield, Jack. *The Wise Heart: A Guide to the Universal Teachings of Buddhist Psychology.* Bantam, 2008.

I sometimes recommend this as a good first foray into the Insight Meditation movement (well, I did once, when someone asked me), although many of Kornfield's books are equally clear and moving.

Academic Papers and Articles

Benz, Stephen. "Taking Sides: Graham Greene and Latin America." *Journal of Modern Literature*, Winter 2003.

Greene, Graham. "The Country with Five Frontiers." *New York Review of Books*, February 17, 1977.

EPILOGUE

Books

Taubman, William. *Gorbachev: His Life and Times*. W. W. Norton & Company, 2017.

    A comprehensive and deeply illuminating biography. Extremely readable.

Kotkin, Stephen. *Armageddon Averted: The Soviet Collapse, 1970–2000*. Oxford University Press, 2008.

    Kotkin's singular and brilliant analysis of the Soviet collapse.

Articles

Cohen, Stephen F. "The Soviet Union's Afterlife." *The Nation*, October 22, 2011.

INDEX

Credit: Douglas Gorenstein

Joseph Weisberg is a television writer, based in New York, best known for creating *The Americans*. He previously wrote the novels *An Ordinary Spy* (Bloomsbury, 2007) and *10th Grade* (Random House, 2002). This is his first non-fiction book.

PublicAffairs is a publishing house founded in 1997. It is a tribute to the standards, values, and flair of three persons who have served as mentors to countless reporters, writers, editors, and book people of all kinds, including me.

I. F. STONE, proprietor of *I. F. Stone's Weekly*, combined a commitment to the First Amendment with entrepreneurial zeal and reporting skill and became one of the great independent journalists in American history. At the age of eighty, Izzy published *The Trial of Socrates*, which was a national bestseller. He wrote the book after he taught himself ancient Greek.

BENJAMIN C. BRADLEE was for nearly thirty years the charismatic editorial leader of *The Washington Post*. It was Ben who gave the *Post* the range and courage to pursue such historic issues as Watergate. He supported his reporters with a tenacity that made them fearless and it is no accident that so many became authors of influential, best-selling books.

ROBERT L. BERNSTEIN, the chief executive of Random House for more than a quarter century, guided one of the nation's premier publishing houses. Bob was personally responsible for many books of political dissent and argument that challenged tyranny around the globe. He is also the founder and longtime chair of Human Rights Watch, one of the most respected human rights organizations in the world.

• • •

For fifty years, the banner of Public Affairs Press was carried by its owner Morris B. Schnapper, who published Gandhi, Nasser, Toynbee, Truman, and about 1,500 other authors. In 1983, Schnapper was described by *The Washington Post* as "a redoubtable gadfly." His legacy will endure in the books to come.

Peter Osnos, *Founder*